Capital Markets and Institutions

PRENTICE-HALL FOUNDATIONS OF FINANCE SERIES

PRENTICE-HALL FOUNDATIONS OF FINANCE SERIES

Ezra Solomon, *Editor*

Capital Markets and Institutions

Fourth Edition

Herbert E. Dougall

C. O. G. Miller Professor of Finance, Emeritus
Stanford University

Jack E. Gaumnitz

Professor of Finance
University of Kansas

PRENTICE-HALL, INC., Englewood Cliffs, New Jersey 07632

Library of Congress Cataloging in Publication Data

Dougall, Herbert Edward.
  Capital markets and institutions.

  (Prentice-Hall foundations of finance series)
  Bibliography: p.
  Includes index.
  1. Capital market—United States. 2. Finance—
United States. 3. Financial institutions—United
States. I. Gaumnitz, Jack E., (date), joint author.
II. Title.
HG181.D59 1980   332.6'0973   79–24895
ISBN 0–13–113670–4 pbk.

Editorial/Production supervision: Marian Hartstein
Manufacturing buyer: Anthony Caruso

Printed in the United States of America

10 9 8 7 6 5 4 3 2 1

PRENTICE-HALL INTERNATIONAL, INC., *London*
PRENTICE-HALL OF AUSTRALIA PTY. LIMITED, *Sydney*
PRENTICE-HALL OF CANADA, LTD., *Toronto*
PRENTICE-HALL OF INDIA PRIVATE LIMITED, *New Delhi*
PRENTICE-HALL OF JAPAN, INC., *Tokyo*
PRENTICE-HALL OF SOUTHEAST ASIA PTE. LTD., *Singapore*
WHITEHALL BOOKS LIMITED, WELLINGTON, *New Zealand*

Contents

Editor's Note

The subject matter of financial management is in the process of rapid change. A growing analytical content, virtually nonexistent ten years ago, has displaced the earlier descriptive treatment as the center of emphasis in the field.

These developments have created problems for both teachers and students. On the one hand, recent and current thinking, which is addressed to basic questions that cut across traditional divisions of the subject matter, do not fit neatly into the older structure of academic courses and texts in corporate finance. On the other hand, the new developments have not yet stabilized and as a result have not yet reached the degree of certainty, lucidity, and freedom from controversy that would permit all of them to be captured within a single, straightforward treatment at the textbook level. Indeed, given the present rate of change, it will be years before such a development can be expected.

One solution to the problem, which the present Foundations of Finance Series tries to provide, is to cover the major components of the subject through short independent studies. These individual essays provide a vehicle through which the writer can concentrate on a single sequence of ideas and thus communicate some of the excitement of current thinking and controversy. For the teacher and student, the separate self-contained books provide a flexible up-to-date survey of current thinking on each subarea covered and at the same time permit maximum flexibility in course and curriculum design.

EZRA SOLOMON

Preface

The aim of the fourth edition is to present an uncomplicated study of the institutions that funnel long-term funds into the capital markets, to assess the demand for funds in these markets, and to analyze the interplay of these forces, particularly as they affect the yields on securities. We have also tried to keep distinct the more recent developments in our ever-changing capital markets and institutions.

No direct attempt has been made to unify the theories pertaining to financial institutions and long-term capital markets. Our effort has been directed more toward helping the reader view the operations and growth of these markets and institutions as a logical process, with the hope that those who are not familiar with financial institutions will gain a better understanding and appreciation of why they are so important in the development of our industrialized society.

The dramatic changes in the capital markets and the investment policies of major financial institutions in the late 1970s have again required us to revise the book substantially. The growing competitive forces, particularly in the market for savings deposits, the high interest rates in 1974 and 1978–79 in an inflationary environment, the continued stagnant stock market, the shifts in holdings of various securities, the growth of newer institutions such as credit unions, and the decline of other institutions such as mutual funds and real estate investment companies are described and analyzed. All tables, where possible, have been updated through 1978 and the data are again aggregated in a master table for the capital market as a whole.

The data have been drawn from a wide variety of sources. Primary sources are used wherever possible. The task of developing flow-of-funds figures has again been eased by use of information compiled by the Federal Reserve in its, *Flow-of-Funds Accounts*.

The authors are indebted for many ideas and much information to a number of persons and organizations, and for data in advance of publication from the National Association of Mutual Savings Banks, the Federal Deposit Insurance Corporation, the United States League of Savings Associations, the American

Council of Life Insurance, the Investment Company Institute, the Securities and Exchange Commission, the staff compiling the *Federal Reserve Bulletin,* and Value Line.

H.E.D.
J.E.G.

Figures

Tables

11111111111111111111111111111111111111111111111111111111111111111111111111111111
11111111111111111111111111111111111111111111111111111111111111111111111111111111
111111111111111111111111111111111111111   11111111111111111111111111111111111111
11111111111111111111111111111111111111111   111111111111111111111111111111111111111
11111111111111111111111111111111111111111   111111111111111111111111111111111111111
11111111111111111111111111111111111111111   111111111111111111111111111111111111111
11111111111111111111111111111111111111111   111111111111111111111111111111111111111
11111111111111111111111111111111111111111   111111111111111111111111111111111111111
11111111111111111111111111111111111111111   111111111111111111111111111111111111111
11111111111111111111111111111111111111111   111111111111111111111111111111111111111
11111111111111111111111111111111111111111   111111111111111111111111111111111111111
11111111111111111111111111111111111111111111111111111111111111111111111111111111
11111111111111111111111111111111111111111111111111111111111111111111111111111111

Nature and Scope
of the Capital Markets

THE economic strength of a nation may be measured in many ways. In part, it may be measured by the value of its accumulated wealth and by the rate at which this wealth grows through the savings and investment process. Or it may be measured in terms of its human and natural resources and its economic institutions. Regardless of the procedure used or the measurement process employed, the economic strength of a nation and the ability of a nation to gain the most from its accumulated resources, of necessity, requires well-developed capital markets and institutions. This first chapter briefly examines some of the dimensions of a capital market, while subsequent chapters expand the discussion of the intermediation process, financial institutions, and financial instruments. It is the latter two categories—financial institutions and instruments—and their associated market environment that form the major focus of this book.

Economic Capital and Capital Formation

National wealth includes all structures, equipment, inventories, land, monetary metals, and net foreign assets. *Economic capital,* in a narrower ˙sense, pertains only to the stock of assets used in production: buildings (but not the land on which they are situated), equipment, and inventories. Consumer durable goods such as automobiles and appliances are not considered economic capital because they yield immediate satisfaction. Although somewhat arbitrary, housing

1

is included because housing can be thought to produce a service. Thus, economic capital owned by individuals consists mainly of residential housing; by business, fixed assets and inventories; and by government, publicly owned facilities.

Capital formation is the growth in the stock of economic capital goods and is generally measured in dollar amounts or as a percentage of gross national product (GNP). Private domestic capital formation is the addition to the stock of capital goods less depreciation of those goods already on hand. The substantial increase in the stock of private domestic capital, both gross and net, for selected years since 1960 is shown in Table 1-1, together the gross national product and the rate of gross capital formation in terms of GNP. As it is the gross investment that must be financed mainly in the capital markets, our main interest lies in that figure. Table 1-1 shows that since 1960 the rate of gross capital formation has ranged from a low of 12.5 percent of GNP in 1975, to a high of 16.2 percent in 1978 with an average of about 14.5 percent.

Except for residential construction, many of the other components of capital formulation have been comparatively low in the 1970s. Contributing to the low rate of gross capital formation in the 1970s were such factors as comparatively high interest rates, international tensions, high cost and uncertainty of energy supplies, foreign competition, higher construction costs, and smaller productivity gains, all of which made it difficult for business to raise prices sufficiently to offset rising costs. The consequence of these developments in the 1970s was often to lower the profitability on new aggregate corporate investment.

The rate of gross capital formation was above average in 1978 as available mortgage money and government housing programs encouraged a sharp rise in residential construction. Corporate profitability and cash flow that encouraged new investment expenditures were also important factors. Table 1-1 also shows the variability from period to period in the major components of gross capital formation. The most volatile of the components tend to be business inventories.

TABLE 1-1. Private Domestic Capital Formation in the
United States, 1960–1978 (billions of dollars)

	1960	1965	1970	1975	1978
Producers' durable equipment	$ 29.5	$ 45.1	$ 62.8	$ 96.4	$ 144.5
New construction (other than residential structures)	18.1	26.1	37.7	53.8	77.6
Business inventories	3.6	9.6	3.8	–10.7	15.5
Residential structures	25.0	31.2	36.5	51.5	107.0
Total gross capital formation	$ 76.4	$112.0	$140.8	$ 190.9	$ 344.6
Capital consumption allowances	47.7	57.5	90.8	161.4	216.9
Total net capital formation	28.7	54.5	50.0	29.5	127.7
Gross national product	$506.0	$688.1	$982.4	$1528.8	$2127.6
Rate of gross capital formation	15.1%	16.3%	14.3%	12.5%	16.2%

Sources: U.S. Department of Commerce, *Survey of Current Business; Federal Reserve Bulletin.*

Actual liquidation of business inventories took place in 1975, which developed as a result of the stockpiling of inventories—especially raw materials—that occurred in 1973 and 1974 due to the energy crisis. Less fear of the energy shortage and readily available raw material supplies at acceptable prices were major factors in the inventory liquidation.

In measuring present and estimated future capital growth, attention often centers on business plant and equipment expenditures. These costs, shown in the first two rows of Table 1-1, amounted to $222.1 billion, or almost 11 percent of GNP, in 1978. The Council of Economic Advisers has suggested that achieving a growth in output of 5 percent per year requires "private investment" to be between 10 and 11 percent of GNP.[1] Since this rate of investment was difficult for our economy to attain in the early 1970s, some effort through lower taxes and the shifting of the tax burden away from taxes on investment has been made in recent tax laws to encourage more business investment. This has generally taken the form of increased tax credits on new equipment expenditures, lower capital gains taxes, and the prospect of some eventual tax relief on the double taxation of corporate dividends. Regardless of the figures used, or the changes in investment expenditures, the need for financing economic goods and services has fostered the growth of the capital markets and the institutions serving this important segment of our economy. As noted earlier, the financing of economic goods, and the institutions and individuals involved in the capital markets, are of primary interest in following chapters.

The Capital Markets: General Character and Definition

There is no such thing as a market for capital, that is, the economic capital goods themselves. But there is a market, or rather a group of markets, for the dollar instruments that represent either title to or claims to capital and to the other resources owned by government, business, and individuals. Just as economic capital represents assets of a more or less permanent nature, *capital* can be used to mean the money value of the instruments of ownership and of long-term claims to assets, and *capital markets* to mean the markets in which these instruments are exchanged.

Capital markets are the complex of institutions and mechanisms through which intermediate-term funds (loans of up to ten years maturity, for example) and long-term funds (longer-maturity loans and corporate stocks) are pooled and made available to business, governments, and individuals, and instruments already outstanding are transferred. As in the case of the money market, the capital markets are local, regional, and national in scope.

Because they deal with instruments representing longer-term funds, the

---

[1] *Economic Report of the President* (Washington, D.C.: Government Printing Office, 1978.

capital markets involve capital in the economic sense. Funds raised through debt instruments by business and individuals are normally invested in fixed assets and inventories. The proceeds of government bonds and corporate shares are often used to finance a variety of expenditures and types of assets. This usage of terms suggests a need to distinguish between the capital markets, or markets for longer-term funds, and the money market, or the market for short-term funds (obligations with a year or less to maturity).[2]

The Money Market

The money market provides for the quick and dependable transfer of short-term debt instruments used to finance the needs of business, government, agriculture, and the consumer. A distinction may be made between the direct, negotiated, or customers' money market and the impersonal, or open, market. The former is found wherever banks and other financial firms supply funds to local customers. It also includes the bank correspondents who funnel funds into larger centers such as New York for direct lending. The open money market is mainly the complex of facilities in New York where idle funds, drawn from all over the country, are transferred through intermediaries. Federal Reserve banks, commercial banks (especially the big "money-market" banks), business corporations with idle funds, insurance companies, foreign investors and borrowers (including foreign banks), finance companies, state and local governments, and individuals all make short-term funds available to other similar institutions, to the United States Treasury, and to securities brokers and dealers for "street" loans. The intermediaries are chiefly Federal Reserve banks, big commercial banks, and government securities dealers. The instruments representing the short-term funds are chiefly federal funds (excess member bank reserves), short-term government securities, bankers' acceptances, and commercial paper.[3]

The Investment Market

The investment market is similar to the capital market except that it encompasses security instruments of all maturities traded in all types of markets. In this book we shall use the term *investors* to mean those who *supply* funds to business, government, and individuals by acquiring debt and equity instruments

---

[2]Traditionally, the money market has been described as the market for short-term debt, with a year or less to maturity, and the capital market as dealing in long-term funds, both debt and equity. These designations leave a category of intermediate-term money represented by debt with from one to five or ten years to maturity. Transactions involving such debt are included in our concept of capital-market activity.

[3]For a more general description of the money market and money market instruments, see R. I. Robinson and D. Wrightsman, *Financial Markets: The Accumulation and Allocation of Wealth* (New York: McGraw-Hill Book Company, 1974), pp. 127–222.

with their savings. The term *investment market* or *financial market* means the entire market for funds, including the stock market, the bond market, the mortgage market, and so on.

Alternatively, the investment market can also be defined to include the market for *primary* and *secondary* securities. The *primary market* involves the sale of new securities for the first time by those needing funds (deficit units) to those with excess funds (surplus units). Hence, a sale of Treasury bills by the U.S. government, a new mortgage by an individual on a home, or new stock issued by a company to institutions and the public are examples of transactions occurring in the primary market. Transactions occurring in the *secondary market* are sales or exchanges involving securities that are already outstanding and held by investors. A sale of existing Treasury bills from one bank to another constitutes a transaction in the secondary market, as do sales of outstanding securities listed on the New York Stock Exchange.

Interrelations of the Money and Capital Markets

Although this book focuses on the capital market, the money and capital markets (or group of markets) are interdependent for the following reasons:

1. Suppliers may choose to direct their funds to either or both markets, depending on their investment policies and on the available rates of return.
2. Users may obtain their funds from either market. For example, a corporation needing funds for additional inventory may borrow short term by selling commercial paper or by negotiating a bank loan. It may also float a bond issue or sell stock for working capital purposes. And, if long-term rates are high, as they were in 1979, the firm might temporarily borrow short-term funds with the expectation of securing lower long-term rates in the future.
3. Funds flow back and forth between the two markets, as when the Treasury refinances maturing bills with Treasury bonds or when a bank lends the proceeds of a maturing mortgage to a business firm on a short-term basis.
4. Some institutions and facilities serve both markets; for example, dealers in short-term federal securities also buy and sell long-term bonds, and commercial banks make both intermediate- and short-term loans.
5. All long-term securities with a maturity date eventually become short-term instruments when held to maturity.
6. Yields in the long- and short-term markets are interrelated. A rise in short-term interest rates reflecting a condition of credit stringency is likely to be accompanied or followed by a more modest rise in long-term rates. Professional investors maintain the normal relationships in the maturity schedule by arbitrage. We should note, however, that money-market rates are more sensitive than longer-term rates and that geographical differences in short-term yields are less pronounced.

Perhaps the chief distinguishing characteristic of the two types of markets is that in the short-term market, as the word "money" suggests, the instruments traded are money or "near money." Federal funds (excess legal reserves of banks) are money. "Near money" instruments are exemplified by short-term governments and commercial paper, the value of which is generally subject to slight price risk. Longer-term instruments on the other hand, issued in or traded in the capital markets, especially the stock market, show considerable price variation.

The Capital Markets: Classification of Characteristics

It is useful to classify the characteristics of the capital markets in several ways.

Major Users: Variety of Types

When funds are made available to those seeking capital, the latter deliver some kind of contract or instrument representing their relationship with the investors. The demand for funds comes from five general categories of users: individuals, corporations, the federal government, state and local governments, and foreign borrowers. Individuals rely on the long-term markets primarily for financing real estate and business transactions.

All longer-term business debts of individuals and unincorporated concerns, together with the equity in farms and smaller firms, should, in a broad sense of the concept, be included as capital-market contracts. Such components, with the exception of mortgage debt and bank term loans, are omitted from our discussion. This somewhat arbitrary treatment seems valid because measurement is difficult and, for the most part, such funds are raised locally and in relatively small amounts. Consumer installment debt used for financing durable goods is also omitted. This omission is consistent with the exclusion of durable goods from the economic concept of capital. We are left, therefore, with the mortgage market, both primary and secondary, as the chief type of capital market insofar as individuals are concerned.

Transactions that involve demand for new funds by business corporations, as well as transfers of outstanding corporate instruments, are exchanged in two main markets—the corporate note and bond market, and the stock market. These markets include both primary and secondary transactions. A market for corporate intermediate-term loans may also be said to exist, but it has no separate identity, being primarily a segment of bank and insurance company loan activity.

As for government securities, our interest lies mainly in the intermediate- and long-term Treasury securities, issued in primary and traded in secondary open markets, and the obligations of state and local jurisdictions, whose market is mainly local and over the counter.

The volume of foreign financing in the American capital markets has become very substantial in the postwar period. The markets for foreign securities are comingled with the domestic corporate bond and stock markets.

Each of these markets has distinctive characteristics of supply and of demand that result in different interest rates and yields. The various segments, however, are interrelated in that they all compete for the supply of funds, and many of the groups seeking funds may choose among the various capital markets to satisfy their financial needs.

Type of Instrument or Contract: Debt or Equity

The instruments that represent funds supplied to and obtained from the capital markets are either debt instruments—personal and corporate notes, corporate bonds, mortgages, and obligations of governments—or equity instruments such as corporate stocks that are sold to raise new funds.

Maturity of Instruments

Somewhat arbitrarily, transactions represented by debt instruments with maturity of a year or less are said to take place in the money or short-term market. This leaves intermediate-term funds (up to five to ten years maturity) and long-term funds for the capital markets. As we have seen, the two markets cannot be completely distinguished.

Degree of Centralization

In the broadest sense the scope of the capital markets is very wide. A market exists wherever a bank or an insurance company makes a term loan, a corporate bond or stock is transferred, a government sells a new bond issue, or a householder borrows money on a mortgage. Capital markets are primarily local and regional, except for federal government securities and the bond and stock markets. Centralization exists, insofar as intermediate-term money is concerned, through the concentration of great banking facilities in very large cities. In recent years geographical barriers have broken down and both the supply of and the demand for long-term and even intermediate-term funds tend increasingly to flow on a national and even international basis in well-developed markets. Nevertheless, some geographical stratification persists. Regional and local markets are particularly important for both issuing and trading in obligations of smaller users of funds—local governments, local businesses, and individuals—and in the stocks of smaller corporations.

Direct versus Open-Market Transactions

When a savings and loan association makes a mortgage loan to a local customer, it is allocating the funds of a number of savers directly to the financing of real estate. The relation between the financial intermediary and the borrower is said to be *direct*. This is also the case for direct borrowing by governments and corporations and for the private sale of corporate shares by the issuer. Thousands of direct transactions occur daily between all types of users and suppliers of funds; these transactions are not centrally reported and are competitive only in a general way. They take place in a vast and segmented market. By contrast, open-market transactions in bonds, stocks, and some mortgages are competitive and immediately influence the market price of funds, as in the case of a national offering of corporate bonds at a known price and yield, or an issue of Treasury securities.

The line dividing direct and open-market transactions is not entirely distinct. In general, the latter are characterized by the use of marketing intermediaries—dealers or brokers who bring together the demand and supply of funds, provide transfer facilities, and "make a market" for various instruments. The known yields prevailing in the organized open markets do, however, influence those determined by direct bargaining.

Primary versus Secondary Transactions

Most transactions in the capital markets represent transfers of existing instruments among investors rather than the raising of new funds. For example, the volume of trading in outstanding securities vastly exceeds the value of new issues. Such mere trading does not represent capital formation. However, the prices and yields at which existing instruments are transferred help to determine the prices of new issues. Thus, when a corporation offers new bonds for money, their after-tax yield must equal or exceed the after-tax yield on outstanding bonds of the same quality and maturity.

The terms *stock market* and *bond market* usually refer to secondary markets for securities. The term *mortgage market* has, until recently, implied mainly a primary market.

Magnitude of the Markets

Later chapters include discussion of the size of capital markets in terms of the assets and obligations of the institutions involved, the magnitude of various sources and uses of funds, and the flows of funds that influence yields. At this point certain selected data (Table 1-2) are presented to indicate the size of the markets in terms of the outstanding instruments that represent longer-term funds. Individual and noncorporate debt other than mortgage debt is omitted.

United States Government debt includes all the direct guaranteed obligations. Marketable debt excludes Savings Bonds and other nontransferable instruments. Net long-term debt of state and local governments excludes sinking funds and intergovernmental duplications. Corporate net long-term debt is debt over

TABLE 1-2. Selected Media in the Capital Markets, at Year End,
1960–1978 (billions of dollars)

	1960	1965	1970	1975	1978
U.S. Treasury debt					
Total	$290	$321	$389	$577	$ 789
Marketable	189	215	248	363	488
Due in over one year	115	121	124	200	259
Federally sponsored agency debt					
(nonguaranteed)	8	14	39	82	109
State and local government debt					
Total	75	107	156	249	301
Long-term securities	67	95	131	214	267
Corporate long-term debt					
Net long-term	139	209	360	611	809[b]
Bonds outstanding (domestic)	85	116	185	292	323
Corporate stock (domestic, at market value)					
Listed	335	573	681	719	866
Traded over the counter[a]	53[b]	181	203	208	262
Mortgage debt					
Total	207	325	473	801	1172
Residential (1–4-family)	142	220	298	491	760

[a]Includes investment company shares.
[b]Estimated.
Sources: *Federal Reserve Bulletin;* Federal Reserve. *Flow-of-Funds Accounts; Treasury Bulletin; Survey of Current Business;* Securities and Exchange Commission, *Statistical Bulletin.*

one year to original maturity and includes: mortgages, term loans, and net long-term trade credit. Corporate bonds outstanding are most important for our purposes. The corporate stock figures include intercompany ownership of shares, but exclude the value of stock of closely held companies.

The corporate stock figures are the most volatile of all the groups. Corporate stock also contrasts with the obligations listed in the other major categories in that it is the only group where the security instrument is not contractual in nature. In viewing the data in Table 1-2 a few observations are in order. First, there has been a rapid rise in the amount of outstanding debt in all the categories. Since 1960, based on percentages, the growth in debt has been the greatest in Federally sponsored agency debt followed by corporate long-term debt and mortgage debt. Percentage wise, state and local debt has grown faster than U.S. government debt since 1960. Nevertheless, the rapid rise in U.S. government debt since 1975 has been very substantial when compared to historical levels on either percentage or absolute terms.

The rapid rise in mortgage debt is attributable to higher real estate construction costs, higher loan-to-value ratios, and expanded ownership of real estate. It is not surprising, in view of the lackluster performance of the stock market, that corporate stock has lost its dominant position as the largest single category in dollar amounts outstanding. Low stock prices have also been a factor in the substantial growth of total corporate debt, as corporations have apparently preferred this latter form of financing, in spite of higher interest rates, to the potential dilution of earnings and delays in receiving monies that often accompany stock issues. Since the common stock figures in Table 1-2 are market values, it is not uncommon to see substantial declines (or rises) in stock values from year to year. As will be seen later, it is the sharp reduction or little appreciation in equity values in recent years that has caused considerable problems for the capital market as a whole.

Net Suppliers and Users of Funds

Table 1-3 shows the total financial assets and liabilities of various sectors including households, businesses, state and local governments, U.S. government, and financial institutions at the end of 1978. It is readily seen that households have been large net suppliers (surplus units) of funds to the financial markets, and businesses and governments have been large borrowers (deficit units) of funds.

Financial institutions are substantial participants in the financial markets. The institutions included as financial institutions in the table are basically the same as those discussed in this book and, in addition, include sales finance companies and one or two other minor institutions. Although financial institutions are net suppliers of funds to the financial market, they essentially "net out" their assets and liabilities in performing an intermediation function. That is, they generally have received funds from individuals and others, issuing their own securities in exchange. In turn, they have taken these funds so received and lent them to government and business.

TABLE 1-3. Financial Assets and Liabilities of Various Sectors, December 31, 1978 (billions of dollars)

Sector	Total Financial Assets	Total Liabilities	Surplus	Deficit
Households	3,385.2	1,207.8	2,177.4	
Nonfinancial business	814.7	1,480.4		665.7
State and local governments	206.3	306.4		100.1
U.S. government	186.2	721.5		535.3
Financial institutions	2,989.4	2,829.5	159.9	
Rest of world	412.1	404.7	7.4	
Total	7,993.9	6,950.3	2,344.7	1,301.1

[a]Includes personal trusts and nonprofit organizations.
[b]Excess of total assets over liabilities consists of gold and corporate shares other than investment company shares less minor discrepancies that are not included in sector assets.
Source: *Federal Reserve Bulletin;* Federal Reserve *Flow-of-Funds 1978 Outstandings.*

At the end of 1978, of financial assets of $2,989 billion held by financial institutions, net credit market instruments held issued by deficit units in business, government, and others amounted to $2,466 billion. On the other hand, of the $2,830 billion in total liabilities, approximately $2,234 billion represented claims due surplus units (primarily households) with asset holdings in the form of demand deposits, time, and savings deposits, and insurance reserves.

The total liabilities for *nonfinancial business* of $1,480 billion for 1978 do not include corporate shares, which represent ownership accounts. When analyzing corporate accountability at the aggregate level, however, it is occasionally useful to include corporate shares in the totals to determine the total amount "owed" to investors. If the $1,025 billion in outstanding corporate shares at the end of 1978 were added to the listed liabilities, the total for nonfinancial business would amount to $2,505 billion or a net deficit of *financial* liabilities exceeding *financial* assets by $1,691 billion.

Financial Institutions and
Financial Intermediaries: Distinction

The terms "financial institutions" and "financial intermediaries," although often used interchangeably, technically are not the same. *Financial institutions,* the broader of the two terms, encompasses not only those institutions involved in the intermediation function described above, but also those that function primarily as brokers or agents in the financial markets by bringing buyers and sellers together through the use of their facilities. Brokerage houses that buy and sell securities for customer accounts are financial institutions, but not financial intermediaries. Insurance companies that sell only term insurance with no savings feature are not functioning as financial intermediaries in the strict sense even though the insurance premiums might be invested in stocks, bonds, or mortgages. A life insurance company that sells policies with a savings feature, such as an ordinary-life policy, is performing an intermediation function when it invests the savings portion in securities or mortgages. Property and liability insurance companies are not intermediaries in the strict sense because they do not issue liabilities in their insurance commitments. Conversely, it could be contended that the substantial surplus and reserve funds that are temporarily invested in capital-market securities would theoretically be returned to policyholders or shareholders after all claims and expenses were paid. In this respect, excess funds over and above expected losses and expenses are technically entrusted to them and they might be considered as intermediaries. While perhaps somewhat arbitrarily, we have included property and liability insurance companies in our discussion of intermediaries.

Financial intermediaries intersperse themselves between surplus units—those units with excess funds—and deficit units that need funds. Intermediaries receive funds from surplus units, paying them a rate of interest on funds left on deposit and supply funds to the deficit units (users) charging a higher rate of interest. Thus, intermediaries relieve the market of primary securities such as mortgages, bonds, and stocks issued by the deficit users of capital and substitute their own—indirect securities or financial assets such as savings certificates, and deposit accounts, whose safety and liquidity warrant a lower interest rate. The spread between the yields paid on primary securities and those paid on indirect securities is the intermediaries' compensation for the special services they perform.

As with most financial intermediaries they are not always performing a pure intermediation function. Yet it is difficult to separate the nonintermediation and intermediation functions of most institutions and, hence, we tend to classify an institution as an intermediary if (1) its primary function is one of intermediation, or (2) the institution is a large factor in terms of total resources committed to the intermediation process.

The more important financial institutions that fit these specifications are savings and loan associations, life insurance companies, mutual savings banks, credit unions, pension funds, and government lending agencies, among others. In addition, we include commercial banks, which, although they perform numerous other functions, are a major factor in the intermediation process and act as financial intermediaries by accepting deposits and purchasing securities such as state and local bonds, Federal government securities, and mortgages.

Classification of Institutions

The instruments or contracts that represent claims to or ownership of assets are issued and traded through a complex of institutions. These institutions serve as channels through which those needing longer-term funds draw on the savings of others. Some savings are invested directly by the savers themselves, and some flow to other users without an intermediary. But for the most part, the savings of millions of saving units flow to other users through a host of institutions. To quote Kuznets, "Financial intermediaries obviate the need for each group of savers to seek out and choose among the wide variety of capital users and, conversely, for each group of capital users to seek out and choose among the wide variety of savers."[4] We may expand this concept to include the transfer of already outstanding marketable instruments. The development of institutions has provided a vastly more effective use of savings and greater liquidity of capital issues.

The American financial system includes a variety of institutions. In this short

---

[4] Simon Kuznets, *Capital in the American Economy: Its Formation and Financing* (Princeton, N.J.: Princeton University Press, 1961), p. 31.

book we direct our attention to those institutions that form a major part of or serve the various capital markets. These may be classified as follows:

Deposit-type institutions:
  Commercial banks; Federal Reserve Banks
  Mutual savings banks
  Savings and loan associations
  Credit unions
Insurance and pension institutions:
  Legal reserve life insurance companies
  Property and liability insurance companies
  Noninsured private pension funds
  State and local government retirement funds
  Federal retirement and insurance funds
Investment institutions:
  Investment companies
  Real estate investment trusts
  Mortgage pools and trusts
Government agencies:
  Federal budget agencies
  Federally sponsored agencies

The common characteristic of these institutions is that their assets consist primarily of financial instruments, a substantial portion of which represents intermediate- or long-term debt or equity of deficit users. The first two groups—deposit and insurance institutions—are further characterized by the fact that their liabilities usually represent contractual obligations to savers.[5] They are real financial intermediaries, receiving funds from individuals, business, and government, and channeling these funds to users on intermediate or long terms. A net increase in their liabilities (and assets), other than from transfers and market revaluation, reflects a net increase in productive capital and an expansion of economic activity.

Investment companies buy securities of many different types, ranging from money market securities to common stocks and long-term bonds, and issue bonds or shares against these portfolios. Real estate investment trusts, as expected, tend to specialize and place most of their funds in direct ownership of real estate properties, in short-term construction loans, and in long-term mortgages.

Federal credit agencies could be classed as a separate institution specializing mainly in mortgage investment. They are discussed in Chapter 8, along with the financing of the federal government proper.

---

[5]The exception is the property insurance group whose obligations are not dollar contracts with savers but services owed to customers.

Certain omissions from the list should be noted. Fraternal life insurance organizations and the insurance departments of mutual savings banks are relatively small in relation to the "legal reserve" companies, and complete historical data are not available. Bank trustees manage a vast aggregate of assets, but they do not own these assets, in the strict sense, and issue no obligations against them. Investment development companies and small-business investment companies are too specialized to be included in a short book. Sales finance companies obtain some funds in the capital markets, but their activities are confined largely to financing consumer durables.

Two financial marketing institutions play a prominent role in the capital markets by serving as middlemen. The first consists of investment bankers and mortgage companies, which merchandise mainly debt and equity instruments. The second includes securities brokers and dealers, securities exchanges, and mortgage brokers, which aid in the transfer of already outstanding instruments. The work of these marketing types is discussed briefly in Chapters 8 to 12.

```
22222222222222222222222222222222222222222222222222222222222222222222222222222222
22222222222222222222222222222222222222222222222222222222222222222222222222222222
2222222222222222222222222222222222222222   222   22222222222222222222222222222222
2222222222222222222222222222222222222222   222   22222222222222222222222222222222
2222222222222222222222222222222222222222   222   22222222222222222222222222222222
2222222222222222222222222222222222222222   222   22222222222222222222222222222222
2222222222222222222222222222222222222222   222   22222222222222222222222222222222
2222222222222222222222222222222222222222   222   22222222222222222222222222222222
2222222222222222222222222222222222222222   222   22222222222222222222222222222222
2222222222222222222222222222222222222222   222   22222222222222222222222222222222
22222222222222222222222222222222222222222222222222222222222222222222222222222222
22222222222222222222222222222222222222222222222222222222222222222222222222222222
```

Nature of the Capital
Formation Process

THE growing institutionalization of the savings and investment process has attracted much attention and, in some respects, has caused a great deal of concern over the last decade. The rapid growth of insurance companies, pension funds, commercial banks, savings and loan associations, and other financial institutions since World War II makes it appear that this phenomenon has occurred only rather recently. Although the rate of growth has varied in the past, the institutionalization of the savings and investment process has been evident at least since the Civil War and, in fact, has paralleled the growth of our industrialized society. This result is not surprising if one assumes that an orderly and complex society necessarily requires a well-developed financial market system. The growth of financial institutions, in whatever form, should be viewed as a logical and rational step in the economic expansion, development, and capital formation process of a highly industrialized society.

This chapter discusses some basic concepts that are helpful in understanding the role of financial intermediaries and individuals in the savings and investment process. The type of industrial environment that is conducive to a favorable growth in financial intermediaries is also discussed. Finally, brief mention is made of the theoretical process that financial intermediaries and individuals undertake in determining what assets to hold or liabilities to assume.

The Capital Formation Process and
the Rise of Capital Markets[1]

Although some goods might be exchanged through barter, in most primitive societies the savers and users of capital were the same. The amount saved by a family or productive unit was generally reinvested in the property and, consequently, there was no need for an intervening third party to hold assets or funds for one unit and lend these funds to another unit. Similarly, it is possible to imagine a modern economy where there is a high level of savings and investment yet where no need for financial intermediaries exists. In this situation each of the economy's spending units—individual, business, or government—would have a balanced budget on income and total spending, and (1) each unit's current income would equal the sum of current expenses plus expenditures for fixed assets, and (2) each unit's saving would exactly match its investment in physical assets. In such an economy of balanced budgets no securities would be issued by spending units, no financial assets would be accumulated, and the savings and investment process would function without the need for financial intermediaries.

On the other hand, it is possible to visualize an economy that is highly conducive to financial intermediaries. In such an economy all current and capital expenditures could be made by units that had no current income, and all current income could be received by units that spend nothing. One group of spending units would have a deficit equal to the amount of its expenditures while the other group would have a surplus equal to its current income. The spending units would tend to issue securities equal in total to the amount of their deficit and the surplus units would tend to accumulate financial securities equal to their surpluses. As a result, security issues and financial-asset accumulations would tend to approximate total GNP or aggregate expenditures and a very favorable environment would exist for financial intermediaries.

In our own economy we have been considerably closer to the first case. That is, with few exceptions, the amount of primary securities issued by spending units in a year has been historically averaging only about 10 percent of GNP. *Primary securities,* viewed in their broadest context, are those issues that represent direct obligations of the spending units and include (1) corporate and foreign bonds, (2) common and preferred stocks, (3) farm and nonfarm mortgages, (4) consumer debt, (5) U.S. government and agency debt, (6) state and local debt, and (7) other miscellaneous debt, such as commercial paper.[2]

---

[1] This discussion follows much of the reasoning contained in John G. Gurley and Edward S. Shaw, *Money in a Theory of Finance* (Washington, D.C.: The Brookings Institution, 1960).

[2] As this book focuses on capital-market instruments and capital-market financial institutions, consumer debt will be excluded from further discussion in subsequent chapters. We include it here to give an overall view of total primary securities, including those issued by individuals, as well as corporations and governments. In addition, certain corporate debts, such as commercial paper and short-term loans, are primary securities but are short-term in

Overall, the percentage of primary securities to GNP throughout the period from 1965-1978 (Table 2-1) has been more than the historical level of 10 percent. In the late 1970s, however, the ratio rose substantially, from 8.3 percent in 1965 to more than 17 percent in 1978.[3] Although the ratio of primary securities to GNP is considerably closer to zero than to 100 percent, it is still sufficient to generate substantial growth for financial intermediaries.

Major categories contributing to the sharp increase in the ratio have been mortgages, government debt (both U.S. and state and local), and consumer debt. The growth in mortgage debt in recent years can be attributed, in part, to the high demands for housing, government housing programs, and the rapid increase in the cost of construction. Heavy government spending leading to large deficits resulted in substantial issues of government debt. Consumer debt increased sharply as family incomes rose, allowing for more capacity to carry additional debt, and fears of further inflation made early purchases advisable. Hence, the rise in the percentage of primary securities to GNP has placed an even greater burden on the financial system, and the need for an efficient and effective system is as important as ever.

Direct and Indirect Securities

As noted previously, in a world of balanced budgets, where each spending unit's current and capital expenditures were financed entirely from its current income, aggregate expenditures in the economy would be internally financed and would approximate GNP. In a world where deficits and surpluses exist among spending units, some expenditures would be financed externally. The extent of such financing would be measured by the sum of the deficits (or surpluses) undertaken (generated) by the spending units. If GNP is $2,100 billion and the sum of all spending units'deficits is $210 billion, 10 percent of GNP is financed *externally* and 90 percent is financed *internally*.

External finance may be direct (primary) or indirect. The distinction between the two forms depends on the nature of the assets held by the surplus units. The financing is called *indirect* if the surplus units acquire claims on financial intermediaries, for example, savings deposits and pension balances. It is *direct* if surplus units acquire claims issued by the deficit users, such as common stocks, bonds, mortgages, and so on, which are not supplied by financial intermediaries.

Although the proportion of GNP that is financed externally has not changed much over the past half-century, the relative proportion of direct and indirect securities representing the total amount of externally financed funds has changed

---

nature and, consequently, not capital-market instruments. Discussion of these latter instruments likewise is not included in later chapters.

[3] In general, the figures in Table 2-1 correspond to the data in other chapters of the book. Slight differences may exist between the figures based on the Federal Reserve's flow-of-funds data and data issued by trade associations or that from other sources.

TABLE 2-1. Net Yearly Primary Security Issues of Spending Units and the Total Issues as a Percentage of Yearly Gross National Product, 1965–1978 (billions of dollars)

Net Issues	1965	1970	1975	1976	1977	1978
U.S. Treasury debt[a]	$ 1.3	$ 12.9	$ 85.8	$ 69.1	$ 57.6	$ 55.1
Federally sponsored agency issues	2.0	8.4	2.2	3.4	6.5	21.2
State and local debt (general)	6.7	8.9	13.2	17.4	24.8	26.3
Corporate and foreign bonds	8.1	23.3	36.4	37.2	36.1	32.1
Corporate stocks	8.0	10.5	10.7	11.9	3.8	3.1
Mortgages	27.4	29.9	57.2	87.1	134.0	145.9
Consumer debt	9.6	5.9	9.4	23.6	35.0	50.5
Other debt[b]	7.5	7.5	8.6	15.3	25.1	36.1
Total primary securities	$ 70.6	$107.3	$ 223.5	$ 265.0	$ 322.9	$ 370.3
Gross national product	$688.1	$982.4	$1,528.8	$1,702.2	$1,899.5	$2,127.6
Primary securities to GNP	10.3%	10.9%	14.6%	15.6%	17.0%	17.4%

[a]Includes budget agency debt.
[b]Excluding bank loans and open-market paper.
Source: Federal Reserve *Flow-of-Funds Accounts*. (Totals may not add, because of rounding.)

TABLE 2-2. Purchases of Primary Security Issues by Individuals and Financial Intermediaries (Representative Years, 1965–1978)

	1965	1970	1975	1976	1977	1978
Total primary securities issued in year	$70.6	$107.3	$223.5	$265.0	$322.9	$370.3
Purchased by private financial intermediaries	61.7	76.5	119.9	191.2	249.6	289.6
Net purchases by individuals and others[a]	8.9	30.8	103.6	73.8	73.3	80.7

[a]Includes households, personal trusts, nonprofit organizations, farms, and nonfinancial corporate business.
Source: Federal Reserve *Flow-of-Funds Accounts*.

significantly. Indirectly financed securities—those issued by financial inter-mediaries—have risen sharply while the proportion that is directly financed—those issued by deficit units directly to surplus units—has dropped substantially. Thus, a growing share of primary issues has been sold to financial intermediaries rather than directly to the surplus units. The implication is that either surplus spending units—mostly individuals—have expressed a preference for the financial inter-mediary issues over the direct issues of deficit units or else they have been in-hibited in their efforts to acquire direct issue securities. In general, it appears that the former holds, although the size of certain direct securities such as mort-gages and the minimum order size for some U.S. government debt securities have been inhibiting factors to direct participation by surplus units. In any event, it appears that surplus units by holding indirect securities have opted for lower returns and lower risk than they might receive otherwise from holding a larger proportion of direct securities.

Table 2-2 shows the relative amounts of primary securities (broad definition) acquired by individuals and by financial institutions. The amount of primary securities purchased by individuals and others declined sharply in the early 1970s (not shown) and, in fact, financial institutions added more primary securities to their accounts than the net increase in amounts issued in 1972 and 1973. The large decline was attributable to purchases of consumer credit ac-counts by banks and sales of securities by individuals and others. In 1975–1978, the acquisition proportions returned to more historic norms but financial institutions still dominated the purchases of primary security issues.

In summary, surplus units have accumulated financial assets in total amounts that, over long periods, have been fairly steady as a percentage of GNP. These accumulations over time, however, have been more and more in the form of indirect financial assets—issues of major financial intermediaries—and relatively less in the form of primary securities such as corporate bonds, stocks, and mortgages.

Financial Intermediaries:
Asset and Liability Structure

This section briefly analyzes the theoretical asset and liability structure of a typical financial intermediary. A changing intermediary structure should be viewed as a logical response by a financial institution in meeting the needs of investors in a competitive environment.[4] Such a structure, however, must neces-sarily be modified according to the constraints imposed by governing authorities.

---

[4] In the discussion that follows and especially when the meaning is clear, the term "investor" will be used interchangeably and to mean both surplus and deficit spending units. Although technically the term "investor" has generally been applied to those who take an active part in the investment process, while "savers" have been considered those who adopt a passive role, the distinction is becoming more obscure and is not of importance to the discussion in this chapter.

Financial Institution Asset and Liability Structure

The formation, growth and the evolving asset and liability structure of financial institutions has been shaped by four major factors: (1) the need to fulfill the demands for funds by users as well as serving as a depository of funds for surplus units, (2) the legal constraints on the various aspects of financial intermediary operations in order to ensure safety of principal, (3) the nature of the markets serving the demand and supply for funds that are amenable to the intermediation function, and (4) increased competition among institutions, resulting in a search for new markets and different financial instruments. Financial intermediaries have grown to fill a basic need in a developing economy, yet they have been substantially influenced and restricted by regulatory agencies established by state and federal governments which have formed legal and implied constraints on various aspects of financial intermediary operations. In succeeding sections the more important of these constraints will be indicated.

Dual Objectives of Regulatory Constraints

Historically speaking, legal constraints have been imposed on financial intermediaries to (1) foster competition in the demand and supply of funds, on the one hand, and (2) to ensure the profitability and financial stability of the institutions on the other. In most respects, these dual objectives are inherently incompatible and public policy has dictated that the two goals should be balanced.

Encouraging too much competition results in marginal firms leaving the industry, which, in a purely competitive environment, is normally viewed as a favorable consequence. Public policy, however, especially since the Great Depression, has deemed this to be too great a burden to bear for those who have entrusted their funds to an institution primarily for safekeeping rather than for profit. As a result, financial intermediaries find themselves in a more regulated market than that experienced by the average industrial firm. The consequence of such regulation is that local monopolies may be fostered, inefficiencies may arise, and marginal firms may remain in business for a much longer time than would normally be the case. The benefit and hope is that, through regulation, the stability and safety of one's principal funds are better assured.

The legal constraints customarily imposed on the institutions in varying degrees pertain to the (1) types of deposits, payments, and contributions they can accept from surplus units; (2) the rate paid on these funds; (3) the services they can offer or operate; (4) the type of assets or claims issued by deficit units that they can hold; and (5) the rates they pay on their deposits or charge to their customers.

Perhaps the most significant development over the last twenty years involving all financial institutions has been the relaxing of the legal restrictions and the general push for more competition. Major reasons for this change in emphasis have been the growing strength of financial institutions and expanded insurance coverage of deposits, which have diminished the need for the safety of principal objective. The relaxation of restrictions has taken the form of (1) increased competition for time and savings deposits; (2) expanded areas of investment, particularly for banks, insurance companies of all types, and savings associations; (3) increased maximum percentages invested in any particular type of asset; and (4) fewer filing requirements and easier entry into new financial areas. Nevertheless, financial institutions are still constrained by numerous laws and traditions that have remained through the years. These constraints have restricted the assets and liabilities of at least some of the financial institutions to an asset and liability structure that they might not prefer. But to others it is a small price to pay for the overall stablility that is desirable in our financial markets.

The Hedging Principle

Operating within the constraints mentioned above, financial institutions are free to choose the asset and liability structure they want to pursue. It is often said that the asset structure of an institution is determined by the liabilities it accepts or that an institution determines its assets, *given* its liabilities. We say that financial institutions are open-ended on their liability structure. That is, they stand willing to accept certain types of liabilities without restrictions on the amounts received. Banks, for instance, are generally willing to accept almost unlimited amounts of several types of savings and checking accounts. Insurance companies accept long-term liabilities in the form of insurance policies, and mutual funds are open-ended in the amount of fund shares they will issue. Presumably, this process continues at least as long as the financial institution can relend or reinvest the funds at a rate of return greater than the cost of obtaining and placing the funds.

The basic rule applied by financial institutions in structuring their assets, given their liabilities, is the *principle of hedging*. If an institution accepts a liability, say, in the form of a deposit that is short-term in nature, it should offset or *hedge* the liability by lending on a short-term basis for the same length of time. In theory, as the asset matures it is used to pay off the debt that comes due at the same time. Presumably, the financial institution is content to make its profit on the spread between the interest rate charged on the loan to the deficit unit (borrower) and the interest rate paid on the liability to the surplus unit (depositor).

Although the concept of hedging as applied to financial asset and liability management is an oversimplification, it is nevertheless helpful in analyzing the financial data in later chapters. The concept is illustrated in Figure 2-1, where panel A shows the perfectly hedged position described earlier, where the asset holding period exactly offsets the time to maturity (holding period) of the liability.

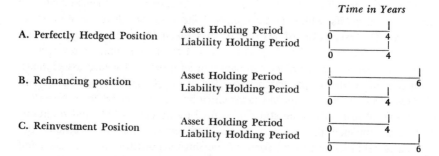

Figure 2-1. Comparison of Asset and Liability Holding Periods, Showing Hedged, Refinancing, and Reinvestment Positions

Even ignoring legal constraints, most institutions probably would maintain only an approximate hedged position in order to have greater flexibility and possibly greater profitability. Lack of an overall hedged position for the aggregate of assets and liabilities held by a financial institution, forces the institution to face either a reinvestment or a refinancing decision. For instance, in panel B, Figure 2-1, the institution accepts a liability for a shorter period of time (four years) than the asset in which it places these funds (six years). When the liability matures, the institution faces a refinancing decision if the funds are withdrawn by the original depositor and not returned to the institution. (In actuality, of course, the institution need only concern itself with the net position after aggregating the maturities and amounts for all assets and liabilities.) Panel C shows that the institution faces a reinvestment decision at the end of four years if the asset matures before the loan is paid off. That is, it must reinvest the funds for two more years until the liability is liquidated. In either case, B or C, the institution is said to be speculating on the differences in asset and liability holding periods and its profit margin may be greater or smaller, depending upon the refinancing or reinvestment rates paid, or received, respectively.

As the latter positions (panel B or C) are not generally acceptable to financial institutions and could result in cash management problems, most firms will attempt to structure their assets and liabilities to conform more or less to the hedged position (panel A). Unfortunately, legal constraints have unwittingly limited some institutions to an unhedged position and, as a result, created unnecessary market inefficiencies.

Although, as noted previously, the hedging concept is far from perfect, it is helpful in understanding a financial institution's asset and liability structure. A preponderance of short-term liabilities normally should be offset by short-term assets, and long-term liabilities should be offset with a substantial amount of long-term assets. This basic understanding of how a financial institution should work should be useful in analyzing long-run changes in financial intermediary asset and liability accounts discussed in later chapters.

TABLE 2-3. Estimated Maturity of Asset and Liability Holdings
of Representative Financial Institutions

Financial Institution	Total Assets/ Liabilities (billions of dollars) 12/31/78	Maturity Structure Based on Initial Holding Period		
			Less than Five Years (%)	Greater than Five Years (%)
Commercial banks	$1,303.9[a]	Assets	80	20
		Liabilities	85	15
Life insurance companies	$ 389.0	Assets	10	90
		Liabilities	12	88
Savings and loan associations	$ 523.6	Assets	12	88
		Liabilities	90	10
Mutual savings banks	$ 158.2	Assets	15	85
		Liabilities	86	14

[a]Last-Wednesday-of-month Series.
Sources: *Federal Reserve Bulletin;* American Council of Life Insurance, *Life Insurance Fact Book.*

Table 2-3 shows the estimated principal asset and liability structures of four representative financial institutions divided into maturities of *five years or less* and those *greater than five years.* The estimated figures in the table are the percentages of assets and liabilities held in each maturity range. The table shows that, as a group, commercial banks have a high percentage of their assets as well as liabilities in short-term instruments. At the end of 1978 it was estimated that about 80 to 85 percent of both their assets and liabilities were of a short-term nature, hence, a substantially hedged position.[5] Similarly, life insurance companies, with a preponderance of long-term liabilities in the form of insurance policies and retirement obligations, also exhibited a substantially hedged position in that a large proportion of their assets (90 percent) were in long-term securities such as stocks, bonds, and mortgages.

The data in the table for savings and loan associations and mutual savings banks suggest a rather poorly hedged position. These institutions have relatively short-term liabilities (savings deposits) and comparatively long-term holdings (mortgages). More than 80 percent of their liabilities are in relatively short term obligations (less than five years), while more than 75 percent of their assets are of a long-term nature (greater than five years). In rapidly changing markets when interest rates are rising, such as in 1974, 1978, and late 1979, when savings and time deposits were transferred on short notice from one institution to another, savings and loan associations and mutual savings banks are likely to

---

[5]Estimates based on Federal Reserve data, including "Ownership of Marketable Securities" and flow-of-funds accounts. Analysis of maturities based on initial maturity period of debt.

experience a cash flow problem, face a "refinancing" decision and hence seek funds from other sources. In the event of savings withdrawals, they will seek additional funds, such as borrowings from Federal Home Loan Banks, or else sharply curtail their lending activities. In either case, the consequences tend to disrupt their operations and the effective functioning of the mortgage market.

The primary reason for the deviation from a hedged position by savings and loan associations and mutual savings banks can be traced to the legal restrictions placed on these institutions in the management of their asset holdings. Although, as we will see later, there has been some relaxation, these constraints have generally restricted savings and loan and mutual savings banks to lending in the mortgage market, which is long-term by nature, while their liabilities—savings shares and deposits—tend to be relatively short-term. Based on the hedging principle, analysis of probable future direction for these institutions would suggest an attempt by mutual savings banks and savings and loan associations to offer either longer-term liabilities or else hold shorter-term assets.

Preferences for Asset Holdings

Another influence on the functioning of our capital markets concerns the selection of assets to hold or liabilities to assume by individuals, firms, or financial institutions. Basically, the participants in the financial markets must choose among the assets to hold and the liabilities to assume as well as choosing whether to invest or spend the funds they have in their possession. It is the interest rate received or paid on the various security instruments and the corresponding rate changes among these instruments that effectively facilitates the process of balancing the demand for funds with the supply of funds consistent with a given level of gross national product.

The Function of Interest Rates
and the Market Clearing Process

Investment or saving, as opposed to current consumption, can be characterized as *present sacrifice* for *future benefit*. As the present is well known, and the future unpredictable, the *certain* present sacrifice is exchanged for an *uncertain* future benefit. In order for investors to hold assets yielding uncertain benefits, they must expect the value of the assets at the end of the holding period to exceed their initial value, assuming the absence of inflation and restrictive markets.

In a similar fashion, firms that borrow large sums either directly from investors or indirectly from financial intermediaries are exchanging a certain present benefit, which could be received by spending the funds so obtained for current consumption, for some future uncertain stream in the expectation of receiving a return over and above the cost of the funds borrowed. In the absence of diversification effects, the rate so received must be expected to exceed the cost of the borrowed funds.

Accordingly, based on the laws of supply and demand, interest rates will continually adjust so that the desired asset and liability balances for individuals, firms, and financial intermediaries, along with the appropriate maturity structure for each asset and liability account, are brought into balance.

The interest rate received on each asset held, or paid on each liability assumed, is a function of the pure time value of money—called the riskless rate—and the degree of uncertainty or risk associated with the given security instrument. Risk includes such things as the risk of default, inflation, expropriation, and so forth. Changes in the time value of money (riskless rate) occur as a result of changes in the consumption and investment preferences of investors. For example, if inflation is an important consideration, surplus spending units could be expected to consume more of their present income for fear of higher prices. Or, alternatively, they would demand a higher interest in order to be persuaded to postpone consumption. This occurred in 1974 and 1978-79 when the high rate of inflation caused interest rates to rise to unprecedented levels.

Two important conclusions follow from this analysis. The rate of inflation and the riskless rate of interest tend to move together because higher rates must be paid to encourage investors to postpone consumption when prices are rising; the longer the prediction period, the greater the uncertainty and, therefore, the higher the risk premium demanded by investors.

The level of interest rates and the adjustment process are important to the effective functioning of financial markets and financial institutions. Any abrupt changes in interest rates are likely to result in more erratic market operations as investors, and others, substantially alter their consumption and/or investment patterns in light of the changes.

The Choice of Asset Holdings

The selection of assets or combination of assets to hold by investors is a function of the expected return of each asset and the associated risk. By associated risk we mean the inherent risk in the asset itself tempered by any diversification factors that reduce the risk that results from combining the given asset with other assets already held in the portfolio. This latter aspect, frequently referred to as the portfolio problem, is that component of risk that can be diversified away by a judicious combination of asset holdings in a portfolio.

In any event, the risk among competing investments is by no means constant over the business cycle and investors will often adjust their portfolios to reflect this change. Holding other factors constant, federal government securities, being riskless instruments, are generally not affected by the business cycle as are other types of securities. When the economy is booming, it is not surprising to see the yields on high-grade corporate bonds move closer (or the yield differential decline) to federal bonds of the same maturity.

In general, investors are assumed to be trying to attain that mix of asset holdings that gives them the greatest benefit. This process more or less continues indefinitely as asset holdings are constantly adjusted to reflect differences in market factors, interest rates, and attitudes toward risk. One of the areas of interest in subsequent chapters is the study of new methods or procedures and new security instruments, as well as changes in the holdings of investors and financial intermediaries as the market participants adapt to changing market conditions. Many of the major shifts that have occurred in asset and liability holdings over the last few years can be traced to changes in the level of interest rates, the number and types of new securities offered, and the degree of competition among financial intermediaries, particularly with regard to the competition for savings. Many of the concepts briefly discussed in this chapter will hopefully prove helpful in analyzing changes and in predicting future directions in the capital markets.

```
3333333333333333333333333333333333333333333333333333333333333333333333333333333333
3333333333333333333333333333333333333333333333333333333333333333333333333333333333
3333333333333333333333333333333333        333     333        3333333333333333333333333333333333
3333333333333333333333333333333333        333     333        3333333333333333333333333333333333
3333333333333333333333333333333333        333     333        3333333333333333333333333333333333
3333333333333333333333333333333333        333     333        3333333333333333333333333333333333
3333333333333333333333333333333333        333     333        3333333333333333333333333333333333
3333333333333333333333333333333333        333     333        3333333333333333333333333333333333
3333333333333333333333333333333333        333     333        3333333333333333333333333333333333
3333333333333333333333333333333333        333     333        3333333333333333333333333333333333
3333333333333333333333333333333333        333     333        3333333333333333333333333333333333
3333333333333333333333333333333333333333333333333333333333333333333333333333333333
3333333333333333333333333333333333333333333333333333333333333333333333333333333333
```

Commercial and Federal Reserve Banks

WE shall first discuss the institutions that accept deposit funds. Their role in the capital markets is to serve as funnels through which savings are invested in intermediate- and long-term instruments. Because of their fiduciary responsibility to depositors, their investment activity is heavily regulated. They are allowed only small holdings of corporate stock and are restricted to "investment-grade" securities in their purchases of corporate and municipal bonds.

Four important deposit institutions are involved in the capital markets: commercial banks, mutual savings banks, savings and loan associations, and credit unions. Commercial and Federal Reserve banks are discussed in this chapter. Federal Reserve banks are not deposit-type institutions, but their special relations with commercial banks, their holdings of federal obligations, their influence on yields, and their general influence on financial markets require our attention, and accordingly, are discussed at the end of this chapter.

Commercial Banks

As of June 30, 1978, there were 14,698 commercial banks in the United States, operating about 50,000 offices, including about 35,000 branches and additional offices. Of this total, 4,616 were national banks, all members of the Federal Reserve System, with total assets of $671 billion; 1,005 state-chartered member banks with $157 billion in assets; and 8,760 state nonmember banks with $327 billion in assets. The rate of growth in total assets in the last decade has been the greatest in *state nonmember banks,* which is also the largest single category in terms of number of banks. Nevertheless, members of the Federal Reserve System still control over 71 percent of all bank assets.

The traditional role of commercial banks has been to furnish short-term funds to individuals, business, agriculture, and government; however, through the years they have become essentially department stores of finance. Their multifunctional role includes substantial activity in the granting of intermediate-term credit through term loans, and long-term credit through the acquisition of government and corporate bonds, and mortgages. More recently, they have expanded into such areas as computer processing for business, leasing, insurance and mutual fund sales, and other businesses that have been closely allied with banking.

Sources of Funds for Capital-Market Assets

No exact relationship exists between specific sources and uses of bank funds. Funds are derived from demand deposits, savings and time deposits, stockholders' investments and firm bank borrowings, including federal funds (which are short-term loans from other banks) and debenture bond issues. Because the turnover of savings and time deposits is so much slower than that of demand deposits (one compared with about sixty times per year), these, together with net worth, comprise the major source for investment in capital-market assets. Time deposits constitute almost 60 percent of total deposits (Table 3-1). Their growth relative to demand deposits has been largely responsible for the shift in bank activity from specialization in short-term financing toward general financing. With few exceptions, time and savings deposits have expanded steadily since the 1950s, reflecting the general growth of savings in the economy, the rising level of interest rates, and the increasing flexibility banks have been allowed by regulatory agencies in competing for these deposits.

Bank growth can be greatly influenced by the limits imposed on time deposits by the regulatory authorities (Federal Reserve Board and Federal Deposit

TABLE 3-1. Demand Deposits, Savings and Time Deposits, and Capital Accounts, All Commercial Banks, at Year End, 1960–1978 (billions of dollars)

	1960	1965	1970	1973	1975	1978[b]
Demand deposits[a]	$156.8	$185.3	$217.3	$273.2	$281.8	$ 418.9
Savings and time deposits[a]	71.6	146.7	229.0	358.2	450.6	630.0
Capital accounts	21.0	30.3	43.0	56.9	69.1	95.5
Total	$249.4	$362.3	$489.3	$688.3	$801.5	$1,144.4

[a]Excluding interbank deposits.
[b]Last-Wednesday-of-Month Series
Source: *Federal Reserve Bulletin.*

Insurance Corporation). In the past, such limits have at times encouraged, and at other times discouraged, the flow of savings to commercial banks, depending on the rates available at other types of savings institutions and in the open money and capital markets. More recently, interest-rate ceilings imposed by the Federal Reserve have been allowed to increase on certain types of selected time deposit instruments, and more flexibility has been introduced into the system through the authorization of money-market time deposits which carry a ceiling rate for commercial banks that is equal to the most recently issued six-month U.S. Treasury bill.[1]

Table 3-1 shows the growth of demand, savings and time deposits, and capital accounts for all commercial banks from 1960 through 1978. The rate of growth in these deposits has accelerated in the last few years as a result of the increased level of savings, higher interest rates, and the intensified competition for savings dollars.

An analysis of the data by bank size and location reveals that time and savings deposits are relatively more important as a source of funds for small and medium-size banks than for large-city banks. At the end of 1978 time and savings deposits amounted to more than 70 percent of total deposits for medium-size and small banks compared to 60 percent of the total for large commercial banks.

The figure for medium-size and small banks represents an increase of over 10 percentage points since 1973. It is an important statistic since medium-size and small banks are the major competitors of savings and loan institutions for savings dollars, and it underscores the intense competition occurring among all savings institutions.

Perhaps the biggest casualties, however, as a result of the competition for time and savings deposits and the rise in interest rates paid on these deposits, have been the stock market and those institutions that primarily invest in the stock market. Individuals, especially, have avoided common stock purchases in favor of higher current yields and lower risk afforded by bonds and time and savings deposits.

---

[1] In July 1979, the maximum annual rate on bank passbook deposits was limited to 5¼ percent; single-maturity time deposits (including certificates of deposit) could pay from 5 percent on less than $100,000 principal with maturities of less than ninety days up to 7¾ percent for maturities of eight years or more. There was no rate limit on single-maturity certificates of deposit in denominations of $100,000 or more. The rate paid on some CD's was up to 12 percent. Savings and loan associations were offering up to 5½ percent on passbook accounts and up to 8 percent on term accounts. In the open market, U.S. Treasury bills brought 9.0 percent and high-grade corporate bonds brought 9.5 percent. The ceiling rate for money market time deposits for savings and loan associations and mutual savings banks was ¼ percentage point higher than that for commercial banks until the treasury bill rate reaches 8¾ percent. The differential is reduced proportionately at 6-month treasury bill rates above 8¾ percent and is removed completely when the treasury bill rate reaches 9 percent or more.

Table 3-1 also shows the growth of capital funds (net worth and debentures) of commercial banks. It is desirable for banks to have an expanding capital base as the national economy grows in order to meet the demands of large borrowers and to provide greater safety to depositors. Maximum loan limits to one borrower as well as the total amount of assets held in buildings and equipment by a bank are usually related to the size of the capital account. Furthermore, the appeal of capital-market assets, with the greater price risk, as compared with money-market assets, is affected by the relative size of the equity cushion. Other factors influencing the equity base include the volatility of demand deposits, the types of loans on the books, the ratio of loans to deposits, the relative yields on short-, intermediate-, and long-term loans and investments, together with such influences as the attitudes of bank examiners, changes in bank legislation, and the general need for liquidity of individual banks and of the banking system as a whole.

Annual Sources of Funds

The annual changes (Table 3-2) in adjusted savings and time deposits and capital help explain the variations in uses of funds of commercial banks. In the past, tight money- and capital-market conditions, such as in 1966 and 1969, seriously impaired growth in savings deposits at commercial banks. This situation was particularly bad in 1969, when total deposits actually declined. The relative and absolute declines in deposit accumulations during these two years were caused by comparatively low maximum rates allowed on bank time and savings deposits, which were not competitive with open-market rates or the rates offered by savings and loan associations, and by the lower rate of savings by individuals. Continued increases in the allowed maximum rates in the 1970s and the elimination of rate ceilings on large denominated CD's helped reverse these trends, and commercial banks have enjoyed unprecedented deposit growth in the 1970s. In fact, the maximum rates paid on commercial bank time and savings deposits in some categories (deposits over $100,000) matched or exceeded those allowed savings and loan institutions.

As commercial banks invest in both money-market and capital-market assets and derive funds from demand deposits as well as from time deposits and capital, annual changes in the latter two sources cannot properly be called a flow of funds for investment solely in longer-term loans and securities. In some periods, after liquidity requirements have been satisfied, funds from demand deposits are invested in capital-market assets. At the same time, in most years a substantial portion of time deposits and capital is held in liquid form. Shifts among assets also take place, even though their totals may not change.

Because it is not feasible to associate specific sources and uses of bank funds, the actual flow of funds into capital-market instruments must serve as our data

TABLE 3-2. Annual Changes in Savings and Time Deposits and Capital,
Commercial Banks, 1970–1978 (billions of dollars)

	1970	1971	1972	1973	1974	1975	1976	1977	1978
Savings and time deposits[a]	$37.3	$41.2	$42.6	$50.1	$50.9	$41.5	$41.6	$49.9	$53.7
Capital accounts	3.0	4.3	5.4	5.5	5.6	5.4	9.0	3.5	1.5
Total	$40.3	$45.5	$48.0	$55.6	$56.4	$46.9	$50.6	$53.4	$55.2

[a]Excluding interbank deposits.
Source: *Federal Reserve Bulletin.*

on such investments (see Table 3-5). For 1970–1978, the flow of funds into capital-market investments was as follows (billions of dollars):[2]

1970	1971	1972	1973	1974	1975	1976	1977	1978
$26.1	$32.8	$37.7	$32.7	$30.7	$39.1	$34.0	$41.5	$53.5

By relating these figures to the previous figures of changes in adjusted time deposits and capital accounts (Table 3-2), we see that the growth in time deposits and capital accounts was greater than the increase in longer-term assets in every year from 1970 to 1978. The longer-term sources thus provided some funds for cash reserves and short-term assets.

Uses of Bank Funds in the Capital Market: General

When the somewhat arbitrary definition *capital-market financing* (equity investments, intermediate-term debt, and long-term debt) is applied to commercial banking activity, the volume of bank operations in the capital markets is found to be very substantial. They include a variety of direct as well as open-market transactions and involve the whole range of users of funds—individuals, business, and government.

Given their size as measured by total assets and their flexibility relative to other financial institutions, commercial banks are easily the most dominant financial institution in our society. Table 3-3, showing the combined assets of all commercial banks, is a somewhat misleading indication of the role that banks play in the capital markets as contrasted with their role in the money market. The data do not distinguish between short- and long-term assets. In addition, there is a constant flow of funds between assets with differing maturities and the flow is influenced by the need for liquidity, by the demand for different types of credit, and by the earnings rates on different credit instruments. Transfers to and from money-market and capital-market assets are both deliberate and automatic. A bank may sell a long-term federal bond and invest the proceeds in a short-term bond or make a short-term loan. Or an opposite transaction—from short- to long-term—may be undertaken. An automatic shift from long- to short-term results from the maturing of loans and investments that, when first acquired, represented intermediate- or long-term credit. In any event, the basic hedging principle as discussed in Chapter 2 would imply that as the average term to maturity increases for the bank's liabilities, assets should also be invested in relatively longer-term securities.

The figures in Table 3-3 indicate the important banking assets. The two major categories of "earning assets"—loans and investments—represent, in part, capital-market financing. Clearly, the data reveal the dominance of loans over

---

[2]Derived from data in *Federal Reserve Bulletin;* Federal Deposit Insurance Corporation, *Annual Reports;* sources in Table 3-5.

TABLE 3-3. Combined Assets of All Commercial Banks, at
Year End, 1960–1978 (billions of dollars)

	1960	1965	1970	1975	1978
Cash assets	$ 52.2	$ 61.0	$ 94.0	$134.5	$ 177.3
Loans					
Commercial and industrial[a]	43.4	71.9	113.4	181.0	221.6
Farm (excluding real estate)	5.7	8.2	11.2	20.2	28.2
Real estate	28.8	49.7	73.3	136.4	214.0[f]
Individuals	26.5	45.7	66.3	107.6	167.2[f]
Securities	5.1	8.5	9.9	11.1	11.0[f]
Financial institutions	7.7	15.5	18.6	42.5	61.0[f]
Other[b]	2.9	7.3	24.0	52.8	32.0[f]
Total loans[c]	$118.1	$202.8	$310.6	$543.0	$735.0
Investments					
U.S. Treasury securities[d]	61.1	59.7	62.0	84.6	97.4
Bonds of federal agencies[e]	1.8	4.6	13.5	34.4	43.5
State and local government bonds	17.6	38.7	69.8	102.7	123.2
Corporate bonds	0.9	0.9	2.6 }	9.1 }	6.6
Other securities	0.6	0.8	0.5 }		
Total investments	$ 82.0	$108.7	$143.4	$230.8	270.7
Other assets	6.0	10.4	22.4	57.7	61.0
Total assets	$258.4	$378.9	$575.4	$966.0	$1,255.0

[a]Includes commercial paper.
[b]Includes federal funds sold and securities for resale.
[c]Total shows net of reserves.
[d]Includes trading account securities.
[e]Includes debt of federally sponsored and budget agencies.
[f]Estimated
Sources: Federal Deposit Insurance Corporation, *Annual Reports; Federal Reserve Bulletin.*

investments as an earning asset. In general, loans are preferred to investments as an earning asset by banks because they normally generate higher returns, are a more active, as opposed to passive, investment, and serve as the primary function of a bank. Investments should be viewed as the *residual* account in the asset category. That is, if loan demand is great, investments will be liquidated and the funds placed in loans. When total loan demand is slack, the opposite effect tends to occur. If loan demand is slack in one category, such as commercial and industrial loans in 1977–1978, banks may first try to make more loans in a strong demand area before placing the funds in an investment security. With demand for real estate loans strong—particularly single-family housing—and consumer borrowing high during most of the late 1970s, banks made substantial loans in these areas. When funds are placed in investments that are not necessary for strict reserve or liquidity requirements, they nevertheless will generally be placed in short-term investments to provide the necessary liquidity should loan demand suddenly increase.

We shall discuss the significance of the intermediate- and long-term portion of each main type of loan and investment, omitting mention of consumer financing, even though some of this (for example, housing improvement loans) may qualify as long-term on a strict maturity basis. In general, the earning assets discussed fall outside the "secondary reserves" of the banks—money-market instruments and short-term federal obligations—held primarily for liquidity rather than for income.

Term Loans

The growth in bank term loans has been an important postwar development. These loans have over one year to original maturity (seldom over ten) and are usually amortized on a regular basis. They form a major part of the commercial and industrial loan figure in Table 3–3 and, to a minor extent, the individuals category. Term loans are frequently used by businesses as alternatives to bond financing because (1) they offer more flexibility in that often they can be pre-paid without penalty; (2) the term loan can be "closed" or approved quicker and can be cheaper overall; (3) no time-consuming and costly registration procedures (which can take up to six months in bond financing) are required; (4) standard sinking fund requirements, refunding provisions, and other restrictions on firm operations, frequently contained in the bond indenture agreement, can be avoided or minimized; and (5) the term loan frequently can be renewed, extended, and otherwise tailored more closely to a firm's needs and current operations.

Term loans are also a desirable replacement for former short-term loans in that (1) they do not have to be continually renewed at maturity as often, and (2) the interest rate may be fixed rather than variable, which aids a firm's financial planning. In making term loans, banks compete chiefly with life insurance companies.

A modified type of term loan that has been increasingly used by business because of its special features that are helpful in periods of volatile capital markets is the revolving credit loan. A *revolving credit loan* is a firm commitment by a bank to lend up to a specified amount over a period of time, normally three to five years. This is a benefit over a line of credit that may be reduced or rescinded in tight money periods if funds are not available. Typically a revolving credit loan is evidenced by a series of short-term notes that may be renewed for the duration of the commitment if necessary. Finally, the notes at maturity may be "rolled over" into a term loan of fixed maturity and amount for a longer period of time. A drawback to this form of financing is that it is frequently of higher cost (about ½ of 1 percent) than a line of credit, and many of these loans have the interest rate fluctuate with the prime rate.

Information on the volume and characteristics of bank term loans is irregular and incomplete. The proportion of term loans to total loans differs greatly among banks; for some large banks it is now over 50 percent. At the end of December 1978, term loans held by large commercial banks (which held 50 percent of all bank loans) totaled $55 billion, or 50 percent of their commercial and industrial loans.[3] At this rate the figure for all banks would be over $110 billion.

Term loans to business offer the advantage of flexibility in particular covenants and in type of security required; this flexibility helps to explain their use in financing working-capital and fixed-asset requirements, especially during periods of buoyant business activity and ample bank credit. Even during periods of credit stringency, the ratio of term to total business loans often increases, and many borrowers, especially smaller firms, turn to these loans when unsecured short-term funds are hard to get.

Finally, large firms waiting for lower long-term rates or more favorable stock market conditions may finance for shorter periods through short-term loans.

Mortgage Financing by Commercial Banks

Table 3–4 shows the composition of bank holdings of mortgages from 1960 through 1978. Commercial banks are one of the major institutions in the mortgage market. They have not committed as many resources to mortgages, how-

TABLE 3–4. Mortgage Loans Held by Commercial Banks, at Year End, 1960–1978 (billions of dollars)

	1960	1965	1970	1975	1978
Farm	$ 1.7	$ 2.9	$ 4.4	$ 6.4	$ 9.0
Residential					
1–4-family	19.2	30.4	42.3	77.0	127.0
Multifamily	1.1	1.9	3.3	5.9	10.9
	$20.3	$32.3	$45.6	$ 82.9	$137.9
Commercial and industrial	6.8	14.5	23.3	46.9	67.1
Total	$28.8	$49.7	$73.3	$136.2	$214.0
Conventional and other	$20.1	$39.3	$62.8	$126.8	
FHA-insured	5.8	7.7	7.9	6.3	214.0
VA-guaranteed	2.9	2.7	2.6	3.1	
Total	$28.8	$49.7	$73.3	$136.2	$214.0

Sources: National Association of Mutual Savings Banks, *National Fact Book*. *Federal Reserve Bulletin*, Federal Deposit Insurance Corporation, *Annual Reports*.

---

[3] *Federal Reserve Bulletin*

ever, as their total asset size might suggest because mortgages are generally long-term instruments that usually carry fixed interest rates which at times are lower than rates in competing money-market instruments. Recently, banks have committed about 15 percent of their total assets to mortgages.

The table also shows that commercial banks have been selective in the type of real estate loans they finance. They have generally favored single-family housing or short-term construction loans. This contrasts with the real estate financing by insurance companies and savings and loan associations, which have much more balanced real estate portfolios. Banks have also preferred conventional private financing over government-guaranteed financing represented by the Federal Housing Administration (FHA) and Veterans Administration (VA) loan programs. Reasons generally given for this preference include the paperwork, time delays, and maximum allowed interest rates on FHA and VA loans, which are frequently below competing market rates and the declining eligibility for some of the programs.

Farm mortgage loans   As a group, banks are far less important in agricultural real estate than are insurance companies and government agencies specifically designed to aid rural housing. At the end of 1978, the $9.0 billion in farm mortgages held by commercial banks represented less than 1 percent of all commercial bank assets.

Residential mortgage loans   Although experiencing a relative decline in mortgage financing compared to other institutions, bank financing of residential real estate has still been substantial in the postwar years reflecting the great expansion in housing activity. Residential one- to four-family mortgage loans held by commercial banks totaled $127 billion at the end of 1978. This was approximately 17.0 percent of the $762 billion of one- to four-family mortgages outstanding in the United States, down from 21 percent in 1950. The share of total FHA-insured, VA-guaranteed loans outstanding held by banks declined from 26 percent in 1950 to less than 5 percent in 1978.

Although the commercial bank position in the mortgage market relative to other institutions has declined in importance, banks are still major factors in certain mortgage market sectors. The postwar increase in single-family residential mortgages held by banks reflects the general rise in demand for home financing, increased yields on this type of asset, the great growth in time deposits, and the expansion of federally underwritten loans. The figures may be somewhat misleading, however, in that much of the mortgage financing by banks is of a short-term nature even though mortgages are usually considered long-term instruments. Banks frequently provide construction lending to builders to build homes or other projects. When the home or project is completed, permanent financing is usually obtained from a savings and loan association or an insurance company.

Commercial bank holdings of multifamily mortgages have remained low, amounting to less than 1 percent of total assets at the end of 1978. There has been some renewed interest in these loans as the growth of high-rise housing, the desire for higher yields, and the rapid growth in bank deposits have caused banks to search for additional loan placements.

In addition to direct lending on mortgages held to maturity, some banks originate loans that they pass along to others. Thus, they help to make the mortgage market national in scope. They also "warehouse" or carry mortgage loans originated by mortgage companies until the latter pass these along to permanent investors, and make short-term loans to real estate investment companies.

Commercial and industrial mortgage loans   Commercial mortgage loans have grown substantially in the last few years and totaled $67 billion at the end of 1978. This figure represents about 32 percent of the total of such mortgages outstanding in the United States. They are the largest commercial mortgage lenders of all the institutions (followed closely by life insurance companies). Hence, in a relative sense commercial mortgages represent the area of mortgage specialization for commercial banks. The growth in commercial mortgages held by banks is attributable in part to (1) the normally higher yields on commercial mortgages as opposed to residential and multifamily mortgages, (2) the need for additional investment outlets by commercial banks, (3) the heavy demand for loans by businesses that causes banks to "reach for security" in order to make the loans through mortgage loans secured by commercial properties, (4) the sharp increase in bank interim construction loans on commercial properties, (5) fewer legal restrictions on corporate mortgages, and (6) their comparatively large size.

Securities Loans

Although securities loans are short-term in nature, they play an important ancillary role in the securities market. They are made to investment bankers to carry new issues through underwriting and distribution, to dealers for the financing of customers' margin accounts, and to individuals for their purchases of securities.

The volume of securities loans fluctuates with changes in margin requirements, securities prices, the dollar volume of securities trading, the volume of new securities, and interest rates. Margin regulation under the Securities and Exchange Act of 1934, the growth of private placements of securities, and the increased reliance by business on internal financing have all reduced the demand for securities credit. Table 3-3 shows that, at the end of 1978, outstanding securities loans of all commercial banks totaled $11.0 billion, or less than 2 percent of total commercial bank loans outstanding. This compared with $17 billion or almost 30 percent of outstanding loans in the autumn of 1929.

Banks also make loans secured by securities collateral—"nonpurpose" loans—for purposes other than purchasing or carrying securities. These are classified as either business or individual loans.

Bank Securities Investments

In addition to loans, investments in the form of bond and note issues held are the second major category of earning assets for commercial banks. Investment assets held by commercial banks amounted to less than 22 percent of total bank assets at the end of 1978 compared to over 60 percent for bank loans. This has not always been the case. In 1950, investments constituted 44 percent of total bank assets with loans amounting to only 31 percent. The relative importance of the two main types of earning assets since 1960, shown in Table 3-3, reveals the continuing shift in emphasis from securities to loans by commercial banks in an attempt to get higher yielding assets.

Most of the investment assets held by commercial banks are comprised of U.S. government securities, federal agency securities, and state and local government bonds.

Bonds other than U.S. obligations, often with two years or less to maturity, constitute the bulk of the investment portfolio of banks. These bonds constitute a residual account that provides income from funds not needed for loans and serve to diversify the assets of the banks. The risk of changing market values is reduced by spacing maturities, although in years like 1974 and 1979, with bond prices at record lows, the potential losses on the sales of bonds contributed greatly to the credit strain and the high level of interest rates. The credit risk (in other than U.S. obligations) is minimized by applying high investment standards, as required by regulation, and by diversification.

The volume of bond investments is affected by seasonal, cyclical, and secular influences, especially the demand for loans and the available yields on securities compared with interest rates on loans. Federal Reserve policy also affects the ratio of investments to loans. In periods of credit restraint, as in 1979, investments are often reduced in order to obtain funds for loan expansion.

United States government securities   Except from the standpoint of income taxation and yield, Treasury obligations are almost ideal bank investments. They involve no credit risk and the least price risk for a given maturity. They can be used as collateral at other banks or at the Federal Reserve banks without penalty rates, have excellent marketability, and are preferred by bank examiners. Shorter maturities provide liquidity as well as safe income, and banks can change the composition of their federal bond portfolios by shifting between short- and medium-term maturities. In periods of credit ease, banks take the initiative in acquiring medium-term securities for income. Primary reserves are ample and may be expanded by using Federal Reserve credit. In periods of credit strain and higher yields (as in 1973-1974 and 1978-1979), securities may be sold to provide loan funds. Such contraction of the investment portfolio is, however, limited by the aversion of the banks to selling the longer maturities at a loss. The reluctance to sell securities at a loss and the tightening of credit by the Federal Reserve helped force the prime rate to a record 15¼ percent in October 1979.

Commercial banks tend to buy short-term federal securities in periods of economic recession when the banks have idle funds, even though yields may be low relative to other government securities in order to preserve their liquidity (Figure 8-1). Conversely, they tend to sell bonds in prosperous years at higher yields and lower prices in order to increase loanable funds. This policy almost inevitably leads to losses on resale, which are, however, allowed as expenses for federal income tax purposes.

Commercial banks by far are the largest private institutional owners of U.S. Treasury securities (see Chapter 8). At the end of 1978 their holdings totaled $97 billion, or 12 percent of gross Treasury debt. About 70 percent of these securities had maturities of five years or less. In periods of high inflation and credit restraint, the yields on federal short-term securities have often matched or exceeded those on longer-term maturities. Hence, there is little purpose in holding long maturities that have substantial price risk because of changing market yields. When declining interest rates are probable, some new funds may be placed in longer maturities to maximize income and allow banks a better asset/liability hedge position. But this situation has generally not prevailed during the 1960s and 1970s.

The rise in bank holdings of federal securities from less than $56 billion in 1974 to more than $97 billion in 1978 was primarily a result of slack business loan demand and high yields in government securities. Federal holdings dropped in 1979 as securities were sold to meet loan demand.

As a percentage of total bank assets, however, federal securities have dipped significantly, from slightly over 35 percent in 1950 to less than 8 percent at the end of 1978.

Much of the relative decline of federal securities held by banks can be attributed to higher after-tax yields that banks can receive on business loans, federal agency securities, and state and local government issues. Furthermore, when loan demand is heavy, federal securities, because of their low yield, are likely to be liquidated first, and, consequently, bank holdings of these securities tend to drop sharply. The process is essentially reversed when loan demand slackens. For example, from the end of 1972 through July 1974, federal securities held by commercial banks declined from $67.7 billion to $53.0 billion or a drop of over 21 percent, yet rose to over $85.0 billion by December 1975, in a period when loan demand was slack.

The bank procedure of buying federal securities when loan demand is slack and selling federal securities when loan demand quickens tends to be cyclical in nature and aggravate interest rate swings, causing rates on federal securities to go higher in high-loan-demand times and lower in slack periods. Nevertheless, it is probably more likely that bank investment policy has influenced the spreads between the prices and yields of different maturities of federal securities more than the yield structure as a whole.

Federally sponsored agency securities   At the end of 1978, commercial banks held $43.5 billion or about 16 percent of their total investments in federally related securities. The yields on these bonds are slightly higher than those of Treasury obligations. However, because of their moral support by the federal government, these obligations have little risk and good marketability. The growth in the amounts of these issues outstanding, together with their higher yields, have undoubtedly contributed to the relative decline of federal securities in bank portfolios alluded to earlier. Changes in the credit financing arrangements instituted in 1974 (see Chapter 8) as well as greater emphasis on programs funded by federal credit agencies promise that these securities will most likely continue as important assets in bank portfolios.

State and local government obligations   "Municipal" bonds constitute the largest single holding in investment securities by banks, and banks are the largest institutional owners of municipal securities with slightly more than 40 percent of total state and local debt (see p. 166). In contrast to the relative decline in federal bond investments, holdings of state and local government bonds have risen 100 percent since 1968 and at the end of 1978 totaled $123.2 billion, or 46 percent of total investments and 10 percent of total assets. This increase reflects a number of factors: (1) the great growth of state and local government borrowing since World War II (banks are the principal market for the bonds of smaller municipalities); (2) the attractive yields of "tax exempts" compared to the after-tax yield on other bonds; (3) the relatively good investment record of these bonds; (4) the variety of serial maturities available; and (5) the increasing activity of banks in underwriting and distributing municipal securities.[4] The chief disadvantage of municipals is their lack of a good secondary market. Most banks, however, hold such securities to maturity and in 1975, when yields on "munis" reached all-time highs and prices reached all-time lows, such a practice was virtually mandatory.

Banks are not limited in the amount of "investment merit" or qualified general obligatory bonds that they are permitted to own because such bonds are backed by the "full faith and credit" of the issuing governing body, which includes the power to tax. Member banks are restricted in investing in qualified state or local revenue bonds up to 10 percent of capital and surplus. This suggests that apparently the regulatory agencies feel that the additional yield does not offset the riskiness of the bonds as the funds for interest payments and principal amortization are based only on the revenues generated from the assets financed through sale of the revenue bonds.

In general, banks emphasize municipal bonds with maturities less than ten years. They do, however, adjust their purchases of tax-exempt securities to meet loan demands and reserve requirements. Changing conditions in these two

---

[4] Banks are permitted to act as principals in underwriting new municipal issues, excluding revenue bonds.

factors, together with the varying supply of state and local bonds resulting from bond elections, have a pronounced short-run effect on municipal bond yields (see Chapter 9). In the long run, the countercyclical tendency of banks to invest in municipal securities when their own liquidity is high (and interest rates are low) rather than when yields are high provides a supporting influence on this market.

Corporate bonds and other securities   At the end of 1978, commercial banks held 6.6 billion in corporate bonds and other securities, constituting about 2 percent of their investments and less than 1 percent of their total assets. This was almost double the amount held in 1972, reflecting the appeal of the very high interest rates in these securities. The lack of bank activity in the corporate bond market is explained by the high standards of quality and marketability required by law and regulation for investment in these obligations, the greater appeal of federal obligations for safety and liquidity, the favorable after-tax yields on state and local government bonds, and by the growth of term loans. The demand for corporate bonds by tax-exempt institutions (for example, pension funds) or by those enjoying lower income-tax rates (such as life insurance companies) has driven down the yields on high-grade corporate bonds to a level where they are unattractive to banks (see p. 178). Larger tissues of high-grade corporate bonds do offer good marketability, but the longer maturities involve more price risk than do alternative investments. Railway equipment obligations, with their serial maturities are, however, attractive to banks, their principal owners.

At the end of 1978, commercial banks held less than 2 percent of all corporate bonds outstanding (see Chapter 10). Except for rare occasions, banks are not permitted to buy corporate stocks as investments.[5] They do, however, influence the prices and yields of stocks through the volume of loans used to purchase or to carry securities and through the discretionary power they have in managing personal trust accounts.

Annual Uses of Funds
in the Capital Market, 1970–1978

The annual net changes in bank holdings of capital-market investments are shown in Table 3-5. The data include all maturities of federal securities. The figures indicate the volatility of investment in U.S. securities, which, as noted earlier, tends to function as the residual account for varying loan demand. Comparing the data with term loans, we see that as loans to business increase

---

[5]Exceptions are ownership of stock in Federal Reserve banks by member banks, stock in affiliates, and a few miscellaneous types. For instance, various statutory provisions explicitly authorize national banks to buy stock of particular organizations, such as safe deposit companies, bank premises subsidiaries, small business investment companies, and so on.

TABLE 3-5. Annual Changes in Capital-Market Assets, Commercial Banks,
1970–1978 (billions of dollars)

	1970	1971	1972	1973	1974	1975	1976	1977	1978
U.S. Treasury securities[a]	$ 7.0	$ 3.2	$ 2.1	$-8.8	$-2.4	$28.7	$17.9	$-0.9	$-5.8
Federal agency securities	3.8	4.0	3.9	7.5	3.6	1.6	1.4	0.9	6.2
State and local government bonds	10.5	12.8	7.1	5.6	5.2	1.6	2.6	9.2	8.3
Term loans to business[b]	2.0	2.0	6.4	8.4	11.0	1.3	-1.1	5.2	10.5 (est)
Corporate and foreign bonds	0.8	1.2	1.4	0.4	1.0	1.8	-0.7	-0.2	-0.3
Home mortgages	0.9	7.6	9.0	11.0	6.6	2.3	8.2	17.2	34.6
Other mortgages	1.1	2.0	7.8	8.6	5.7	1.8	5.7	10.1	
Total	$26.1	$32.8	$37.7	$32.7	$30.7	$39.1	$34.0	$41.5	$53.5

[a]Interbank items deducted.
[b]To nonfinancial corporations.
Sources: Federal Deposit Insurance Corporation, *Annual Reports*; *Federal Reserve Bulletin*; Federal Reserve *Flow-of-Funds Accounts*. Term loans from Bankers Trust Company, *Credit and Capital Markets* (New York, annual). (Some columns do not add to totals because of rounding.)

sharply, U.S. security holdings tend to diminish, and vice versa. Continued high investment in municipal bonds is generally attributed to the tax-exempt features of these securities, which because of limited marketability tend to be held by banks to maturity. The high dollar amounts invested by banks in mortgages in the 1970s can be traced, in part, as noted earlier, to business firms needing funds and hence, a willingness to mortgage their assets, if necessary, in order to secure the loans. Commercial and residential loans usually provide interim construction financing.

The variation in savings and time deposits materially influences the investment policies of banks. In such years as 1972, banks were able to supply rising demands for business, housing, and consumer credit without liquidating federal securities and were able at the same time to record increases in their holdings of state and local government bonds and mortgages. In 1973, 1974, and 1979, however, liquidation of Treasury securities occurred in order to increase investment in higher-yielding assets to cover the higher interest costs on savings accounts, to accommodate the demand for loans, and to aid the liquidity management of banks.

In the 1950s and 1960s tight money conditions, such as those in 1966 and 1969 resulting in high interest rates, usually caused a sharp drop in banks' deposits. This was a direct result of the interest-rate ceiling on time and savings deposits imposed by bank regulators. In the 1970s ceiling rates were relaxed substantially and numerous types of new certificates with varying interest-rate restrictions were introduced. The result of this relaxation has been an unprecedented growth in bank time deposits in the 1970s, much higher rates on time deposits among all competing institutions and ultimately, higher interest rates, in general, on bank loans of all types.

Banking Developments and Competition

The 1970s could well be remembered as the decade of sharply increased competition among financial institutions. Undoubtedly, one of the major influences was the Hunt Commission (see Chapter 4), whose recommendations in 1971 were a catalyst for many of the changes now taking place. Most, if not all, of these changes have especially affected the banking community whose response to the breaking down of barriers between different types of institutions and less regulation has been in many directions. While it is not the purpose of this book to discuss any of these changes in detail, some of the more important developments that have a significant impact on how banks conduct business in the capital market deserve mention.

Bank Holding Companies and Implications for Banking

Historically speaking, banking laws have prohibited banks from engaging in nonbanking activities. The justification was that the fiduciary responsibility of banks in protecting depositors' funds and the need for bank soundness was so overriding as to require laws confining commercial banks to banking only, and prohibiting them from engaging in extraneous businesses, such as owning and operating industrial firms. It was feared that if this was not done, pressures might force banks to make loans to favored customers of subsidiary businesses or make unreasonable loans to businesses they own.

To avoid and otherwise obviate certain provisions of the laws, many banks formed holding companies that held the stock of the subsidiary bank. The holding company itself, then, was free to acquire other firms and engage in any other type of business. Only the bank, being a subsidiary engaged in banking, was bound by the banking laws.

This loophole was closed by the Bank Holding Company Act of 1956 that essentially reestablished the traditional separation of banking and nonbanking activities by prohibiting a bank holding company from acquiring any shares of any company that was not a bank. Recognizing, however, that a strict interpretation of the laws could be too damaging, the act allowed bank holding companies to engage in business activities that were *closely related to banking.* In general, this was interpreted to mean (1) investing in companies that furnish or perform services directly for the bank holding company, such as auditing or investment counseling firms; (2) acquiring companies or buying stock in firms such as safe deposit companies; or (3) acquiring shares of firms whose activities are solely of a financial, fiduciary, or insurance nature and are "closely related" to the banking business, such as firms writing credit life insurance for a bank's customers.

In the 1956 act and in an amendment in 1966, Congress specifically exempted one-bank holding companies, feeling that including them would conflict with the objective of fostering local ownership of unit banks, as local banks are frequently owned by people engaged in other forms of business. A problem with the one-bank holding company exemption rose in the late 1960s during the surge of conglomeration and the merger wave when several industrial firms acquired only one large bank and hence were exempt from the law. The loophole grew to such magnitude that the assets of one-bank holding companies soon exceeded the assets of those covered by the Banking Holding Company Act.

A growing fear that the conglomerate firms were going to acquire many of the large banks provided the catalyst for an amendment to the act in 1970 that closed the loophole and placed one-bank holding companies under the act's control. As a result, one-bank holding companies can now engage only in banking and in activities closely related to banking and, in some cases, if they plan to hold the bank they must dispose of some previously acquired businesses.

At the same time, however, the amendment (1970) considerably broadened the Federal Reserve Board's interpretive powers in determining which activities are closely allied with banking. So far the board's decisions have given banks considerable latitude in engaging in businesses such as insurance, investment counseling, courier services, and leasing activities, such that in the future these activities could add significantly to the operating income of banks. Traditionally, banks have relied on income from loans to individuals and businesses and on investment income to supply the bulk of operating revenues. These two sources typically have provided better than 85 percent of bank income (Table 3-6), while other income amounted to only about 15 percent. In 1978, despite rapid growth in loans and investment securities held by banks, income from other sources rose to 17.2 billion, or about 16 percent of bank operating income.

The implication of these figures and the favorable interpretations by the Federal Reserve Board pertaining to "closely allied activities" under the Banking Holding Company Act is that banks are increasingly expanding their nonbanking functions, which means increasing competition for other financial intermediaries. This is consistent with the general government policy of encouraging increased competition among all financial intermediaries by removing traditional legal barriers or modifying existing policies.

The existence of bank holding companies has caused additional problems for bank regulators, especially the Federal Reserve. Of concern to the Federal Reserve is the number of banks—primarily those controlled by multibank holding companies—that are withdrawing as members of the Federal Reserve System. Since national banks must be members of the Federal Reserve System, withdrawing as a national bank means turning in the charter and being rechartered as a state bank. (Withdrawal from the System by a state bank is less formal and more direct.) The amount of assets held by members of the Federal Reserve has declined from 79 percent of total assets for all banks in 1974 to 72 percent in 1978. With fewer banks as members it obviously makes effective monetary policy through Federal Reserve actions just that much more difficult and places a greater burden on the remaining members of the System especially as it affects their earning assets. Hence it is not surprising that the Federal Reserve has advocated legislation that would require all commercial banks to be members of the Federal Reserve System.

Withdrawals have occurred because the cost of membership versus the benefit has been too great. In many cases the underlying cause has been the current structure of the banking system and the bank holding company form.

The costs faced by a member of the Federal Reserve System are primarily the reserve requirements, which are non-interest-earning deposits. Member banks can count only vault cash and cash on deposit—drawing no interest—at the Federal Reserve as reserves. Although Reserve requirements for nonmember banks differ from state to state, they frequently are lower than the Federal Reserve as a percent of total deposits and, in addition, such items as correspondent bank balances and some categories of earning assets are usually counted in the reserve base. Thus, the net result of withdrawing is usually a freeing up of reserves to reinvest in higher-yielding earning assets.

TABLE 3-6. Sources of Income of Insured Commercial Banks 1965–1978 (billions of dollars)

	1965		1970		1975		1978	
	Amount	Percent	Amount	Percent	Amount	Percent	Amount	Percent
Interest on loans[a]	$11.2	66.7%	$23.9	65.7%	$45.5	68.6%	$ 79.6	70.0%
Interest on securities	3.5	20.8	6.6	21.3	12.2	18.4	16.4	14.5
Service charges and fees	1.2	7.0	2.0	6.1	3.2	4.9	5.0	4.4
Other income[b]	.9	5.5	2.1	6.9	5.4	8.1	12.2	11.1
Total operating income	$16.8	100 %	$34.6	100 %	$66.3	100 %	$113.2	100%

[a]Includes income from federal funds.
[b]Other income includes trust department income, income from trading accounts, and from other sources.
Source: *Federal Reserve Bulletin.* (Some figures may not add to totals because of rounding.)

The benefits of Federal Reserve membership that are often advanced are check clearing, money (wire) transfer, collection and courier services, vault privileges, rediscounting and borrowing privileges, and automatic clearing houses. However, most of these services can be performed by a large bank in competition with the Federal Reserve, and consequently a member of a multibank holding company can often have its banking needs filled by the lead bank of the group and little is to be gained through Federal Reserve membership. As expected, it is primarily banks of multibank holding companies that are withdrawing their charters from the Federal Reserve.

Despite the substantial changes affecting commercial banking through the growth of multibank holding companies, the evidence so far indicates that holding companies have been beneficial for the general public. Competition has intensified and a wider range of banking services has been offered whenever affiliates of holding companies have been established.[6] Also, research has indicated that there is a definite tendency for the profitability of a bank to increase as bank size increases.[7]

Competition for Deposits: Flexible Rate Notes and Electronic Funds Transfer Systems

To encourage more competition among financial institutions and to allow them to compete effectively for funds during tight money periods against other borrowers such as government and business, a number of savings instruments have been devised by financial institutions. Most of these instruments in one form or another allow interest rates to vary on a periodic basis or are indexed to the interest paid on a money-market instrument such as a six-month Treasury Bill.

Flexible Rate Notes

Several major banks offered flexible-rate notes beginning in 1974. Although receiving a less than enthusiastic reception from banking authorities and strong opposition from other financial institutions, about $1 billion of these notes were initially sold. The notes guaranteed the holder a specified return, usually for a minimum of six months, and then a variable return based on the general level of interest rates thereafter until maturity. The flexible-rate notes allowed the investor to hedge his investments against rapidly changing interest rates while at the same time committing his funds for longer periods of time of up to about two years. Another form of a flexible rate note is the rising-rate note, wherein the interest rate earned increases every year for five years. Unlike other notes,

[6] Norman N. Bowsher, "Have Multibank Holding Companies Affected Commercial Bank Performance," Federal Reserve Bank of St. Louis *Review,* April 1978, pp. 8–15.

[7] Edward C. Gallick, "Bank Profitability and Bank Size," Federal Reserve Bank of Kansas City *Monthly Review,* January 1976, pp. 11–16.

this security can be held to maturity or redeemed at the end of any anniversary date. The rate received is an average of the yearly rates paid.

Effective in June 1978, commercial banks, savings and loan associations, and mutual savings banks began offering two additional types of deposit certificates. In each case the nonbank thrifts were initially allowed to pay up to ¼ of 1 percent more. The money-market certificate (MMC) which has been a tremendous success—over $32 billion in bank deposits alone as of January 1979, is a short-term, variable-rate, nonnegotiable instrument with a minimum denomination of $10,000 and a six-month maturity. The ceiling rate on this instrument is adjusted weekly for new deposits and is equal to the average (auction) yield on new six-month Treasury bills (thrifts pay ¼ of 1% higher up to 8¾ percent). The second type of instrument is the long-term, fixed-ceiling certificate, which pays 7¾ percent interest if held up to eight years (8 percent maximum for thrifts). Currently there are no minimum denominations on this certificate

In order to bring savings-account rates closer to money market rates, a four-year certificate is authorized with rates tied to the average yield on four-year Treasury securities. The maximum rate paid on these certificates is one percentage point less for thrifts, and 1¼ percent less for commercial banks, than the average four-year Treasury rate.

As noted earlier, the purpose of flexible-rate certificates was to enable financial institutions to more effectively compete for customers' deposits, particularly during tight money periods when Regulation Q ceilings normally caused depositors to transfer funds into higher-yielding federal and corporate securities. In this manner it was felt that funds would be more readily available for housing and nonresidential construction. When first offered the MMCs were yielding slightly over 7½ percent. Subsequently, the Treasury bill rate rose to almost 10 percent in December 1978 and concern was expressed that due to the high rates, mutual savings banks and savings and loan associations would not roll over the certificates at maturity and the housing market would decline accordingly. However, at maturity most of the certificates were renewed (at 10 percent or better) as the thrifts stayed in the market. Many of the funds, though, were not placed in mortgages as expected; instead, they were placed in higher-yielding certificates of deposit at other commercial banks, often obtaining a spread greater than 1 percent. Hence, the outcome was similar to past credit crunches, although not nearly as bad; namely, during tight money periods, funds available for new mortgages tend to decline. In addition, Federal Reserve action in March 1979 removed the ¼ of 1% differential spread in favor of thrifts when rates reach 8¾ percent.

Electronic Fund Transfer Systems (EFT)

To speak of a single electronic funds transfer system is an oversimplification. There are a number of different systems in various phases of development or use, and changes, it seems, are made on almost a weekly basis. The common factor in these systems is that they speed the transfer of funds by communicating information relating to payments by electronic means rather than by check or other forms of paper instruments. Thus, EFT systems are replacing manual processes with electronic data processing and speeding the flow of funds through high-speed data transmission. The advent of EFT promises to make banking and savings easier and more convenient for customers but at a cost that may be too high for many. Furthermore, several legal questions remain that may affect the final course of EFT systems.

Much of the rapid development in EFT banking, particularly teller machines, is a direct result of the speed and aggressiveness with which the thrift institutions have been promoting and expanding their services (see Chapter 4). For the sake of simplicity EFT systems can be grouped into three categories: teller machines, point-of-sale systems, and automated clearing houses. Although perhaps not directly involved in the capital markets, EFT systems are discussed here because they affect competition among other institutions, which in turn influences investment strategy in the capital market.

Teller machines are machines through which routine banking services may be conducted. These machines can be located on the bank's premises or, more likely, at some convenient location in a shopping center or supermarket. The machines may be manned or automatic and vary in complexity. Automatic teller machines (ATMs) typically include receiving deposits, dispensing funds from checking or savings, receiving payments, transferring funds between accounts and responding to balance inquiries. The convenience of being open 24 hours a day in a neighborhood center is a strong feature of this service.

As of November 1979, commercial banks have been allowed to offer what, in effect, are interest-paying checking accounts. Although payment of interest on checking accounts is still technically forbidden by law, the new automatic transfer service (ATS) essentially accomplishes the desired result (although legal challenges still remain). Nonbank thrifts, through negotiable order withdrawal and pass card accounts (Chapter 4), have essentially been offering similar services for a longer period of time, even though such plans are not available to all thrifts nationwide.

Under the ATS a bank automatically transfers money from a depositor's savings account to his checking account (or reverses this procedure), as needed, to pay for checks written. The transfer, in essence, enables a customer to earn interest on his checking dollars. That is, by placing money into the bank's transfer account a person can earn more interest on dollars that would normally be used for checking account balances. There are costs that are charged for this service, however, such that small depositors will gain little, if anything. Those likely to benefit are the ones that normally keep high minimum checking account balances on hand as a matter of preference.

Point-of-sale (POS) *systems* allow customers to transfer funds directly to merchants in order to make purchases. Rather than writing a check that may take three or four days to clear and be credited to the merchant's account, transfers are made immediately. The benefit of a large-scale POS system to the capital markets is that funds should be released sooner to those firms or institutions that customarily place funds in the money and capital market. Although the money market would tend to benefit most, there undoubtedly would be some spillover effects into capital-market investments.

The *automatic clearing house* (ACH) is analogous to a traditional clearing house in that it represents a system for the interbank clearing of debits and credits. The main difference is that all transfers are done electronically. The system is particularly useful in payroll, retirement, social security, dividend accounts, or any other similar transaction that is periodic in nature and tends to be a fixed payout. The greatest benefit of an ACH to the capital market in particular and financial institutions in general is one of efficiency. Hence, an ACH should be viewed as simply another development in the evolution of our financial system.

International Growth and Foreign Competition

Another significant development occurring over the last two decades but intensifying in the 1970s has been the growth in international banking. Most of the large banks in the United States have substantial earnings that are derived from overseas branches and in some cases the foreign operations exceed the domestic operations. These large banks are just as comfortable in dealing in overseas loans and investments, Eurodollars, and foreign currency as they are in domestic functions. While a discussion of international banking is beyond the scope of this book, in the future banking will have to be viewed with more of an international flavor. That is, banks will tend to make loans to their best, most creditworthy borrowers regardless of where they are located. Or they will invest in the securities that offer the highest return commensurate with risk. On the other hand, federal officials have cautioned the big banks that unsupervised bank lending to developing countries could lead to chaos.

The international scope of banking extends to the domestic front. There are about 100 foreign banks operating 400 offices in the United States. They account, for example, for about one-fourth of all commercial loans made in New York and California. Foreign banks are unsupervised by the federal government. They can branch into several states, which is not allowed to domestic banks, and they are not bound by the reserve requirements of the Federal Reserve System. Thus, they can lend out a larger percentage of their funds. In order to meet this competition, several large banking institutions have advocated nationwide branch banking and, in fact, many of them currently have large customer servicing offices in major metropolitan cities. It would be a small step to expand to a full-service bank. Others have advocated direct Federal Reserve control over foreign banks. In any event, regulation and the role of foreign banks promise to present problems for domestic banks and the Federal Reserve in the future.

As noted in Chapter 2, a pure financial intermediary essentially borrows from depositors at one rate of interest and relends the funds at a higher rate of interest to those who need funds. Presumably, the intermediary makes sufficient money from the interest-rate spread to pay expenses and make some profits. The increasing volatility in the capital markets that has been reflected in widely varying interest rates over the business cycle and which eventually led in part to the flexible-interest-rate instruments on customers' deposits has upset the traditional role of the financial intermediary, affecting his interest-rate spread. That is, if rates are fixed on the lending side but allowed to vary on the deposit side, banks are in a position to speculate on the interest-rate spread, which is contrary to the operations of a purely financial intermediary. Thus, it should come as little surprise that if the interest rate is flexible on the deposit side, financial intermediaries should try to free up the asset side by making loans or investments that fluctuate with interest-rate levels.

One of the significant developments in the 1970s has been the shifting of the risk of interest-rate fluctuations from the depositors and financial intermediary to the borrower. In the past, depositors were generally paid a low, fixed rate that remained the same regardless of inflation and interest-rate levels in general, and borrowers tended to pay a rate that did not fluctuate with market levels except

TABLE 3-7. Income and Expenses of All Insured
Commercial Banks (percent of average assets)[a]

Item	1974	1975	1976	1977	1978
Gross interest earned[b]	6.19%	5.45%	6.38%	6.46%	7.24%
Gross interest expense	3.55	2.85	3.47	3.54	4.17
Net interest margin	2.64	2.60	2.91	2.92	3.07
Noninterest income[b]	0.70	0.81	0.72	0.71	0.74
Loan loss provision	0.23	0.33	0.32	0.26	0.25
Other noninterest expense	2.17	2.23	2.44	2.45	2.49
Income before tax	0.94	0.85	0.88	0.92	1.06
Taxes[c]	0.21	0.17	0.21	0.23	0.29
Other[d]	0.01	0.01	0.03	0.01	-0.02
Net income	0.72	0.69	0.70	0.71	0.76
Cash dividends declared	0.28	0.29	0.27	0.26	0.27
Net retained earnings	0.44	0.40	0.43	0.45	0.49

[a]Average of beginning- and end-of-year fully consolidated assets net of loan loss reserves.
[b]Beginning in 1976, interest on balances with banks was reported separately; prior to that it was an undefined component of other noninterest income. In 1976, it amounted to 0.39 percent of average assets.
[c]Includes all taxes estimated to be due on income, on extraordinary gains, and on securities gains.
[d]Includes securities and extraordinary gains or losses (-) gross of taxes.
Source: *Federal Reserve Bulletin, Insured Commercial Bank Income in 1978*, pp. 692-706.

as a function of the level of interest rates at the time the loan was contracted for. Now almost the opposite has occurred, with the borrower and the lender paying and receiving rates, respectively, that are in some form or another tied to changes in interest-rate levels. Thus, most of the risk for interest-rate fluctuations has now been passed to the borrower. Approximately 60 percent of the commercial and industrial loans outstanding in 1978 were of the flexible type, wherein the interest rate charged was tied to the prime rate.

One might think that as banks have passed the risk of interest-rate fluctuations to the borrower through flexible-rate loans, their net interest margin—the difference between the interest rate received and rate paid—would remain about the same or decline because of reduced risk. As shown in Table 3–7, however, this result has not occurred. The table shows that the net interest margin rose substantially during tight money periods, reaching a high of 3.07 in 1978, which is considerably above the historical average of slightly over 2 percent. It appears that the interest from the earning assets—primarily loans—was used to offset higher loan losses and much higher expenses in bank premises (as reflected in the other noninterest expense line, Table 3–7), which was attributed to larger occupancy and equipment expenses.

Federal Reserve Banks

Capital-Market Functions

Although the Federal Reserve Banks have their greatest direct influence in the short-term money market, some discussion of them is pertinent to our study, on several grounds: (1) these institutions invest some of the funds representing member bank and Treasury deposits in intermediate- and long-term credits and so may be classed as financial intermediaries; (2) the Reserve Banks are the largest institutional owners of U.S. government obligations; (3) their credit policy has an important impact on the prices and yields of long-term securities and mortgages; (4) their open-market operations in Treasury securities now involve longer-term obligations; and (5) as fiscal agents for the Treasury, they play an important role in the marketing of federal securities.

Sources of Federal Reserve Funds

Member bank deposits, Treasury deposits, Federal Reserve notes, and capital accounts provide the funds for the investments of the banks in securities and other assets. Member banks are required (1978) to hold reserves ranging from 7 to 22 percent of their demand deposits depending on asset size—7 percent for banks with less than $2 million in demand deposits up to 22 percent for reserve city banks. They hold 3 percent of savings and from 3 to 6 percent of time deposits—depending on term to maturity—at the Federal Reserve Banks of their districts, less some vault cash counted as reserve. At the end of 1978, member bank reserves on deposit totaled $31.2 billion, or about 20 percent of Federal Reserve assets. Their increase reflects the growth of bank deposit liabilities. The size of reserve accounts is also influenced by the composition of the deposits of the member banks (demand versus time).

Federal Reserve notes outstanding totaled $103.3 billion, or 68 percent of assets at the end of 1978; capital stock and other capital accounts totaled $2.8 billion, or 2 percent of total assets. It is appropriate to think of the liabilities of the central banks as the result of asset acquisition rather than vice versa. "Federal Reserve funds" are supplied by Federal Reserve Bank credit outstanding (U.S. government securities held, discounts and advances, and float), gold stock, and Treasury currency outstanding, and are absorbed by currency in circulation (including Federal Reserve notes), deposits (including reserves of member banks), and minor accounts. In any consolidation of banking system funds, that is, where funds of commercial and central banks are combined, the member bank reserve deposits at the Federal Reserve Banks are eliminated to avoid double counting. Such deposits are not additions to the deposits of the member banks on which they are based. For this reason we omit any annual sources of funds data for Federal Reserve Banks similar to the data presented for other institutions.

All liabilities of Federal Reserve Banks should be considered as very short-term, so their assets must be highly liquid. For this reason, the chief impact of the Reserve Banks on the capital markets is more indirect (through other financial intermediaries) than direct.

Uses of Funds: Ownership of United States Government Obligations

The Federal Reserve Banks play a direct role in the capital market through their holdings of federal and agency securities (the only securities they own). Federal securities held have increased from $78.5 billion in 1973 to more than $114 billion at the end of 1978. Annual changes in ownership of direct, federal debt and federal agency debt in the period 1970-1978 were as follows (billions of dollars)[8]:

	1970	1971	1972	1973	1974	1975	1976	1977	1978
U.S. Treasury obligations	$5.0	$8.1	$-0.3	$8.6	$2.0	$7.4	$ 9.1	$5.8	$7.7
Obligations of federal agencies	—	0.4	0.6	0.7	3.2	1.0	0.9	1.4	-0.4
	$5.0	$8.5	$ 0.3	$9.3	$5.2	$8.4	$10.0	$7.2	$7.3

---

[8] *Federal Reserve Bulletin;* Federal Deposit Insurance Corporation, *Annual Reports.*

All federal securities held are fully marketable, and maturities of five years or less constituted almost 80 percent of total holdings at the end of 1978. This indicated little activity by the Federal Reserve officials in influencing rates on long-term debt.

Unlike private lending institutions. Federal Reserve Banks do not seek the highest yields. Investment decisions are based on factors such as money supply, market stability, and so on, rather than the availability of profitable outlets for their funds.

Influence on Market Yields

The chief influence of the Reserve Banks in the long-term capital markets is through the impact of their credit policy as directed by the Federal Reserve on the loan and investment activities of banks and other financial intermediaries. Changes in the reserve requirements of member banks in the discount rate on targeted federal funds rates and in the volume and direction of open-market operations (purchase or sale) of federal securities (almost continuous) all influence the size of member bank reserve deposits and thus encourage the contraction or expansion of member bank lending activity. All except the first of these types of credit control have a specific influence on bank loan rates and other short-term rates in the money market. They influence the volume and yields of intermediate-term loans and mortgages as a part of total bank loans.

The immediate impact of changing Federal Reserve credit policy is felt on short-term interest rates. Increases in the discount rate and in the targeted federal funds rate were designed to stiffen short-term market rates as part of the program for curbing credit expansion. The most sensitive short-term rates, those on Treasury bills, serve as bellwether rates for other short-term instruments.

The most continuous tool of credit control is open-market operations. From 1953 through 1961, the purchases and sales of Treasury obligations directed by the Open Market Committee (OMC) were concentrated on "bills only." It was felt that any change in short-term interest rates would, through arbitrage and substitution, eventually make itself felt in yields on longer-term Treasury obligations and on other bond yields. In 1961, the "bills only" policy was abandoned in favor of direct intervention in the long-term markets. But the extent of such intervention has been modest, and, in fact, since 1968 the actions of the OMC have been directed almost entirely to the short-term market.

Occasional attempts have been made by the OMC to adjust long-term rates while not appreciably affecting short-term rates or pushing short-term rates in the opposite direction. The OMC in conjunction with the Treasury undertook an "operation twist" in 1962–1964, where short-term rates were nudged upward (chiefly through the Treasury policy of emphasizing the sale of short maturities), and long-term rates were held firm, in keeping with the Administration's desire to encourage domestic economic growth. During this period (1962–1964) the

Federal Reserve Banks substantially increased their holdings of long-term federal bonds to aid in this objective. In 1973–1974 and again in 1978–1979, the policy shifted toward short-term securities as short-term rates were kept high to help combat inflation. In October 1979, Treasury Bills yielded over 12.9 percent.

Changes in the general level of interest rates affect the prices of long-term instruments more than those of short-term assets and also lead to shifts among types of assets on the part of investing institutions.[9] A restrictive credit policy that eventually results in higher long-term yields encourages institutions to shift from Treasury issues to higher yielding mortgages, corporate bonds, and municipal bonds. However, if the flow of savings funds is declining, such shifts are discouraged by the risk of price losses. The volume of forward commitments in mortgages also declines as institutions wait for higher yields in the future.

Marketing Federal Securities

The Federal Reserve Banks participate directly in the marketing of federal securities. They receive the applications of banks, dealers, and others for new issues of federal securities, allot them in accordance with Treasury instructions, deliver them, receive payment, and credit the Treasury accounts (see Chapter 8). The Banks redeem federal securities as they mature, pay interest coupons, and otherwise service the debt.

---

[9] A change from an 8 percent to a 9 percent yield would cause the price of a one-year obligation selling at par to drop to 99.06; a twenty-year 8 percent bond selling at par would decline to 90.80.

```
4444444444444444444444444444444444444444444444444444444444444444444444444444444
4444444444444444444444444444444444444444444444444444444444444444444444444444444
444444444444444444444444444   444   444444444444    4444444444444444444444444444
444444444444444444444444444   4444   44444444444    4444444444444444444444444444
444444444444444444444444444   44444   444444444    44444444444444444444444444444
444444444444444444444444444   444444   4444444    444444444444444444444444444444
444444444444444444444444444   4444444   44444    4444444444444444444444444444444
444444444444444444444444444   44444444   444    44444444444444444444444444444444
444444444444444444444444444   444444444   4    444444444444444444444444444444444
444444444444444444444444444   444444444        444444444444444444444444444444444
444444444444444444444444444   4444444444      444444444444444444444444444444444
4444444444444444444444444444444444444444444444444444444444444444444444444444444
4444444444444444444444444444444444444444444444444444444444444444444444444444444
```

Nonbank Thrift Institutions

THIS chapter discusses three nonbank thrift institutions, mutual savings banks, savings and loan associations, and credit unions. MSBs and S&L's are similar in many respects, especially in regard to their emphasis on mortgages and their similarities in structure, regulation, taxation, and savings plans. Credit unions, although differing substantially in asset structure and investment strategy from mutual savings banks (MSBs) and savings and loan associations (S&Ls), are discussed here because of their dramatic increase in size, the recent liberalization of lending practices, and their competitiveness for the savings dollar.

In the past there has been a good deal of discussion on the problems facing thrift institutions in their competition for savings, particularly with respect to commercial banks. With the general liberalization of lending practices and the flexibility created by regulatory authorities in the competition for deposits, however, many of the distinctions between these arch rivals have begun to disappear. To be sure, significant differences still exist, but the general trend is obviously toward more similarity among all financial institutions in the services they offer to the general public. Some of the remaining problems facing MSB and S&L institutions in their quest for greater flexibility and profitability are discussed later in the chapter.

It is easy to get the impression that MSBs and S&Ls are so similar that they can be discussed as one institution. Actually, there are considerable differences regarding their respective asset size and investment policies that warrant a separate discussion of each institution. We shall examine the general nature and functions, and sources and uses of funds for each institution, including credit unions, before turning to the joint problems faced by all of them in competing with other financial institutions.

Mutual Savings Banks

General Nature and Functions

At the beginning of 1979 there were 467 mutual savings banks chartered in seventeen states (mostly in the Middle Atlantic states and New England), with total assets of $158.2 billion. Nearly three-fourths of the banks were located in three states (New York, Massachusetts, and Connecticut) that held over four-fifths of the combined assets. Although chartering of mutual savings banks is currently limited to seventeen states, their investment operations have been national in scope. They can lend and hold mortgages (often limited to 20 percent of assets) on properties located in the thirty-three non-savings-bank states. In addition, there is no limit on the amount of their holdings of government-underwritten or mortgage-backed securities (see Chapter 12).

Mutual savings banks are the only deposit institutions functioning solely under state charter. They are owned by depositors, who receive all earnings after provision for adequate reserves. Management is in the hands of boards of trustees. Ancillary activities include the sale of life insurance by banks in New York, Massachusetts, and Connecticut.

Sources of Investment Funds

Savings deposits provide the funds for over 90 percent of the assets. The balance consists of general reserve accounts, including contingency reserves and undivided profits, and other liabilities, such as short-term borrowings. The ratio of general reserve accounts to deposits is the basic measure of safety. For all MSBs it averaged 7.0 percent at the end of 1978 (Table 4-1). This ratio tends to fall during periods of rapid deposit expansion and good loan demand, and rise when the opposite holds.

From 1955 through 1978, the total deposits of mutual savings banks increased

TABLE 4-1. Combined Deposits and Reserve Accounts of
Mutual Savings Banks, at Year End, 1965-1978
(billions of dollars)

	1965	1970	1975	1978
Deposits (savings and time)	$52.4	$71.6	$109.9	$141.1
General reserves	4.7	5.7	8.4	10.9
Total	$57.1	$77.3	$118.3	$152.0

Sources: *Federal Reserve Bulletin;* National Association of Mutual Savings Banks, *National Fact Book of Mutual Savings Banking* (New York, annual).

from $28 billion to more than $141 billion, representing a compounded growth rate of over 7 percent per year. Deposit growth, however, particularly since 1966, has been very erratic, tending to be high when overall interest rate levels are relatively low, when MSBs are paying about 1 percent more than commercial banks on savings deposits, or when rates paid on savings deposits have been increased by all institutions. Deposit growth has been low, or even declining, when opposite conditions hold in the financial markets. In 1973-1974 and in 1979, for example, losses of deposits to other types of investments were caused by high interest rates on competing securities.

During the postwar period, growth of MSB deposits fell behind the growth in savings accounts of commercial banks, the reserves of life insurance companies, and sharply behind the growth of accounts in savings and loan associations. This stems from mutual savings banks' lack of national exposure, from the specialized functions they perform, from the slow economic growth in the New England area, and from the lower interest rates paid on deposits.

To meet the competition of commercial banks and other institutions, MSBs and S&Ls have been allowed to offer differentiated time deposits with varying yields depending on the amount deposited, the length of maturity, and the six-month Treasury bill rate.

Deposit Flows and Fluctuations

The annual increases in deposits and net worth accounts from 1970 through 1978 are shown in Table 4-2. As noted earlier, these increases have changed sharply from year to year even though during this period substantial funds have been provided for capital market investments.

The decline in deposit flows from $10.1 billion in 1972 to only $4.9 and $3.0 billion in 1973 and 1974, respectively, was chiefly attributable to the turbulence in the money and capital markets that culminated in the "credit crunch" of 1973 and 1974. Available funds dried up, and with commercial banks paying higher rates on certificates of deposit and on "wild card" certificates, and with higher rates on open-market securities, individuals transferred savings from thrift institutions to government securities and other financial institutions as interest rates rose to historic levels. To meet severe strains on

TABLE 4-2. Annual Changes in Deposits and Reserves,
Mutual Savings Banks, 1970-1978 (billions of dollars)

	1970	1971	1972	1973	1974	1975	1976	1977	1978
Deposits	$4.5	$ 9.7	$10.1	$4.8	$3.0	$11.2	$13.0	$11.1	$8.9
General reserves	0.2	0.4	0.6	0.6	0.4	0.5	0.6	0.9	0.9
Total	$4.7	$10.1	$10.7	$5.4	$3.4	$11.7	$13.6	$12.0	$9.8

Sources: National Association of Mutual Savings Banks, *National Fact Book of Mutual Savings Banks* (New York, annual); Federal Reserve *Flow-of-Funds Accounts*.

liquidity and earnings in 1973 and 1974, mutual savings banks drew upon the significant reserves built up in previous years and sold U.S. government securities.

In 1975 and 1976, as a result of declining open-market interest rates, individuals reversed the procedure and shifted substantial funds from open-market instruments into savings accounts. For these years combined deposits of mutual savings banks increased by over $24 billion. In 1978-1979 money tightened considerably and interest rates rose to unprecedented levels, exceeding, in many cases, even the previous highs recorded in 1973-1974. However, although deposit growth at MSBs moderated substantially, reasonably good positive flows were still obtained as the flexibility from new deposit certificates allowing for higher rates to be paid enabled MSBs to effectively compete for investors savings.

Despite increases in the level of earnings in the late 1970s, the reserves of MSBs have not kept pace with the growth in deposits. In part this can be explained by higher taxes, which restricted capital buildup as a result of the 1969 Tax Act, and by government action, which encouraged deposit growth through lower reserve ratios, bank borrowings, and higher ceiling rates on deposit certificates.

Annual sources of funds for capital-market investment   Deducting from the figures in Table 4-2 the net changes in cash and miscellaneous assets produces the following annual sources of new funds available for investment in capital-market assets (billions of dollars):

1970	1971	1972	1973	1974	1975	1976	1977	1978
$3.6	$9.4	$10.0	$4.6	$3.1	$10.5	$11.9	$11.2	$8.7

Such data on net changes do not represent the amount of funds actually used in capital-market transactions. The amortization of mortgages and the maturing of bonds, together with investment income, produce substantial additional funds for reinvestment.

General Investment Policy

The basic purposes of savings banks require that conservative policies of lending and investment be followed. Although deposits turn over slowly, some degree of liquidity must be maintained. The importance of the ultimate safety of assets explains the legal requirements that govern investment in securities and mortgages in the various states.[1] These regulations specify the eligible instruments, the standards of quality applied to each (except federal obligations, which automatically qualify), and the limitations on some major instruments as

---

[1] For a convenient discussion of legal lists, see National Association of Mutual Savings Banks, *Mutual Savings Banking: Basic Characteristics and Role in the National Economy*, a monograph prepared for the Commission on Money and Credit (Englewood Cliffs, N.J.: Prentice-Hall, Inc., 1962), Chap. 5.

percentages of total assets or total deposits. In most states the prudent-man rule applies; this rule, in theory, permits broad discretion but in fact results in the acquisition of high-grade investments. Legal restrictions limit the demand for certain securities (such as industrial bonds) and for mortgages, especially those originating out of state. These limitations restrict the flow of funds through the national capital markets and contribute to the differential yields among different categories of investments. Compared to savings and loan associations, however, mutual savings banks have consdierably more latitude in their choice of investments.

Table 4–3 shows the amounts and distribution of industry assets for selected years beginning in 1965. During this period, major shifts took place in the investment powers of savings banks and in their role in the capital markets. Their most important impact is seen in the decline in the relative position of federal securities and mortgages as a result of improved yields among alternative capital-market instruments, especially corporate bonds.

In 1950, federal securities amounted to $10.8 billion, or 48 percent of mutual savings banks assets. At the end of 1978 on an asset base of over $158 billion, they totaled only $4.6 billion, or less than 3 percent of total assets.

The primary beneficiary of the decline in federal securities investment was mortgages, which rose from $8 billion in 1950 to $95 billion at the end of 1978. The percentage of assets held in mortgages rose from 36 percent in 1950 to a high of 76.2 percent in 1965 but has since declined to 60 percent at the end of 1978. Thus, although the absolute amount invested in mortgages by mutual savings banks has continued to increase yearly since 1965, there has been a relative decline in the percentage of new funds placed in mortgages.

The data in Table 4–3 do not reveal the interim cyclical changes in flow of funds into assets that reflect variations in relative yield differentials among alternative capital-market instruments, especially the differences between the changing yields on corporate and municipal bonds and the relatively inflexible yields on mortgages. During periods of credit stringency, such as 1973, 1974, and 1978, the emphasis on new investment was in corporate bonds rather than mortgages, as rates on the former investments approached or exceeded those on the latter. MSBs have placed large amounts of their new funds into corporate bonds as yields have remained high. The liquidity offered by corporate bonds compared to mortgages is another contributing factor. More recently, mutual savings banks have been adding amounts of tax-exempt state and local issues in response to sharply increased income taxes. With rising income tax rates for mutual savings banks as a result of the 1969 Tax Act, tax-exempt securities should continue to grow as an investment holding.

The relative importance of major types of assets varies considerably among banks, domiciled in different states because of differences in legal list requirements, strictness of supervision, need for liquidity, rate of supply of funds, and local investment opportunities. For example, of the major states, the banks in

TABLE 4–3. Combined Assets of Mutual Savings Banks: Amounts and Percentages, at Year End, 1965–1978
(billions of dollars)

	1965		1970		1975		1978	
	Amount	Percent	Amount	Percent	Amount	Percent	Amount	Percent
Cash assets	$ 1.0	1.5	$ 1.3	1.6	$ 2.3	1.9	$ 3.7	2.3%
Mortgage loans (net)	44.4	76.2	57.8	73.2	77.2	63.8	95.2	60.2
U.S. Treasury obligations	5.5	9.4	3.2	4.1	4.7	3.9	5.0	3.2
Bonds of federal agencies[a]	0.8	1.4	2.2	2.8	6.1	5.0	13.4	8.5
State and local government bonds	0.3	0.5	0.2	0.2	1.5	1.2	3.3	2.1
Corporate bonds	2.9	5.3	8.3	10.5	17.5	14.5	21.6	13.7
Preferred stocks	0.4	0.7	0.7	0.9	2.9	2.4	} 4.9	3.0
Common stocks	1.0	1.8	1.8	2.3	1.5	1.2		
Other assets	1.8	3.2	3.5	4.4	7.4	6.1	11.1	7.1
Total	$58.2	100 %	$79.0	100 %	$121.1	100 %	$158.2	100%

[a]Includes federally sponsored and federal budget agency securities.
Sources: *Federal Reserve Bulletin*; National Association of Mutual Savings Banks, *National Fact Book of Mutual Savings Banking* (annual).

Connecticut have the highest percentage of assets in mortgages and those in Pennsylvania the highest percentage in corporate securities, while those in Maryland have the highest percentage in U.S. government securities. A major drive for the federal chartering of mutual banks was to broaden and unify investment powers and to make funds available in a wider national market.[2]

Securities Investments

Historically speaking, savings banks have played a relatively minor role in the securities markets, which include bonds of all types and stocks. More recently, however, these securities have grown in importance because of their high relative yields so that they now (1978) constitute about 30 percent of total savings bank assets compared to only 16 percent in 1965. As noted earlier, within this group there has been a gradual shift away from low-yielding federal securities toward a new emphasis on corporate bonds. Lower liquidity reserve requirements than for commercial banks have meant less need for cash, and hence secondary reserves could consist of longer-maturity bonds. The pressure for ultimate safety requires high standards for corporate bonds; however, shifting between bonds and mortgages occurs depending upon the availability of funds and changes in the relative yields on the different investments.

Unlike life insurance companies, which acquire large amounts of corporate bonds by private placement, savings banks obtain these securities mainly in the open market and so turn to that market for funds when resale is indicated.

United States government securities   Federal obligations were typically held for safety, liquidity, and income. They reached their peak of popularity at the end of World War II because of the efforts of the banks to aid in war financing and the lack of a good supply of mortgages and corporate bonds. The great postwar movement into the higher-yielding mortgages reduced the combined holdings of Treasury and federal agency obligations from 63 percent of total assets in 1945 to only 3 percent at the end of 1978.

Savings banks have traditionally held federal securities for liquidity rather than for earnings. Federal securities with a maturity of five years or less constitute more than 78 percent of total federal securities held (1978).

Corporate bonds   Holdings of corporate and foreign bonds have increased both relatively and absolutely in the postwar period. At the end of 1978 they totaled $21.6 billion, or $13.7 percent of total assets. This was almost three times the holdings of corporate bonds in 1970 and was second only to the growth in mortgages during this time (but mortgages declined to less than 60 percent of

---

[2]National Association of Mutual Savings Banks, *National Fact Book of Mutual Savings Banking.* 1978

total assets). The high rate of interest paid on corporate bonds in recent years has been responsible for the continued relative shift from mortgages to bonds. As of December 1978, the composite rate on corporate bonds was 9.64 percent versus an average rate of 9.95 percent on new home mortgages. Because of their liquidity compared to mortgages, corporate bonds serve as secondary liquidity sources and often are sold in periods of outflows such as in 1973-1974.

Other securities investments Holdings of other securities investments by savings banks represent a small percentage of total assets. Municipal bonds have increased in importance as savings banks sought to minimize the effects of the 1969 Tax Act. These securities, although representing only 2 percent of total assets at the end of 1978, have more than quadrupled in size since 1973. Similarly, federal agency securities have increased in importance because of their high yields, low risk, and increasing abundance, as federal programs have encouraged functions financed by federal agencies. The purchase of corporate stocks was fostered in 1951 by the imposition of income taxation on mutual savings banks, giving dividend income (which is 85 percent tax exempt) a special appeal, and by changes in state laws that made modest amounts of selected common stocks eligible for purchase. At the end of 1978 savings banks held $3.0 billion in common stock and $1.9 billion in preferred stock. Given the fiduciary responsibility of savings banks, however, it is not likely that preferred or common stock, regardless of the potential yields, will ever amount to anything more than a token investment for savings banks.

Mortgage Investments: General Policy

Sound mortgages as part of a larger portfolio are good investments for savings banks except in times when high interest rates cause disintermediation, resulting in cash flow problems. Normally, liquidity is provided by holdings of federal securities and by careful management of cash flows. When disintermediation occurs, sales of all kinds of investments, including mortgages in the secondary market, are frequently necessary to generate the needed liquidity. At the end of 1978, mutual savings banks held $95.2 billion, or 8.1 percent, of the total outstanding mortgage debt of $1,170 billion and $62.3 billion, or 8.2 percent, of the $759.6 billion of the one- to four-family residential debt outstanding. Real estate loans constituted 60 percent of their combined assets in 1978, a drop of thirteen percentage points since 1970 (see Table 4-3). Slower growth than other financial institutions and the diversity of investment opportunities have been responsible for relative decline of MSBs in the mortgage market.

The postwar increase in mortgages (Table 4-4) reflects a number of factors: (1) the increase in deposits and, therefore, of assets; (2) the great postwar demand for housing credit; (3) the development of federally guaranteed loans; (4) the relatively attractive yields on mortgages as compared to other securities;

TABLE 4-4. Mortgage Loans Held by Mutual Savings Banks, at Year End, 1965–1978 (billions of dollars)

	1965	1970	1975	1978
Farm	a	$ 0.1	$ 0.1	$ 0.1
Residential:				
1–4-family	$30.2	$37.5	$50.0	$62.3
Multifamily	10.1	12.4	13.8	16.5
	$40.3	$49.9	$63.8	$78.8
Commercial and industrial	4.3	7.9	13.4	16.3
Total	$44.6	$57.9	$77.2	$95.2
Conventional and other	$19.4	$29.8	$50.4	$69.2
FHA-insured	13.8	16.1	14.4	14.2
VA-guaranteed	11.4	12.0	12.4	11.8
Total	$44.6	$57.9	$77.2	$95.2

aLess than $100 million.

Sources: *Federal Reserve Bulletin;* National Association of Mutual Savings Banks, *National Fact Book of Mutual Savings Banking* (annual). Some figures do not add to total due to rounding.

(5) the liberalization of regulations governing investment in mortgages whereby loan-to-value ratios for conventional mortgages have risen to 80 percent and more in most states; (6) the growth of private mortgage insurance; and (7) the increasing practice of out-of-state lending, which has been facilitated by greater use of local mortgage company correspondents.

In the past, mutual savings banks sought to maximize earnings (and hence the rate paid to depositors) by setting as high a ratio of mortgages to total assets as regulations and local demand would allow and by seeking outside outlets for mortgages funds. This has changed somewhat as mortgage yields no longer exceed the levels of several other competing investments.

Residential and Commercial Mortgages

Residential loans have typically accounted for better than 80 percent of total mortgage holdings by savings banks, with commercial mortgages representing the remainder. At the end of 1978, residential mortgages totaled $79 billion and commercial and industrial mortgages $16 billion (Table 4-4). The percentage of commercial mortgages in the portfolio has risen in the 1970s as a result of the higher interest rates generally available on these mortgages compared to residential mortgages.

Mutual savings banks are second only to the Federal National Mortgage Association as a source of federally underwritten home loans. At the end of 1978, they held $26 billion of FHA-insured and VA-guaranteed mortgages, or 15 percent of the combined total. These mortgages have declined in importance since 1968 as savings banks have placed more funds in conventional loans. Prime reasons for this shift were (1) the "maximum" rates allowed on FHA and VA loans, which tended to lag behind conventional rates and were less than the going mortgage market; (2) the delay and extra paperwork in closing FHA and VA mortgage loans; and (3) the rise of conventional mortgage insurance, which allowed high mortgage-to-value ratios, offsetting a previous FHA and VA advantage, with little risk to savings banks.

The increase in the contractual rate on government-insured loans to 11½ percent in 1979 was designed to maintain investment in federally sponsored liens, but continued increases in market yields left these liens in a poor competitive position (see Figure 12-1). Efforts have been made to reduce the paperwork and processing delays on government-insured loans. However, since the private sector can now offer most of the benefits of government-insured loans with respect to down payments and insurance guarantees, it is expected that savings banks will continue to prefer the private market and place much of their mortgage funds in conventional mortgages.

The continuing development of the secondary mortgage market, especially in insured mortgages, provides another useful outlet for mortgage funds. In this manner MSBs can be more geographically diversified while obtaining a guaranteed return.

Annual Uses of Funds in the Capital Market

The data in Table 4-5 show the annual changes in capital-market investments for 1970-1978. The comparatively low net changes in 1970 and again in 1974 reflect the credit squeezes of those years. Large increases in total funds flows in 1971-1972 and 1975-1978 reflect the slowed economy and lower rates on securities, competing directly with savings deposits. The sharp rise in competing rates in 1974 and in 1978 led to the predictable decline in mutual savings banks growth.

Again, the data show a preponderance of total funds placed in mortgages, with commercial mortgages receiving considerable sums because of the higher rates paid. High purchases of corporate bonds in 1970-1972 turned to net sales of $1 billion in 1973 as savings banks met liquidity requirements and mortgage commitments, but then returned in 1975 and 1976 as high yields made these securities preferred investments.

Savings Banks in the National Capital Markets

Although savings banks are chartered in only seventeen states and Puerto Rico, they have asserted some influence in the mortgage market at the national level. Interstate lending, formerly dominated by life insurance companies, has achieved major proportions. As noted previously, at the end of 1978, approximately $25.0 billion, or 26 percent, of the savings banks mortgage portfolios

TABLE 4-5. Annual Flow of Funds into Capital-Market Assets of Mutual Savings Banks, 1970-1978
(billions of dollars)

	1970	1971	1972	1973	1974	1975	1976	1977	1978
U.S. Treasury securities	$-0.1	$0.1	$ 0.2	$-0.5	$-0.4	$ 2.2	$ 1.1	$ 0.1	$-0.9
Federal agency securities[a]	0.4	0.8	1.1	0.1	0.2	1.7	2.9	2.6	1.8
State and local government securities	–	0.2	0.5	–	–	0.6	0.9	0.4	0.5
Corporate and foreign bonds	1.2	3.9	2.1	-1.1	0.9	3.5	2.8	1.2	0.3
Corporate stocks	0.3	0.5	0.6	0.4	0.2	0.2	0.1	0.4	0.1
Home mortgages	1.1	1.2	2.6	2.6	0.7	0.8	2.9	4.6	4.5
Other mortgages	0.7	2.7	2.9	3.1	1.5	1.5	1.2	1.9	2.4
Total	$ 3.6	$9.4	$10.0	$ 4.6	$ 3.1	$10.5	$11.9	$11.2	$ 8.7

[a]Includes federally sponsored and federal budget agency securities.

Sources: National Association of Mutual Savings Banks, *National Fact Book of Mutual Savings Banking* (annual); Federal Reserve *Flow-of-Funds Accounts*. (Some columns do not add to totals because of rounding.)

were held in the 33 non-savings-bank states. Most out-of-state loans are acquired from mortgage companies that retain the servicing of the loans (see Chapter 12). Relaxed regulations permitting out-of-state loans, together with the growing use of correspondents, have done much to break down geographical barriers. Many smaller banks confine their lending operations to their local communities. But the larger Eastern banks are active exporters of capital to capital-deficient areas such as the Southwest and the West.

In addition, savings banks have been actively participating in the national mortgage market by purchasing substantial amounts of Government National Mortgage Association (called "Ginnie Mae") securities (see Chapter 12). These securities are backed by government-insured (FHA and VA and Farmers Home Administration) mortgages and hence are fully guaranteed by the U.S. government. The mortgages are pooled and a covering security is issued. The principal and interest on the Ginnie Mae security is paid by the repayments from the underlying pool of FHA and VA mortgages. Holdings of these investments by savings banks totaled $10 billion in 1978. This represents the second largest investment in GNMA-guaranteed mortgage-backed securities among financial institutions.

Savings and Loan Associations

Savings and loan associations are the most important single source of home mortgage credit and, in addition, the only major financial institution whose express purpose is to make home mortgage loans. They typically hold more than 80 percent of their assets in mortgages of all types. At the end of 1978 mortgages totaled $432.9 billion, or 82 percent of their total assets of $523.8 billion. Hence, associations operate almost exclusively in the long-term markets, with activity confined mostly to the financing of local housing.

As we will see later, this heavy emphasis on mortgages, especially during tight money, high-interest-rate periods, has caused considerable problems in the past for these associations and their functioning in the capital markets. It is not surprising that their recent efforts have been aimed at greater flexibility in the capital markets and reducing their dependence on mortgages as an almost singular source of revenues. Additional efforts have been made toward achieving a better hedged position between their assets and liabilities, and by issuing flexible-rate deposit certificates and emphasizing valuable-rate mortgages.

General Nature and Functions

Savings and loan associations are organized under both federal and state charters. The savings accounts of all federally chartered associations are insured (to $40,000 per account) by the Federal Savings and Loan Insurance Corporation. State-chartered associations may also join the corporation. Federal and insured state associations are regulated by the Federal Home Loan Bank and state regulatory departments.

At the end of 1978 there were 2,000 federally chartered associations with assets of $298 billion and 2,723 state-chartered associations with assets of $225 billion. This represents a decline of 1,724 state associations and an increase of 127 federal associations since 1960. The consolidation in associations has been the result of mergers, liquidations, and conversions by many state associations to federal charters.

All federally chartered associations were initially organized as mutual associations without stockholders. In the past, some mutual associations converted to stock associations in order to sell shares to the public. In 1963, a moratorium was placed on conversions and the moratorium was extended on several occasions except that some associations were allowed to convert to stock ownership under a test program.

Many associations desire to convert from mutual, or depositor-owned, associations to stock corporations so they can raise capital by selling stock. This could be helpful during tight money periods when interest rates are high and disintermediation is likely to occur or when deposit growth is high and additional reserves are needed. However, the mechanics of conversion and the windfall profits on conversion led many to resist conversion attempts, and in 1977 the Federal Home Loan Bank Board placed a freeze on conversions.

Stock associations are legal in twenty-two states, and in 1977 there were 747 associations in existence before the moratorium was declared. Three states—California, Ohio, and Texas—control over 74 percent of all stock association assets. At the end of 1978 stock associations held 20 percent of the assets of all savings and loan associations.

General Sources of Funds

In a significant step, in 1968, federally chartered associations (and state-chartered mutual associations where state laws permitted) were allowed classification as "deposit institutions." Holders of "savings accounts" were to be considered creditors in every sense of the term. (Depositors would, however, retain their voting privileges.) Previously, depositors were considered "savings shareholders" and payments made to savers had to be referred to as dividends or earnings. Consequently, a dividend once declared had to be the same for those depositors with equal sums on deposit. The new ruling applying to all associations allowed deposits to be differentiated according to maturity and the amount of deposit such that higher rates could be paid, for example, to those who agreed to keep the funds on deposit for a specified time period.

In addition, a new ruling, in 1971, allowed for flexibility in passbook savings interest rates. Associations can now pay interest at less than the regular rate for several kinds of passbook accounts. Formerly, an association had to pay its declared rate on all passbook accounts.

Savings accounts of associations amounted to $431.0 billion at the end of 1978, about four times the $110 billion at the end of 1965. This amounted to 35 percent of savings balances in all deposit institutions. Major factors contributing to this substantial increase were (1) the introduction of flexible rates and several new types of savings accounts, (2) aggressive promotion, (3) a savings rate of individuals of about 6.0 percent of disposable income, (4) rising rates paid on savings accounts relative to competing institutions, and (5) poor investor experience in the securities markets, particularly common stocks.

The introduction of the certificate account as a second major type of savings instrument—besides the passbook account—greatly aided the growth in total deposits. Certificates are issued in fixed amounts for a specified maturity and earn a higher interest rate than is paid on passbook accounts. Most of the increase in deposits since 1968 has been accounted for by increases in certificate accounts. In 1968, certificates accounted for 23 percent of total savings deposits, with the remaining 77 percent in passbook accounts. By the end of 1978, certificates had grown to over 68 percent of total savings.

Savings accounts of $431 billion constituted 82 percent of total liabilities and net worth in 1978. Other liabilities were: advances from Federal Home Loan Banks and other debt, $43.0 billion, up sharply from $20.6 billion in 1975; and miscellaneous liabilities, including loans in process and property taxes held in escrow, $20.6 billion. Net worth totaled 29.0 billion.

The protection to savings and loan account holders afforded by reserves and capital (6.8 percent of savings accounts in 1978) is somewhat less than that provided by commercial banks (see Chapter 3). However, safety is better measured by the quality and liquidity of assets than by the dollar relationship of assets to liabilities.[3]

Another growing source of funds in addition to growth in deposits, mortgage payment inflows, and Federal Home Loan Bank borrowings is the sale of mortgages or the issuance of mortgage-backed bonds. The development of a good secondary mortgage market enables S&Ls to better adjust their cash flows. Mortgage-backed bonds are similar to a typical bond except that they are backed by collateral in the form of a specified pool of mortgages. The mortgaged-backed security is the direct obligation of the issuing S&L, and hence the bonds carry

---

[3] Beginning in 1966, the Federal House Loan Bank Board (FHLBB) required that associations with adjusted net worth (actual net worth less an allowance for delinquent mortgages) between 8 and 10 percent of specified assets (conventional loans plus 20 percent of FHA and VA loans) to allocate 5 percent of net income to reserves each year. These regulations were substantially revised during 1971 and 1972. Required reserves are now equal to a minimum of 5 percent of total savings, but these can be accumulated over a period of time. Furthermore, required reserve allocations can be suspended by the FHLBB, especially when associations have difficulty in meeting the requirements because of a heavy inflow of savings, or when they want to encourage mortgage lending. Additional changes were made in computing the net worth requirement; the major change tied the net worth requirement to the amount of risk exposure in the assets. The higher the percentage of risky assets in the portfolio, the higher is the net worth requirement.

no federal insurance or guarantee. Mortgage-backed bonds may be issued in amounts up to 5 percent of total savings deposits. In 1978 about 1 billion mortgage-backed securities were issued.

Annual Sources of Funds

Annual sources of net funds for 1970-1978, derived by changes in balance sheet items, are shown in Table 4-6. The data reflect a similar pattern to that of mutual savings banks, in that savings flows decline in tight money periods such as 1973 and 1974 and increase substantially in periods of monetary ease and when personal savings increase. The rapid rise in savings flows in 1971-1972 and in 1975-1977 was also aided by changes in the rates paid on savings accounts.

Borrowing from the Federal Home Loan Banks varies according to (1) money situations, (2) demand for mortgages, (3) savings flow, and (4) government programs encouraging home building. In tight money periods such as 1973 and 1978, S&Ls borrowed heavily from the FHLBs, which helped to offset the drop in savings inflows. In periods of monetary ease and slack mortgage demand, the process is usually reversed, with association borrowings reduced, such as in 1971 and 1976.

Deducting annual changes in cash and miscellaneous assets from the figures in Table 4-6 provides data on the funds available for capital-market investment (billions of dollars):

1970	1971	1972	1973	1974	1975	1976	1977	1978
$10.4	$26.0	$33.9	$27.2	$19.1	$35.5	$49.5	$61.9	$56.7

Uses of Funds: General Investment Policy

That savings and loan associations are primarily mortgage-lending agencies is revealed by Table 4-7, which shows the composition of industry assets from 1965 through 1978. The percentage of total assets invested in mortgages by associations has remained rather constant at about 83 percent since World War II. This is in contrast to mutual savings banks, who built up their mortgage portfolios in the 1950s and 1960s from a low of about 36 percent in 1950 to a high of 76 percent of total assets in 1965, which has since declined to about 60 percent at the end of 1978. It also reflects the legal restrictions that constrain savings and loans largely to investment in mortgages. Associations added considerably to their cash and liquid investment in 1973 and dropped the mortgage portfolio to 81 percent of total assets from 85 percent in the previous year. The prime reasons for this were (1) higher yields on acceptable legal investments compared to mortgage loans, (2) concern by associations regarding disintermediation as interest rates generally rose in the last half of 1973 and in the first three quarters of 1974, (3) changing reserve requirements, and (4) a slack mortgage demand caused by high interest rates and overbuilding in multifamily units.

TABLE 4-6. Sources of Net Funds, Savings and Loan Associations, 1970–1978
(billions of dollars)

	1970	1971	1972	1973	1974	1975	1976	1977	1978
Savings accounts	$10.9	$27.8	$32.6	$20.2	$16.0	$42.8	$50.2	$51.0	$44.3
Net worth	1.0	1.2	1.5	1.9	1.4	1.2	1.7	2.1	2.4
Borrowing	1.2	-2.0	0.7	7.2	7.8	-4.2	-1.7	8.8	15.5
Loans in process	0.6	2.0	1.2	-1.5	-1.4	1.9	1.9	3.1	0.8
Total	$13.7	$29.1	$36.0	$27.9	$23.8	$41.8	$52.1	$55.9	$63.0

Sources: United States League of Savings Associations, *Savings and Loan Fact Book* (annual); *Federal Reserve Bulletin*; Federal Reserve *Flow-of-Funds Accounts*. (Some columns do not add to totals because of rounding.)

71

TABLE 4-7. Combined Assets of Savings and Loan Associations, Amounts and Percentages, at Year End, 1965-1978
(billions of dollars)

	1965		1970		1975		1978	
	Amount	Percent	Amount	Percent	Amount	Percent	Amount	Percent
Cash	$ 2.9	2.2%	$ 1.8	1.0%	$ 8.1	2.4%	$ 7.9	1.5%
Mortgage loans								
1–4 family	94.2	72.7	125.0	70.9	223.9	66.2	355.3	67.8
Other	16.1	12.4	25.4	14.4	54.7	16.2	77.6	14.8
U.S. Treasury securities	7.4	5.7	6.8	3.9	5.4	1.6	8.9	1.7
Federal agency securities[a]	0.8	0.6	4.1	3.3	17.2	5.1	27.4	5.2
State and local government securities	–	–	0.1	0.1	1.1	0.3	1.4	0.3
Miscellaneous liquid investments	–	–	1.8	1.0	5.3	1.6	11.7	2.2
Consumer loans	1.4	1.1	2.1	1.2	6.5	1.9	9.9	1.9
Federal Home Loan Bank stock	1.3	1.0	1.5	0.9	2.6	0.8	4.0	0.8
Other assets	5.5	4.3	7.5	4.3	13.4	3.9	19.7	3.8
Total	$129.6	100 %	$176.2	100 %	$338.2	100 %	$523.8	100 %

[a]Includes securities of federally sponsored agencies and federal budget agencies.
Sources: *Federal Reserve Bulletin*; Federal Reserve *Flow-of-Funds Accounts*; United States League of Savings Associations, *Savings and Loan Fact Book* (annual).

Similar situations pertaining to high interest rates occurred in 1978 and 1979 as the threat of inflation and a restrictive money supply drove rates to new highs. Savings and loan associations were not nearly as affected by disintermediation as in previous years, however, as new flexible-rate deposit certificates allowed them to effectively compete for savings dollars. Coupled with a strong mortgage demand, S&Ls were able to keep mortgage commitments relatively high.

The generally low liquidity ratios of saving and loan associations combined with their poor unhedged position in assets and liabilities—short-term liabilities, long-term assets—would be a matter of deep concern if it were not for the availability of funds from the regional Federal Home Loan Banks. Borrowing by associations from the FHLBs increased by $12.0 billion in 1978. Outstanding obligations due the banks totaled $30.3 billion at the end of 1978, an all-time high. This represented almost 7.4 percent of savings balances held by associations, up from 4 percent in 1968.

All federally chartered associations and most state-chartered associations, together representing 98 percent of the assets of the industry, are members of the Federal Home Loan Bank system. Loans from the Federal Home Loan Banks are used to smooth irregularities among savings inflow, withdrawals, and mortgage-lending activity. Reliance on the bank of their district varies greatly among associations. In addition to lending to member S&Ls at varying rates of interest, the banks serve as general regulatory agencies. Their policies,with respect to the amount of credit extended and the rates charged, as well as their dictates on reserves and maximum interest to be paid on member savings accounts, have a very substantial influence on member lending policies.

Liquidity requirements are also determined by the seasonal pattern of deposits and withdrawals and by the flow of cash derived from maturing mortgages. These factors differ considerably among associations, but the average association experiences strong seasonal inflows in January, June, July, and December. Outflows are typically greatest in January, April, July, and October and are closely related to interest payment periods. The saver tends to wait until after the interest payment period before withdrawing his funds.

This withdrawal/deposit procedure tends to be disruptive to the association mortgage lending policies, as they must continually focus on estimated net flows to avoid liquidity problems. The willingness of FHLBs to lend funds and the different maturities offered by the associations on savings accounts have helped to ease the liquidity problem and smoothed the net flow of funds from month to month, which is important to associations who need a fully invested position in mortgages or high-yielding, liquid securities in order to pay the high promised yields on savings deposits and still earn a modest profit.

Finally, an important and constant-to-increasing source of cash to associations are mortgage inflows. These flows are received by associations from (1) payments on amortized principal, (2) mortgage prepayments, and (3) loan liquidations resulting from sale of mortgaged properties. In addition, associa-

TABLE 4-8. Major Sources of Cash for All Savings and Loan Associations, 1970-1978
(billions of dollars)

	1970	1971	1972	1973	1974	1975	1976	1977	1978
Net savings receipts	$11.0	$27.9	$32.7	$20.2	$16.0	$42.8	$50.6	$ 51.0	$ 44.9
Mortgage portfolio inflows	14.8	23.0	30.1	30.9	27.4	34.2	46.8	63.5	68.9
Net income after interest	0.8	1.2	1.6	1.9	1.4	1.3	2.2	3.2	3.8
	$26.6	$52.1	$64.4	$53.0	$44.8	$78.3	$99.6	$117.7	$117.6

Sources: Federal Home Loan Bank Board, *Source Book* (annual); United States League of Savings Associations, *Savings and Loan Fact Book* (annual).

tions also achieve liquidity by selling whole loans and loan participations from their existing mortgage portfolios in the secondary mortgage market.

Cash flows from the existing mortgage portfolios of associations which include loan repayments and portfolio sales have been significant in recent years and have served to dampen the effects of wildly fluctuating net savings flows. Table 4-8 shows the flow of funds from these two major sources: net savings and mortgage portfolio inflows. The sharp drops in net savings receipts in 1972 and 1974 were indicative of the tight money situation that existed during these times. The significant rises in inflows in 1971-1972 and 1976-1977 were a result of the large net savings inflow and the high level of mortgage activity and portfolio sales. The large increase in outstanding mortgages coupled with high interest rates on these loans, making mortgage amortization payments larger, contributed to the substantial increases in portfolio inflows in 1975 and 1976. Tight money and disintermediation of savings from S&Ls led to only moderate increases in mortgage portfolio inflows and a modest decline in net savings receipts in 1978.

Mortgage Lending

The spectacular postwar rise in total mortgage investments has been a result of a national emphasis on home ownership; increases in population, personal income, and savings; and the concomitant increase in financial institutions to support this growth.

Table 4-9 shows that the bulk of mortgage loans financed by associations continues to be conventional loans on one- to four-family housing units. At the end of 1978, loans on one- to four-family homes constituted 82 percent of total mortgages and 68 percent of total assets.

TABLE 4-9. Mortgage Loans Held by Savings and Loan Associations, at Year End, 1965–1978 (billions of dollars)

	1965	1970	1975	1978
Residential				
1–4-family	$ 94.2	$124.5	$223.9	$356.2
Multifamily	7.6	13.8	25.5	36.0
	$101.8	$138.3	$249.4	$392.2
Commercial and other	8.5	11.5	29.2	40.7
	$110.3	$149.8	$278.6	$432.9
Conventional	$ 98.8	$131.2	$248.0	$403.9
FHA-insured	5.1	10.2	14.6	13.2
VA-guaranteed	6.4	8.4	16.0	15.8
Total	$110.3	$149.8	$278.6	$432.9

Sources: *Federal Reserve Bulletin;* United States League of Savings Associations, *Savings and Loan Fact Book* (annual). *Federal Land Bank Board Journal.*

Savings and loan associations specialize in amortized, conventional residential loans for the following reasons: (1) the associations are geared by law and tradition to local lending; (2) local demand in most areas has been sufficient to absorb the increase in local savings attracted by the favorable rate paid on accounts; (3) associations are permitted a high loan-to-value ratio on conventional loans (up to 95 in some cases); (4) the paperwork, rate limitations, and government supervision of FHA and VA loans limit the appeal of this form of financing; and (5) the growth of private mortgage insurance essentially gives conventional lending the low down payment/large mortgage possibilities previously available only through government financing.[4]

The aversion of associations to government supported loans should not be overshadowed by the increases in FHA and VA loans in the 1970s. The increase during these years was caused primarily by the large savings inflows, association purchases of government-backed loans in the secondary market, and higher maximum rates and loan fees on government mortgages. Savings and loan associations still tend to avoid origination of FHA and VA loans.

Associations have supplied the largest share of total home financing. In 1978, they held $356 billion, or 47 percent, of the national total of $760 billion of loans on one- to four-family dwellings.

Association loans on multifamily structures and on commercial and industrial properties have expanded in recent years, reflecting a search for diversification and higher-yielding assets, as well as increased demand by business enterprises for long-term financing.

More recently, lending authority for associations has been broadened to include loans for acquisition and development of residential land, and for participation in mortgages held by other institutions.

Association loans to consumers for nonmortgage purposes, although closely allied to home ownership, expanded rapidly in the 1970s so that at the end of 1978 they totaled over $11 billion, or 2.2 percent, of total assets. These loans include financing for mobile homes, home improvement loans, and loans secured by savings accounts.[5] Consumer loan growth in recent years can be attributable to liberalization of federal and state regulations governing thrift associations and the higher yields associated with these investments.

Other Investments

For safety and liquidity, federally chartered associations invest in federal securities, obligations of federal agencies, and the four top grades of state and municipal bonds. Depending on loan demand, the proportion of these holdings

---

[4]In 1979, the FHLBB authorized federal associations to make conventional loans of 95 percent of value on single-family homes in amounts up to $60,000 and loans of 80 percent but less than 90 percent of value in amounts up to $75,000. (Maximum dollar amounts are 50 percent higher in Alaska, Guam, and Hawaii.)

[5]Current regulations permit associations to invest up to 10 percent of their assets in

to total assets had been in the neighborhood of 6 to 9 percent for several years. The emphasis in these obligations has been on short- and intermediate-term maturities to reduce price risk and to offset the long maturities of the mortgage portfolio.

Liquidity requirements were substantially revised by an amendment to the Federal Home Loan Bank Act. Regulations now specify the required liquidity ratio as a percentage of total withdrawable savings account balances and short-term borrowings. Acceptable liquid investments include cash, demand and time deposits held at commercial banks, deposits at the FHLB, federal securities, and government agency issues. By law, the board is allowed to vary the required reserve ratio from 4 to 10 percent.

In 1978, the required ratio was 6.5 percent, yet qualifying liquid assets totaled over 8.5 percent of total assets, thus reflecting the high yields on these securities and the anticipated liquidity problems from disintermediation in early 1979.

Annual Uses of Funds in the Capital Market

Annual data on long-term uses of funds for 1970–1978 are shown in Table 4–10. The rate of acquisition of new home mortgage loans rose sharply in the 1970s, reflecting the growth in institutional savings and the increase in housing starts, even though higher mortgage interest rates during some periods tempered demand for housing. In 1971 and 1972, years of relative monetary ease, there was a sharp recovery in lending volume compared to 1970, and home mortgage funding to that date reached an all-time high. The $17.1 billion, $24.7 billion, and $21.5 billion net addition to home mortgages in 1971, 1972, and 1973, respectively, were between two to three times the net additions for any previous years. Volume fell off in 1974 as a result of a decline in deposits and high interest rates that cut mortgage demand, but moved up sharply thereafter to new highs in 1975–1977 as rates moderated and demand remained strong. In spite of higher mortgage rates in 1978, home mortgage funding dropped only slightly as housing demand remained strong and S&Ls were able to attract additional funds.

Throughout the period, amounts invested in other mortgages, including commercial mortgages, increased also, reflecting the high rates obtainable on these loans and the demand from commercial borrowers. Undoubtedly, some of the demand for loans from commercial borrowers in the 1970s was a "spillover" effect from other markets, where unsecured loans were difficult to obtain and interest rates to corporate borrowers remained high.

The rapid rise in ownership of federally sponsored agency securities was the result of higher liquidity requirements under new FHLB Board rules, and the generally high yields on these bonds compared to mortgages and U.S. government debt securities.

---

loans on mobile homes. These loans are generally made to consumers to finance purchase of new or used units or to mobile home dealers to help carry inventories.

TABLE 4-10. Annual Flow of Funds into Capital-Market Assets, Savings and Loan Associations, 1970-1978 (billions of dollars)

	1970	1971	1972	1973	1974	1975	1976	1977	1978
Treasury securities	$-1.3	$-0.8	$-0.5	$-1.6	$ –	$ 1.2	$ 3.7	$-1.3	$-0.6
Federal agency securities[a]	1.9	3.0	2.4	2.3	1.2	4.1	0.7	4.9	5.6
State and local government securities	–	–	–	–	0.3	0.6	0.1	0.1	-0.1
Home mortgages	6.8	17.2	24.7	21.5	13.9	23.2	37.3	49.9	43.9
Other mortgages	3.0	6.6	7.2	5.0	3.7	6.3	7.6	8.3	7.9
	$10.4	$26.0	$33.9	$27.2	$19.1	$35.5	$49.5	$61.9	$56.7

[a]Includes federally sponsored and budget agency securities.

Sources: United States League of Savings Associations, *Savings and Loan Fact Book* (annual); Federal Reserve *Flow-of-Funds Accounts*. (Some columns do not add to totals because of rounding.)

Influence of Monetary Policy

Since savings and loan associations specialize in mortgage assets with long-term maturities and are not controlled by the same reserve requirements as those for commercial banks, it was often thought that monetary policy had little effect on association operations. Reasons advanced for this thesis were that (1) once committed, the rate earned on a mortgage remains unchanged; and (2) rates paid to savers, the same to both new and old, change only at intervals that may be months or even a year or two apart. Thus, it was concluded that much of the associations' asset and liability base was "locked in," with variations in market rates resulting from tighter or easier Federal Reserve policy affecting only new lending and savings activity—the earned and paying rates—whose changes normally lagged behind open-market yields anyway.

The sobering experiences of many associations since the mid-1960s, particularly during tight money periods, have tended to refute this hypothesis and have led to the conclusion that monetary policy does indeed have a significant effect on association operations, although such effects may be more indirect.

A tight monetary policy affects the volume of new housing starts and new mortgage commitments as well as increasing the cost of borrowings from the Federal Home Loan Banks, which in turn must obtain their own funds at open-market yields.

Furthermore, the significant changes in competition for savings deposits with commercial banks and with other securities has had a major impact on association operations. When money is tight and interest rates, including those paid on savings deposits, rise, the heavy commitment to long-term mortgages at fixed rates tends to work against savings associations. That is, because the S&Ls are "locked in" at a specified interest rate or are operating in a market that is interest-rate-sensitive, they are limited—legally and competitively—by the rates they can pay on savings accounts. If rates rise on other competitive securities, substantial disintermediation is likely and association operations may be seriously affected. To mitigate this effect, associations have opted for variable-rate mortgages or flexible-rate deposit certificates.

Role in the National Mortgage Market

Savings and loan associations operate mainly in local markets. Unlike other lenders—mutual savings banks and life insurance companies in particular—they have not made frequent use of agents or correspondents in originating or servicing their loans. Associations do, however, contribute to a national flow of funds in several ways. They purchase and sell mortgages from other associations, commercial banks, insurance companies, mortgage companies, and brokers, and they participate with each other and with other lenders in large loans. In 1978, insured associations purchased $11.0 billion worth of loans and participations, and sold $15.5 billion worth. In addition, by borrowing from Federal Home Loan Banks, associations tap national sources of capital for local employment. Also, savings funds are attracted from out-ot-town areas where yields on deposit investments are lower. For instance, California associations have aggressively advertised on a national basis to attract funds by offering the highest yields available. The fact that most accounts are insured (to $40,000) by the Federal Savings and Loan Insurance Corporation is a major factor in inducing investors to shift funds to distant associations.

Until recently, savings and loan associations had not been active in the general secondary-mortgage market. However, the rapid development of the secondary mortgage market (see Chapter 12), with improved marketability of conventional mortgage loans as well as FHA and VA loans and new mortgage-backed securities, indicates an alternative of considerable importance to savings association in the future.

Credit Unions

Credit Unions (CUs) have not generally been considered serious participants in the capital market, because most of their activities have been restricted to short-term consumer lending. Legislation passed in 1977, however, made it possible for CUs to make mortgages up to thirty years in maturity (ten-year maximum previously), and home improvement and mobile home loans lasting up to fifteen years. Hence, CUs at least have the legal approval to deal extensively in the capital market, although from a hedging (Chapter 2) as well as a return perspective, their asset preference should remain primarily in the consumer loan area. In fact, some credit unions that made mortgage loans under the relaxed rules have withdrawn from the market, in the belief that it takes too much money to stay in the market and that smaller consumer loans are more appropriate. Nevertheless, CUs are discussed in this book for the first time because of their growing similarity to other financial intermediaries, especially in asset and liability holdings, and their rapid growth in the 1970s, which makes them an important factor in the competition for savings.

Asset Size and Structure

In the 1970s, CUs have been the fastest growing of all financial institutions and, although small by comparison to other major institutions in the late 1960s, they have since grown to where assets exceeded $62 billion at the end of 1978. Table 4-11 shows the assets and liabilities of all CUs for selected years from 1965 through 1978. The data indicate the preponderance of consumer loans in CUs assets. The largest item in consumer credit is auto financing. The figures also show modest increases in holdings of home mortgages and U.S. government securities, but it is too soon after the liberalization of loans on mortgages in

TABLE 4-11. Combined Assets and Liabilities of Credit Unions, at Year End, 1965–1978 (billions of dollars)

	1965		1970		1975		1978	
	Amount	Percent	Amount	Percent	Amount	Percent	Amount	Percent
Assets								
Federal CUs	$ 5.2	49.1%	$ 8.9	49.4%	$20.2	53.2%	$34.7	55.4%
State CUs	5.4	50.9	9.1	50.6	17.8	46.8	27.9	44.6
Total	$10.6	100 %	$18.0	100 %	$38.0	100 %	$62.6	100 %
Loans outstanding								
Federal CUs	$ 3.9	48.2	$ 7.0	49.6	$14.9	53.2	$28.6	55.2
State CUs	4.2	51.8	7.1	50.4	13.3	47.2	23.2	44.8
Total	$ 8.1	100 %	$14.1	100 %	$28.2	100 %	$51.8	100.0%
Savings								
Federal CUs	$ 4.5	48.9	$ 7.6	49.0	$17.5	53.0	$29.3	55.3
State CUs	4.7	51.1	7.9	51.0	15.5	47.0	23.7	44.7
Total	$ 9.2	100 %	$15.5	100 %	$33.0	100 %	$53.0	100 %

Sources: *Federal Reserve Bulletin*; National Credit Union Administration, *Annual Reports.*

1978 to get an idea of the eventual interest in mortgage holdings. When temporary excess funds are available on a short-term basis, CUs often place the funds into higher-yielding savings and loan deposits and liquidate these balances when new consumer loans are made. At the end of 1978, CUs were the third largest institution, after commercial banks and finance companies, in supplying consumer credit.

Similar to commercial banks and savings and loan institutions, CUs can be either state- or federally chartered. Federal credit unions currently account for about 55 percent of all credit union assets versus 45 percent for state-chartered CUs. Since 1970, federal credit unions have been regulated by the National Credit Union Administration, while individual states regulate state-chartered institutions. All CUs are mutual organizations in the sense that they issue no capital stock and have not sought borrowing sources for liquidity or asset expansion. The introduction of savings share insurance in 1970 has contributed substantially to the attractiveness of CU shares.

Credit unions are comprised of groups of people who share a common bond, such as employment, educational, religious, social, or other. CUs can usually offer higher interest on shares or charge a lower rate on loans because they are tax-exempt, the officers serve on a voluntary basis, and much of the premises and office space may be provided free of charge by the employer. More recently, CUs have been authorized to offer six-month money-market certificates on the same terms and basis as S&Ls. In addition, some CUs are now authorized for "share draft" accounts, which allow withdrawal of funds via third-party payments. All of these changes closely parallel those allowed other institutions, such as commercial banks, savings and loan associations, and mutual savings banks. Hence, it is not surprising that considerable agitation—such as the taxation of CUs—has been directed toward CUs by the other institutions.

Competition among Savings Institutions

Savings Trends

At least since the 1950s, there have been a number of developments in the competition for savings that have tipped the scales in favor of one financial institution or another. The effect of these changes has had a differential effect on savings growth in general, and on the savings and profitability experience of nonbank thrift institutions in particular.

As discussed earlier (chapter 3), commercial banks are the primary competitors of nonbank thrift institutions. Table 4–12 shows the annual change in savings deposits for savings associations, mutual saving banks, commercial banks, and credit unions. The table shows the fluctuating year-to-year changes in total savings, and the improvement in savings gains in recent years by all institutions but especially commercial banks and savings associations.

TABLE 4-12. Annual Changes in Time and Savings Deposits, 1960-1978
(billions of dollars)

Year	Savings Associations[a]	Mutual Savings Banks[b]	Commercial Banks[c]	Credit Unions[d]	Total
1960	$ 7.6	$ 1.4	$ 4.1	$0.5	$ 13.6
1961	8.7	1.9	9.9	0.5	21.0
1962	9.4	3.1	14.3	0.5	27.3
1963	11.1	3.3	11.9	0.9	27.2
1964	10.6	4.2	13.7	0.9	29.4
1965	8.5	3.6	20.0	1.0	33.1
1966	3.6	2.6	13.3	0.8	20.3
1967	10.6	5.1	23.7	1.2	40.6
1968	7.4	4.2	20.6	1.1	33.3
1969	3.9	2.6	-9.4	1.4	-1.5
1970	10.9	4.4	37.3	1.7	54.3
1971	27.8	9.8	41.2	2.9	81.7
1972	32.6	10.2	42.6	3.4	88.8
1973	20.2	4.7	50.3	2.9	78.1
1974	16.0	3.1	56.8	3.0	78.9
1975	42.8	11.2	29.6	5.5	89.1
1976	50.2	13.0	41.1	5.9	110.2
1977	51.0	11.1	54.8	7.9	124.8
1978	44.3	8.9	65.8	6.2	125.2

[a]All types of savings.
[b]Regular and special savings accounts.
[c]Time and savings accounts of individuals, partnerships, and corporations.
[d]Credit union shares and member deposits.
Sources: Federal Reserve *Flow-of-Funds Accounts;* Federal Home Loan Bank Board; Federal Deposit Insurance Corporation; U.S. Department of Commerce; National Association of Mutual Savings Banks; CUNA International, Inc.; and United States League of Savings Associations.

From 1956 through 1960, savings associations added a total of $30.1 billion in net new savings while commercial banks added only $20.8 billion. From 1961 through 1973, however, the success in attracting savings was dramatically reversed as commercial banks recorded net new savings of $287 billion while savings and loan associations attracted only $166 billion. Since 1974, the competition for savings has evened up, with S&Ls attracting a net increase of $204 billion through 1978 compared to $248 billion for commercial banks.

The improved performance of commercial banks since the early 1960s was, for the most part, a direct result of the relaxation in laws restricting interest payments on savings deposits and the general encouragement by regulatory agencies in fostering more competition for savings deposits. Interest rates on savings deposits of all types were allowed to rise, while the differential on maximum rates paid by commercial banks and savings and loans was reduced. In the past (1950s), when S&Ls paid considerably higher rates than commercial banks and aggressively sought savings funds, commercial banks were seriously hindered in their efforts to attract deposits. When maximum rates were liberalized and the interest rate differential narrowed, commercial banks did considerably better, largely at the expense of savings and loan associations. In the 1970s, continued rate competition generally benefited all savings institutions at the expense of other investment alternatives, especially the stock market.

Figure 4-1 shows the average annual yields paid on savings deposits by savings associations, mutual savings banks, and commercial banks. The figure reveals the narrowing spread in rates paid by the three institutions from 1960 until 1970, when commercial banks paid higher average interest rates on their savings and time deposits than did S&Ls.

In 1960 the average annual yield on savings accounts in savings associations was 3.75 percent compared to 2.5 percent for commercial banks; in 1974 the yields were 5.98 and 6.93, respectively, a reversal in favor of commercial banks. In 1978, the average yield on savings for S&Ls was 6.53 percent compared to 5.99 percent for commercial banks. Comparing rates and flows, it is apparent that in order for S&Ls to attract deposits about equal in amount to commercial banks, they need to pay higher average rates. It is not clear, however, whether this is or is not desirable, particularly since, based on assets, commercial banks as a group are more than twice the size of all S&Ls. Other factors, such as availability of funds for housing and the impact of monetary policy, are also important considerations.

Credit unions and mutual savings banks also experienced variable growth in deposits throughout the 1970s, but at substantially different rates. CUs were the fastest-growing institution, while MSBs, because they are located primarily in the New England area, which is experiencing only moderate population and

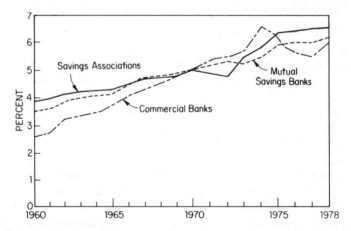

Figure 4-1. Average Annual Yield on Savings at Major Financial Institutions

Sources: Federal Home Loan Bank Board; Federal Deposit Insurance Corporation; National Association of Mutual Savings Banks; United States League of Savings Associations.

economic growth, recorded significantly lower deposit growth rates, although when measured in absolute terms they are larger than flows into CUs.

Profitability Trends

A result of increased competition for savings was an initial reduction in savings and loan associations' relative profitability. In the decade ending in 1964, the average rate of return on net worth for S&Ls amounted to 11.6 percent. In the period 1965-1973, the return on net worth dropped to 8.3 percent. On the other hand, commercial banks' average net income after security gains and losses improved during the same period from 9.0 percent on net worth to 10.8 percent. In recent years S&Ls have reversed their position and performance. In 1977, profit after taxes on net worth was 14.4 percent for S&Ls compared to 9.65 for commercial banks. Mutual savings banks have customarily experienced rates of return on net worth (general reserves) that are lower than those for either CBs or S&Ls. In 1965, MSBs earned only 3.38 percent on net worth. By the late 1970s, the rate earned on net worth of 8.1 percent in 1977 had improved considerably but still remained considerably below that of CBs and S&Ls.

As noted above, the Hunt Commission studied the problem of savings regulations. Its report concluded that rate regulations should be retained and that thrift institutions, including savings banks and associations, should be allowed a rate advantage on savings deposits until legislation was passed allowing broader lending powers for thrift institutions. Although a rate differential is not currently required by law, the typical *maximum* differential in favor of thrift institutions since the time of the report has been reduced to ¼ of 1 percent on savings certificate accounts up to $100,000. There are, however, no maximum rates for any institutions on time deposits of $100,000 or more. More recently, the Federal Reserve Board approved an acquisition by a bank of an inactive industrial loan company to be operated as a subsidiary. Funds are being solicited without regard to the Fed's Regulation Q—interest-rate ceiling. To many this is a bold attempt at eventually abolishing the interest-rate differential and removing the interest-rate ceiling imposed by Regulation Q.

Some of the other recommendations have been partially adopted and previous rulings regarding investments and loans by savings associations modified in light of the Hunt Commission report. For example, most S&Ls and MSBs can now make many types of consumer loans, and the maximum lending terms have been extended for such loans as those for mobile home purchase and home improvement. As noted earlier, credit unions have also been allowed to liberalize loan programs, especially in residential mortgages. Thus, there is little doubt that the public attitude at this time is one of favoring open and freer competition among financial institutions for savings deposits, loans, and investments. In this regard, the public is doing nothing more than reaffirming the role of an intermediary discussed in Chapter 2, namely, that of accepting funds from surplus units and reinvesting them at a higher rate in earning assets, and doing it in the most efficient manner.

With proper safeguards, it appears that financial institutions will continue to have wider latitude in determining the earnings assets in which the funds entrusted to them are invested.

```
55555555555555555555555555555555555555555555555555555555555555555555555555555555555
55555555555555555555555555555555555555555555555555555555555555555555555555555555555
555555555555555555555555555555555555   5555555555555   555555555555555555555555555555
5555555555555555555555555555555555555   5555555555   555555555555555555555555555555
5555555555555555555555555555555555555   555555555   555555555555555555555555555555
5555555555555555555555555555555555555   5555555   555555555555555555555555555555
5555555555555555555555555555555555555   55555   555555555555555555555555555555
5555555555555555555555555555555555555   555   5555555555555555555555555555555555
5555555555555555555555555555555555555   5   5555555555555555555555555555555555
555555555555555555555555555555555555555   55555555555555555555555555555555555555555
55555555555555555555555555555555555555   555555555555555555555555555555555555555555
5555555555555555555555555555555555555   5555555555555555555555555555555555555555555
55555555555555555555555555555555555555555555555555555555555555555555555555555555555
55555555555555555555555555555555555555555555555555555555555555555555555555555555555
```

Insurance Companies

THIS chapter discusses legal reserve life insurance companies and property and
liability companies. These two institutions perform quite distinct functions,
draw on different sources of funds, and employ their funds somewhat differently
in the capital market. Many holding companies and insurance groups, however,
control firms that provide both types of service.

Life Insurance Companies

Nature and Functions

Life insurance companies are one of the largest media for individual savings in
the United States. Their total assets have grown from $64 billion in 1950 to
$390 billion at the end of 1978 and consist chiefly of a variety of capital-market
instruments. Their annual rate of asset growth approximates 9 percent per year
compounded.

Life insurance companies provide financial protection for beneficiaries against
death and longevity, that is, life insurance and annuities. They are classed as
financial intermediaries since the policies they issue (other than renewable term
and industrial) have included in the premium a reserve or savings element that
represents an amount in excess of the need for current death losses. The excess is
invested and compounded to cover death losses at later ages. The level annual
premiums on annuities include amounts accumulated to provide a life income
based on actuarial life expectancy.

Thus, life insurance companies perform two major functions: (1) protection of beneficiaries against premature death (insurance) and unusual longevity (annuities) of the policyholders, and (2) investment of funds representing policy reserves (and other funds) in a wide variety of capital-market instruments.

General Relations to the Capital Market

Because the contracts of life insurance companies involve, for the most part, long-term liabilities, the savings they accumulate are placed mainly in capital-market rather than money-market instruments in order to be sufficiently hedged on assets and liabilities. Except for those held for liquidity purposes, the securities and mortgages in the investment portfolio are ordinarily held to maturity as long as they meet required standards of quality. Investment policy emphasizes long-term safety and the achievement of a return that produces the rates built into premium calculations at which reserves must be compounded.

At the end of 1978, about $323 billion, or 83 percent, of the total assets of life insurance companies consisted of capital-market instruments, including federal, state, and municipal bonds; corporate and foreign bonds; mortgages; and corporate stock.

Capital-market investments have been growing at the rate of about $25 billion each year. The net premium and investment income plus funds from maturing bonds and mortgages, provides an annual discretionary cash flow of about $35 billion, making the industry a very potent factor in capital markets.

Sources of Funds

The major sources of external funds are the accumulating reserve liabilities derived from net premium income and the compounding of investment income. Between 1960 and 1978, policy reserves grew from $98 billion to over $300 billion. Accumulated policy "dividends" (rebates), reserves for future dividends, and other obligations provide additional funds. The total of these last three sources grew from $11 billion to $52 billion in the same period. Net worth accounts, including special and unassigned surplus and the capital stock accounts of stock companies, increased from $10 billion to $26 billion. As most of these sources represent long-term obligations, capital-market assets are appropriate investments.

The annual sources of new funds for capital-market use from 1965 through 1978 are derived by deducting from the annual increase in total assets, the changes in miscellaneous assets, net cash, real estate, and policy loans (billions of dollars):

1970	1971	1972	1973	1974	1975	1976	1977	1978
$6.2	$10.4	$12.9	$14.0	$12.1	$17.6	$23.7	$27.1	$28.6

Cash flow from sale of securities and maturing mortgages is also available for reinvestment.

Before examining actual investment policy, we should note the major factors stemming from the nature of the business and its regulation that determine the general character of the investments.

(1) Contracts with policyholders are essentially long-term obligations. Although some mature every day, the cash drain can be forecast with considerable accuracy, as can the cash inflow from net new premiums, the maturing and sales of securities and mortgages, contract cancellations, and investment income. Most life insurance contracts provide for an accumulation of cash surrender values payable or loaned on demand. However, experience with policy loans and liquidation of cash values shows that only under extreme conditions (as during the early 1930s) are large permanent withdrawals likely to occur. And for the growing insurance company, steady cash inflow more than exceeds the cash drain for death benefits, expenses, and withdrawals.

The emphasis can therefore be placed on acquisition of long-maturity instruments. The general practice is to hold these to maturity, unless changes in market yields cause shifts in broad categories of investments or unless a loss of quality of individual investments requires their liquidation.

(2) Some liquidity is required to provide for day-to-day needs, to meet large emergency death losses, and to permit changes among investment categories without sudden sale of assets. Liquidity is provided by working cash balances, federal bonds, and amortization of mortgages and loans.

(3) Premiums are written on the assumption of a minimum rate of return at which funds representing reserves will be compounded (for example, 5 to 5½ percent). A steady and adequate yield is therefore required. Investment policy must emphasize fixed-income assets of high quality and stable income. It is also desirable to earn a rate of return in excess of the "guaranteed" rate and so distribute premium rebates in the form of "dividends."

(4) Their position as trustees of savings requires that life insurance companies invest funds for ultimate safety. This is achieved by restricting investments to instruments that meet the standards of quality established by policy and regulation. Diversification by type of investment, industrial category, maturity, and degree of marketability is also a means of protecting against losses of principal.

(5) Actuarial commitments require insurance companies to remain fully invested, keeping cash balance to the minimum set by estimated cash inflows and outflows. This requirement explains the use of forward commitments for business loans and mortgages; it also explains the use of mortgage company correspondents to originate and service mortgages in capital-seeking areas to which surplus funds can be directed (see Chapter 12).

(6) Valuation of assets for statement purposes has a considerable effect on investment policy. Mutual companies are permitted to build up only limited surplus accounts, and competition prevents stock companies from accumulating

large excess premium deposits. Substantial declines in asset values must therefore be avoided. Quality must be emphasized, and bond accounts so managed as to prevent large writedowns of assets because of shifts in market rates of interest.

(7) Life insurance income is not tax-free, although the federal income tax rate is substantially less than that applying to business corporations. The increase in the effective rate from 7 to 8 percent in 1959 to 21 to 22 percent in 1978 has led to some interest in the obligations of state and local governments.

(8) Because commitments to policyholders are in fixed dollars, little attention need be paid to actual or potential inflation. Rising operating costs can be met by gradual changes in premiums. Common stocks and real estate are acquired more for their greater long-run income than for their potential value as inflation hedges. (This is not true of pension fund commitments, however, as future payments are usually tied to wage and salary levels, implying a need for inflation protection.)

(9) The effect of state regulation on life insurance investments is important enough to warrant special discussion.

Regulation

Life insurance companies operate under state charter. There is no dual federal charting of life insurance companies such as exists in commercial banking, savings and loan associations, and credit unions.

In all fifty states, the investments of life insurance companies are affected by regulations that specify the eligible investments that can be acquired and the standards of quality that holdings in each permitted category must meet.[1] Companies domiciled in one state and doing business in others must conform to the standards required of domestic insurers insofar as locally generated reserves are concerned, as well as those of the state of domicile. Corporate bonds must meet standards as to type and value of collateral or interest coverage or both; the latter requirement is stricter for unsecured obligations. Conventional mortgages have maximum loan-to-appraised-value ratios (as high as 75 percent on one- or two-family dwellings in New York and some other states). Preferred stocks must meet specified tests of dividend coverage and payment. Common stocks, now permitted in limited amounts in the majority of states, must ordinarily be listed and meet specified earnings and dividend tests. Income-producing real estate is restricted as to type and use of property.

Individual states establish what percentage each category of investments may be of total assets and also restrict the percentages of assets invested in the obligations of one (private) borrower. Geographic limitations on investments also

---

[1]For a convenient discussion of regulation and a summary of the specific regulations in nineteen representative states, see Life Insurance Association of America, *Life Insurance Companies as Financial Institutions,* a monograph prepared for the Commission on Money and Credit (Englewood Cliffs, N.J.: Prentice-Hall, Inc., 1962), Chap. 5 and Appendix.

apply, as do requirements in a few states that a certain percentage of reserves be invested in instruments originating in that state. Fortunately, the latter requirement is not widespread, as it would prevent companies from directing their funds to the areas of greatest need and best yields.

Annual Investment Policy

Table 5–1 shows the combined assets and percentages of legal reserve companies by major categories from 1965 through 1978.

United States government securities   In 1945, direct Treasury obligations totaled $20.6 billion, or 46 percent of total life insurance company assets. Since that time holdings of Treasury securities have declined in both amount and percentage such that at the end of 1978 they represented only $4.8 billion, or a little over 1 percent of total assets and 0.6 percent of total federal debt outstanding. Intermediate- and long-term maturities account for more than 90 percent of life insurance company holdings in federal securities.

The primary beneficiaries of the movement away from federal securities in the last three decades have been corporate bonds and mortgages of all types. The reason for this big shift can be traced to the higher yields available on these latter securities. One of the factors contributing to the accord between the Treasury and the Federal Reserve banks in 1951, when the prices and yields of Treasury securities were "unpegged" (see Chapter 8), was the massive sales of federal securities by insurance companies. In the later 1950s and the 1960s, net sales of federal securities continued at a varying pace depending on the availability and yields on alternative investments.

Foreign Government and International Agency Securities

At the end of 1978, life insurance companies held $8.8 billion in Canadian and international agency securities. Ironically, the $7 billion in Canadian bonds held by U.S. life insurance companies was greater than their holdings in direct federal securities. The higher after-tax yields available on Canadian and international securities are reasons for ownership.

State and local government bonds   The holdings of American state and local government bonds have risen modestly in the last two decades. At the end of 1978 state and local obligations amounted to $6.4 billion, comprising less than 2 percent of total insurance company assets.

Because they are in effectively lower tax brackets than other financial institutions, the tax-exempt feature of state and local issues is less appealing to insurance companies. Consequently, insurance companies have shown a distinct

TABLE 5-1. Combined Assets of Legal Reserve Life Insurance Companies, Amounts and Percentages, at Year End, 1965–1978 (billions of dollars)

	1965 Amount	1965 Percent	1970 Amount	1970 Percent	1975 Amount	1975 Percent	1978 Amount	1978 Percent
U.S. Treasury securities	$ 5.1	3.2	$ 4.0	1.9	$ 4.7	1.6	$ 4.8	1.2
Federal agency securities[a]	0.2	0.1	0.5	0.2	1.4	0.4	6.5	1.7
American municipal bonds	3.5	2.2	3.3	1.6	{4.5	1.6	6.4	1.6
Canadian municipal bonds	1.9	1.2	2.8	1.4				
Foreign central government bonds	0.9	0.6	0.6	0.3	4.5	1.6	8.8	2.3
Corporate bonds[b]	58.6	37.0	73.1	35.3	105.8	30.8	156.0	40.0
Mortgages	60.0	37.8	74.4	35.9	89.2	36.6	105.8	27.2
Preferred stocks	2.9	1.9	3.5	1.7	7.8	2.7	10.5	2.7
Common stocks	6.2	3.8	11.9	5.7	20.3	7.0	25.0	6.4
Policy loans	7.7	4.8	16.1	7.8	24.5	8.5	30.2	7.7
Real estate	4.7	3.0	6.3	3.0	9.6	3.3	11.8	3.0
Cash and other assets	7.2	4.5	10.8	5.2	17.0	5.9	24.1	6.2
Total assets	$158.9	100 %	$207.3	100 %	$289.3	100 %	$389.9	100 %

[a]Includes securities of federally sponsored agencies and budget agencies.
[b]Includes foreign corporate bonds.
Source: American Council of Life Insurance, *Life Insurance Fact Book* (annual).

preference in their investment policies for the higher yields on corporate bonds and mortgages.

General obligation bonds of American state and local governments do not have as much appeal to insurance companies as revenue bonds which may sell at yields often equal to those on fully taxable high-grade corporate bonds. At the end of 1978, revenue bonds constituted about 70 percent of insurance company holdings of American municipal bonds. Life insurance companies share of American state and municipal long-term securities amounted to about 2 percent of all state and local long term debt.

Corporate bonds   Corporate bonds are attractive to insurance companies because of their superior yield, quoted prices (save for those acquired through private placement), marketability, long-term nature and variety. One of the important features of insurance company investments since World War II has been the increase in corporate bond holdings. In 1945, these totaled $10.1 billion, or 22.5 percent of total assets. By 1978, they had increased to $156 billion and 40 percent of total assets. The funds for this expansion were provided in the early years by the switch from U.S. government bonds and later by the large growth in net cash flow.

The composition within the bond portfolio has undergone a marked change. The waning investment quality of railway bonds led to the decline in their percentage of total assets from 4.9 percent in 1950 to about one percent in 1978. Utility bond holdings have increased in absolute amount, but have declined to around 10 percent of total insurance company assets (from 12 percent in 1950). The increase in holdings reflected the postwar expansion of the utility industries, especially gas and electric power, and their improved investment status. They have become relatively less important in recent years because they are usually issued through competitive bidding, in which insurance companies seldom participate.

The industrial bond category has grown substantially from less than 2 percent of life insurance company assets in 1950 to 27 percent in 1978. This growth reflects the upgrading of the investment status of industrial obligations—especially in such rapidly growing fields as oil, chemicals, and finance—and the fact that the great bulk of high-grade issues are acquired through direct placement, in which life insurance companies play the leading role (see Chapter 10). The industrial bond category also includes long-term loans which are similar to, but with longer maturities than, bank term loans.

A more recent bond investment growing in popularity since 1975 among insurance companies is the "Yankee bond." Yankee bonds are bonds issued by foreign companies or governments sold in the United States and denominated in dollars. Foreign companies like the U.S. capital market because it can handle large financings with ease and longer-term maturities are more readily obtainable than in Europe. In addition, since the issues are dollar-denominated, it gives stronger currency companies the hope of paying off the debt in cheaper dollars.

Also, Yankee bonds are preferred by several insurance companies because rates are anywhere from ½ to 1½ percent higher than on comparable domestic bonds, and often the issues of foreign companies are directly or indirectly backed by the full faith and credit of their foreign government. In 1977 and 1978 about $4.0 billion of these securities were issued with insurance companies purchasing slightly more than 50 percent of the new issues.

Mortgages   The large holdings of mortgages by the life insurance industry (see Table 5-2) reflect the following characteristics of these assets: (1) relatively attractive yields (1 to 2 percent above high-grade bonds); (2) safety as required by regulation; (3) long-term maturities; (4) steady amortization of principal, which contributes to liquidity; (5) growing geographical diversification through the use of the mortgage correspondent and wider-spread direct investment; (6) growing diversity of types; (7) the special appeal of FHA-insured and VA-guaranteed loans; (8) loan-to-value ratios on conventional residential liens as high as 75 percent in some states; (9) rising real estate value increasing the safety of mortgages on property; and (10) an opportunity to structure apartment and industrial mortgage loans to include participation in the equity or profits of the underlying assets. These advantages are somewhat offset by the costlier management, the poorer marketability of mortgage investments as compared with listed securities, the risks associated with investments as compared with listed securities, and the risks associated with investment in new construction or new properties with sharply higher costs.

Total mortgage investments have increased annually since World War II and

TABLE 5-2. Mortgage Loans Held by Legal Reserve Life Insurance Companies, at Year End, 1965–1978 (billions of dollars)

	1965	1970	1975	1978
Farm	$ 4.8	$ 5.6	$ 6.8	$ 10.4
Residential				
1–4-family	29.9	26.7	17.6	14.4
Multifamily	8.4	16.0	19.6	19.0
	$38.3	$42.7	$37.2	$ 33.4
Commercial and other	16.9	26.1	45.2	62.0
Total	$60.0	$74.4	$89.2	$105.8
Conventional and other	$41.6	$57.7	$77.4	$ 96.5
FHA-insured (nonfarm)	12.1	11.3	7.9	6.1
VA-guaranteed	6.3	5.4	3.9	3.2
Total	$60.0	$74.4	$89.2	$105.8

Sources: *Federal Reserve Bulletin;* American Council of Life Insurance, *Life Insurance Fact Book* (annual); United States League of Savings Associations, *Savings and Loan Fact Book* (annual); National Association of Mutual Savings Banks, *National Fact Book* (annual).

have risen from $16.1 billion, or 25 percent, of total assets in 1950, to over $105 billion, or 27 percent, of total assets in 1978. The rate of net mortgage growth has been about $5 billion yearly since 1965, depending on the demand for mortgages and the level of interest rates. If rates are high, mortgage demand tends to diminish, resulting in only moderate increases in mortgages outstanding. Thus, characteristically, annual investment in residential mortgages has been irregular and has followed the cyclical rises and falls in housing starts (for example, large increases in 1964, 1968, and 1971–1973 and decreases in 1966, 1969, and 1974).

Moreover, mortgages compete primarily with bonds as an alternative outlet for insurance company funds. The ebb and flow of funds into federally supported mortgages has also been irregular, varying with relative interest rates on competitive investments. Investment in federally underwritten loans has seen the most variation because their nominal interest rates are pegged and changed only at rather long intervals. Life insurance companies have not been enthusiastic about buying such investments at a discount when the nominal rate is inadequate (see Chapter 12).

Unlike other financial institutions investing in mortgages, life insurance companies have recently placed increasing amounts in multifamily and commercial mortgages at the expense of single-family housing. Table 5–2 shows that investment in one- to four-family units by insurance companies declined sharply, from $26.7 billion in 1970 to $14.6 billion in 1978. The primary reason for this shift was the emphasis on higher yields and the small size of single-family mortgages. Other reasons were the relative decline in housing starts, competition for mortgages from other institutions (most notably, savings and loan associations), and the increase in policy loans made at low rates of interest that forced a search for higher-yielding investments.

Insurance companies have particularly favored multifamily and commercial properties because substantial funds can be placed conveniently in large projects and the expected yields are often high. In 1979, it was common for loans on commercial properties to carry an 11½ percent interest rate, plus a percentage of the equity or profits from the project while rates on single-family homes were in the vicinity of 10¾ percent. The holdings of commercial mortgages (26.1 billion in 1970) rose to 62.0 billion in 1978, representing 58 percent of all mortgages held by life insurance companies.

As a group, life insurance companies are the fourth most important institutional owner of residential mortgages, behind savings and loan associations, commercial banks, and mutual savings banks. Like other institutions, they have also tended to prefer conventional loans to government-guaranteed FHA and VA loans. FHA-insured and VA-guaranteed loans fell from 41 percent of mortgage assets in 1950 to less than 10 percent in 1978 as insurance companies sought higher yields and lower loan-processing costs.

Farm mortgage investments totaled $10.4 billion at the end of 1978, or less than 3 percent of total assets. Nevertheless, the industry is the largest private institutional owner of such loans, holding 14 percent of total farm mortgages at the end of 1978.

Life insurance companies rely heavily on local mortgage correspondents for the origination of their mortgage loans. Customarily, about 40 percent of their total mortgages have been obtained in this fashion. (The contribution of mortgage companies to a growing national market in mortgages and to greater geographical uniformity in interest rates is indicated in Chapter 12.)

Corporate stocks   The traditional lack of investment by insurance companies in common stocks has been attributed to the need for a steady and secure income, and safety of principal. In addition, there is not a strong need for inflation hedges. Tradition and law, which restrict common stock investment to a small percentage of assets or of policyholders' surplus and limit the amount of investment in any one company also discourage greater holdings of this type of asset.

Except for market declines, however, holdings of common stocks have increased steadily in amount, for several years. This figure was $10.3 billion in 1968, grew to $21.8 billion at the end of 1972, declined to $19.6 at the end of 1973 in a sharp market drop, and then recovered to $25 billion at the end of 1978. These figures reflect the appreciation or depreciation in market values as well as investment policy. Preferred stocks, whose appeal is for current income, totaled $10.5 billion, or less than 3.0 percent of total assets at the end of 1978.

The interest of life insurance companies in common stocks is likely to increase in the future. Indirect interest derives from participation in the operation of mutual (open-end) investment funds. Direct interest reflects the mounting importance of insured pension plans invested in equities, with the portfolios segregated from general assets, and the relaxation of state rules to permit a higher proportion of life insurance reserves to be invested in equities. Also, in 1976 many states allowed for the first time the issuance of individual variable life insurance policies. Although variable annuities or other policies whose ultimate payments to the beneficiary fluctuate based on market performance are questionable from a pure insurance viewpoint, these types of policies may be beneficial to those who desire a chance for maximum return as well as some form of insurance coverage.

Although about $25 billion in common stock is no small amount, it suggests that the influence of life insurance companies in the stock market lags far behind that of others. At the end of 1978, insurance companies owned only about 4 percent of the value of stocks listed on all stock exchanges.[2]

Annual Uses of Funds

The annual capital-market uses of life insurance company funds from 1970 through 1978 are shown in Table 5-3. The influences indicated earlier in this

---

[2]See Table 11-5 for total of all listed stocks.

TABLE 5-3. Annual Flow of Funds into Capital-Market Assets, Life Insurance Companies, 1970–1978
(billions of dollars)

	1970	1971	1972	1973	1974	1975	1976	1977	1978
U.S. Treasury securities	$-0.1	$-0.2	$ –	$-0.4	$-0.1	$ 1.4	$ 0.6	$ 0.3	$-0.6
Federal agency securities[a]	0.1	0.2	0.1	–	0.2	0.4	0.9	1.6	2.3
State and local government bonds (domestic)	0.1	–	0.1	0.1	0.3	0.8	1.1	0.5	0.2
Corporate and foreign bonds	1.8	5.6	7.7	6.2	4.5	10.2	15.7	18.3	17.4
Corporate stocks	2.0	3.6	3.5	3.6	2.3	1.9	3.0	1.2	1.1
Home mortgages	-0.9	-2.1	-2.3	-1.9	-1.4	-1.4	-1.5	-1.4	-0.2
Other mortgages	3.2	3.2	3.8	6.3	6.3	4.3	3.9	6.6	8.4
Total	$ 6.2	$10.4	$12.9	$14.0	$12.1	$17.6	$23.7	$27.1	$28.6

[a]Includes securities of federally sponsored agencies and of budget agencies.
Source: American Council of Life Insurance, *Life Insurance Fact Book*; (annual); *Federal Reserve Flow-of-Funds Accounts*. (Some columns do not add to totals because of rounding.)

chapter are clearly revealed by the data: the sell-off of federal bonds and home mortgages, and the steady accumulation of corporate bonds, and commercial and multifamily mortgages.

As insurance companies are well hedged on their asset and liability accounts, the changes shown in Table 5-3 are largely a result of their efforts to place funds in assets yielding higher returns while holding the maturity of the assets more or less constant.

From 1970 through 1978, corporate bonds accounted for over 56 percent of the increase in capital-market assets at balance-sheet value and multifamily and commercial mortgages, for 26 percent.

Influence in the National Capital Markets

Life insurance companies direct between $35 billion and $40 billion of new and internal funds into the capital markets each year. They are the dominating force on the demand side for corporate bonds and are second only to commercial banks in the commercial mortgage market. Their decisions concerning investment of capital significantly affect yields in these markets. Likewise, changes in market yields influence the direction of their funds toward different categories of assets.

In the late 1960s and early 1970s, the movement toward all-purpose financial combines included the acquisition, by a number of life insurance companies or their parents, of mutual fund management companies, mortgage banking firms, and property insurers. The consolidated statements of such groups lose the characteristics of life insurance companies, and their flows become less and less typical of the insurance industry.

Property and Liability Insurance Companies

Nature and Scope of Industry

The property and liability insurance group contains over 2,000 companies, with assets in excess of $128 billion (1977), consisting mainly of capital-market securities. Unlike life insurance companies, property and liability companies do not collect savings. They sell a service, and their liabilities do not represent firm dollar obligations to policyholders. They acquire their assets almost exclusively in the secondary markets. Their aggregate resources include a very respectable percentage of outstanding government and corporate instruments, and so investment policies exert an influence on the market for outstanding long-term securities. Although our discussion pertains to the whole industry, two important subclassifications are often recognized: (1) mutual and stock companies, and (2) insurers of property loss due to events such as fire, and insurers of personal liability.

Mutual companies do not issue stock but are owned by their policyholders. Their net worth is appropriately called "policyholders' surplus." The net worth of stock companies (capital stock and surplus) also constitutes protection to policyholders and so is also called policyholders' surplus, using the term in a broad sense. The distinction between the two types of ownership has an important influence on investment policy.

Insurers against loss to property from fire and other causes sell contracts that provide for indemnification of damage losses up to the limits of the policy. The actual losses depend on the cost of repair or replacement. Casualty insurance companies (auto, workmen's compensation, and so on) are primarily concerned with losses caused by injuries to persons and by damage to property of others. Many casualty companies also write fidelity and surety insurance.

"Multiple-line" companies, offering a variety of lines of property or casualty insurance or both, are found in both the mutual and stock categories.

Two minor types of organizations are *reciprocal exchanges*—cooperatives formed to provide coverage for members at cost—and *domestic Lloyds*—associations of unincorporated individuals that underwrite unusual risks.

Sources of Funds

Investment funds are derived mainly from (1) premium income allocated to two types of reserves for possible payment to policyholders—reserve for losses and reserve for unearned premiums, (2) increases in policyholders' surplus consisting of capital (stock) and surplus and voluntary reserves of stock companies, and guarantee funds, net surplus, and voluntary reserves of mutuals. Loss reserves represent liability for claims that have been filed and that are anticipated (a 60 to 65 percent loss ratio is assumed). Premiums are collected in advance and are not fully earned until the policies expire (one, three, or five years for fire, one year for casualty), so the unearned premium reserve represents the amount that would be returned to policyholders for the unexpired terms if all policies were canceled.

In addition to the above, funds are also obtained from investment income and principal reductions on securities held. However, in the past, investment income has generally been viewed as a source of revenue to cover underwriting losses that may occur, and for dividend payments. Hence, if the combined expense and loss ratio—underwriting losses plus expenses divided by earned premium income—is more than 100 percent, some of the investment income is ostensibly earmarked to offset the losses.

Dividend payments have not kept pace with the growth in earnings as insurance companies have sought to retain funds to build up capital and surplus. More recently, property and casualty companies have broken a long-standing tradition of relying on internal growth and are now offering debt and equity securities in public markets in an effort to expand their business lines more rapidly. More-

TABLE 5-4. Reserves and Net Worth, Property and Liability Insurance Companies, 1965-1977 (billions of dollars)[a]

	1965	1970	1975	1977
Loss reserves				
Stock companies	$ 8.7	$14.0	$22.3	$ 42.3
Mutuals	3.4	6.6	8.6	12.1
	$12.1	$20.6	$30.9	$ 54.4
Unearned premium reserves				
Stock companies	$ 8.3	$11.2	$15.9	$ 20.6
Mutuals	2.3	3.3	4.3	6.1
	$10.6	$14.5	$20.2	$ 26.7
Policyholders' surplus				
Stock companies	$13.7	$14.0	$18.4	$ 27.1
Mutuals	3.1	4.0	5.7	8.5
	$16.8	$18.0	$23.1	$ 35.6
Total reserves and net worth	$39.5	$53.1	$74.2	$116.7
Total assets				
Stock companies	$31.3	$42.6	$69.7	$ 99.6
Mutuals	9.4	14.1	20.0	28.9
	$40.7	$56.7	$89.7	$128.5

[a]Not including reciprocal and Lloyds companies.

Source: Alfred M. Best Co., Inc., *Best's Aggregates and Averages, Property-Casualty* (annual).

over, the added capital base will allow the firms greater protection against rapid inflation, cyclical losses, and a lag in rate changes in areas where they are experiencing poor underwriting results.

The actual net worth of a company is often higher than reported because part of the unearned premium reserve represents funds in excess of actual need. Acquisition costs have already been incurred, and the risks could be reinsured for less than the prepaid premium. Typically, analysts transfer 35 to 40 percent of this reserve in calculating adjusted actual net worth.

The distinction between reserves and policyholders' surplus is important in determining investment policy. The data in Table 5-4 show the amounts and relative proportions of these accounts, along with total assets for selected years from 1965 through 1977. The data exclude reciprocal and domestic Lloyds companies but represent about 97 percent of the industry in the United States.

Annual Sources of Funds, 1970-1978

The annual sources of new funds from 1970 through 1978 are shown in Table 5-5. The increase in unearned premium reserve accumulation, particu-

TABLE 5-5. Sources of Funds, Property and Liability Insurance Companies, 1970–1978
(billions of dollars)

	1970	1971	1972	1973	1974	1975	1976	1977	1978 (est.)
Unearned premium reserves	$1.7	$1.1	$1.3	$1.2	$0.9	$1.6	$ 3.3	$ 3.5	$ 3.1
Loss reserves	2.2	2.7	3.7	3.8	4.1	5.0	7.8	9.9	11.5
Policyholders' surplus[a]	1.3	2.4	2.5	2.0	1.1	0.3	2.3	6.3	7.7
Total	$5.1	$6.2	$7.6	$7.0	$6.2	$7.0	$13.4	$19.7	$22.3

[a]Net of changes in market values of assets; net worth is unadjusted.
Sources: Alfred M. Best Co., Inc., *Best's Aggregates and Averages, Property-Casualty* (annual); Bankers Trust Company, *Credit and Capital Markets* (annual). (Certain columns do not add to totals because of rounding.)

larly in 1970 and 1976, reflects favorable loss experience and higher insurance rates. After deducting the annual changes in cash and miscellaneous assets from the figures in Table 5-5, the following sums were available for capital-market use (in billions of dollars):

1970	1971	1972	1973	1974	1975	1976	1977	1978
$4.0	$6.2	$6.7	$5.8	$4.4	$5.9	$12.4	$19.3	$19.8

Uses of Funds

Two major functions are performed by property and liability companies: underwriting of risks and investment of funds in a diversified portfolio of securities. The substantial holdings of federal securities and other high-grade assets reflect the obligation of the companies to meet all underwriting losses when incurred. Unlike life insurance companies, property and liability companies are unable to estimate future claims with a high degree of accuracy.

Table 5-6 shows the combined percentage distribution of the assets of property and liability companies from 1965 through 1977. The data conceal substantial variations within the industry resulting from factors discussed below, but it is interesting to note that since 1975 the percentage composition of assets for all property and liability companies as a group has changed appreciably. There has been a relative decline in holdings of U.S. government securities and common stock, which has been absorbed by additional investments in municipal and corporate bonds.

The investment policies of property and liability companies contrast sharply with those of life insurance companies. The table shows that, despite recent trends, property and liability companies invest substantial sums in corporate stocks and very little in mortgages, while the opposite holds for life insurance companies. A greater need for liquidity by property and liability companies helps to explain the differences in security holdings. There are also differences, however, in the investment policies of mutual and stock property and liability companies themselves, which are briefly discussed below.

Factors Affecting Investment Policy

Differences among sources of funds play an important part in investment policy. Reserve liabilities have short and intermediate maturity, depending on the length of policies (one to five years). If an insurance company were to stop writing new business, it would pay out on existing claims approximately the amount of its loss reserves plus that portion of unearned premium credited to loss reserves as the policies neared expiration. This payment coverage would require substantial liquidity. Actually, however, most companies can meet both expenses and losses from new premium income which relieves the pressure for liquidity, but does not remove price risk from the portfolio. The possible need

TABLE 5-6. Combined Assets of Property and Liability Insurance Companies, Amounts and Percentages, at Year End, 1965-1977
(billions of dollars)

	1965		1970		1975		1977	
	Amount	Percent	Amount	Percent	Amount	Percent	Amount	Percent
U.S. Treasury securities	$ 6.0	14.4%	$ 5.0	8.5%	$ 7.9	8.4%	$ 14.3	11.3%
Federal agency securities[a]	0.5	1.2	0.4	0.6	0.4	0.4	0.6	0.5
State and local government bonds								
General	5.7	13.6	8.4	14.5	13.9	14.9	17.3	13.7
Revenue	5.5	13.2	8.4	14.5	19.1	20.5	31.7	25.0
Corporate bonds	2.6	6.2	8.1	14.0	11.6	12.4	18.9	15.0
Preferred stock	1.1	2.6	1.6	2.8	3.0	3.2	3.8	3.0
Common stock	14.1	33.7	16.0	27.6	20.2	21.7	17.9	14.1
Mortgages	0.1	0.2	0.2	0.4	0.2	0.2	0.3	0.2
Premium balances	2.6	6.2	4.3	7.5	7.6	8.1	10.1	8.0
Cash	1.3	3.1	1.4	2.4	1.7	1.8	2.2	1.7
Other assets	2.3	5.5	4.2	7.2	7.7	8.2	9.5	7.5
Total	$41.8	100.0%	$58.0	100.0%	$93.3	100.0%	$126.6	100.0%

[a]Includes federally sponsored agency and budget agency securities.
Source: Alfred M. Best Co., Inc., *Best's Aggregates and Averages, Property-Casualty* (annual).

to sell securities in large amounts to meet calamitous losses requires not only an equity cushion, but also limited vulnerability to fluctuations in the market value of portfolio assets.

Previously, common stock holdings provided sufficient liquidity and growth to make these instruments easily the preferred holdings by property and liability companies. However, the bad experience with stock prices in the 1970s, the sharp rise in interest rates paid on alternative investments, and the rapid rate of inflation have caused the insurance companies to look for alternative investments. In retrospect, many companies found that heavy commitments in common stocks in the late 1960s and early 1970s placed too much risk in the portfolio and contributed to the double-barreled effect on company operations. That is, property and liability company earnings tend to suffer cyclical swings roughly paralleling the business cycle. When the economy is down, underwriting experience is likely to be bad, as moral risk factors and lagging rate increases take their toll. Unfortunately, this is normally the time when the stock market is also performing in lackluster fashion. Thus, poor market performance tends to follow poor underwriting experience, and good market performance follows good underwriting experience, which can lead to highly cyclical earnings. To moderate the cyclical earnings, many property and liability companies have switched from common stock holdings to corporate and municipal bonds that offer high and steady returns. Other factors determining investment policy are discussed below.

Type of organization   Mutual companies lack the investment of stockholders as a cushion against losses in asset value. Policyholders' surplus belongs to the clients rather than to proprietors, and consequently the investment policy of mutual companies is more conservative than that of stock companies. Bonds and preferred stock constituted 18 percent of total assets at the end of 1977. The relative importance of federal bonds has, however, declined substantially in the postwar period.

Type of business written   Property insurance policies may cover terms as long as five years and tend to have highly variable losses, whereas liability policies typically cover one year and losses are more stable from year to year. Consequently, companies writing property insurance often need greater liquidity even though the average liability settlement has increased substantially.

Regulations for safety   State laws governing investments vary considerably. In general, they require (1) investment in high-grade bonds of funds representing reserves, and minimum levels of policyholders' surplus or capital; (2) adequate diversification, and (3) observance of quality standards (for example, for stocks, a certain dividend history).

Sources of funds   Ability to meet all claims under any conditions requires avoidance of substantial price risks. Premiums are collected in advance, and funds representing reserves must be available at all times. In 1977, cash plus premium income in process of collection plus bonds equaled 9.7 percent of total assets. Loss reserves and unearned premiums represented 63 percent of total liabilities and surplus.

The proportion of liquid assets has declined in recent years. This decline reflects chiefly the increase in the book (year-end market) value of stocks held, together with a decline in the relative importance of safety in terms of federal and corporate bonds.

Tax relief   Stock companies pay the corporate income tax rate on net investment income and net underwriting profits. Mutuals are taxed on substantially the same basis.[3] As a result, high-yielding corporate bonds and tax-exempt direct obligations of state and municipal governments and tax-free revenue bonds are in favor. Stock companies hold a smaller percentage in these assets because of the larger relative importance of common stocks in their portfolios.

Need for inflation protection   At the end of 1977, stock companies had 13 percent and mutuals 16 percent of their total assets in common stocks. The slight increase in common stock holdings in recent years reflects the need for price appreciation as protection against increasing costs of repair and replacement. In addition, 85 percent of dividend income is tax-exempt. Nevertheless, there is a wide variation in policy; some companies emphasize common stocks, while others own relatively small amounts.

Liquidity   Liquidity needs are provided by cash and high-grade bonds. Recently, the main interest in federal bonds has been in the short- and intermediate-term categories because of their lesser price risk and because their yields are (in 1978) slightly above those of long maturities (see Chapter 8).

Volume of business and loss experience   Both rapidly rising volume of premiums written and an adverse record of underwriting losses require a conservative investment policy. The combination of insurance and investment "exposure," together with the other factors mentioned above, sets the pattern for the individual company.

Annual Uses of Funds, 1970–1978

The data in Table 5-7 show the net disposition of funds in capital-market assets in recent years. Federal bonds were not attractive to property and liability

---

[3] Mutual companies are permitted to establish pretax protection against loss accounts in an amount equal to 1 percent of insurance losses during the year and 25 percent of ordinary underwriting income for a period of five years. Mutual companies that elect to distribute their underwriting profit to policyholders are allowed full deduction for these "dividends."

TABLE 5-7. Annual Flow of Funds into Capital-Market Assets, Property and Liability Insurance Companies, 1970–1978
(billions of dollars)

	1970	1971	1972	1973	1974	1975	1976	1977	1978 (est.)
U.S. Treasury securities	$ –	$ –	$ 0.1	$–0.1	$ 0.4	$ 2.5	$ 3.1	$ 3.1	$ 0.8
Federal agency securities[a]	0.1	-0.2	-0.1	–	0.3	0.2	0.3	0.3	0.2
State and local government securities	1.3	3.5	4.4	3.3	1.9	2.4	5.1	10.2	13.8
Corporate bonds	1.5	0.3	-0.7	-0.2	2.0	2.1	3.8	3.4	2.5
Corporate stocks[b]	1.1	2.5	3.0	2.8	-0.2	-1.3	0.1	2.3	2.5
Total	$4.0	$ 6.2	$ 6.7	$ 5.8	$ 4.4	$ 5.9	$12.4	$19.3	$19.8

[a]Includes securities of federally sponsored agencies and of budget agencies.
[b]Stocks are shown net of change in market values.
Sources: Alfred M. Best Co., Inc., *Best's Aggregates and Averages, Property-Casualty* (annual); Bankers Trust Company, *Credit and Capital Markets* (annual). (Certain columns do not add to totals because of rounding.)

companies until 1976 when higher rates and lack of alternative investment outlets made these securities worthwhile holdings. The major emphasis, however, has been on tax-free state and municipal bonds. Net acquisitions of corporate stocks (mostly common) rose modestly in the late 1970s.

Corporate bonds have drawn increasing investor funds as their attractive yields have compared favorably with other capital-market instruments.

Property and casualty insurance companies, with $127 billion in assets, of which $105 billion consisted of securities at the end of 1977, are not nearly as large as the other major institutions—commercial banks, life insurance companies, and savings and loan associations—in asset size. Yet, because of their specialization in limited types of securities, they are a significant institutional factor in the stock market and in the market for state and local government obligations.

```
6666666666666666666666666666666666666666666666666666666666666666666666666666666666666
6666666666666666666666666666666666666666666666666666666666666666666666666666666666666
66666666666666666666666666666666    6666666666666   666    6666666666666666666666666666666666
66666666666666666666666666666666    66666666666   6666    6666666666666666666666666666666666
66666666666666666666666666666666    666666666   66666    6666666666666666666666666666666666
66666666666666666666666666666666    6666666    666666    6666666666666666666666666666666666
66666666666666666666666666666666    66666    6666666    6666666666666666666666666666666666
66666666666666666666666666666666    666    66666666    6666666666666666666666666666666666
66666666666666666666666666666666    6    666666666    6666666666666666666666666666666666
66666666666666666666666666666666    6666666666    6666666666666666666666666666666666
66666666666666666666666666666666    666666666    6666666666666666666666666666666666
6666666666666666666666666666666666666666666666666666666666666666666666666666666666666
6666666666666666666666666666666666666666666666666666666666666666666666666666666666666
```

Pension and Retirement Plans

DURING the postwar period, pension and retirement plans of all types have become important investors in the capital markets. In this chapter we are concerned chiefly with trusteed (noninsured) private pension funds and state and local government retirement funds. A shorter section on federal retirement funds is also included.

As the liabilities of pension funds are long-term commitments to employees, it is not surprising, from a hedging viewpoint, that all types of long-term capital market instruments are found in the growing accumulations of retirement systems. Historically, private pension funds placed emphasis on common stocks in an attempt to attain higher returns for their investment portfolios, which would help reduce the retirement expense burden. Poor stock market performance in the late 1960s and in the 1970s, however, has caused many companies to commit most of their new pension fund monies to high-yielding short- and long-term debt instruments to the exclusion of common stocks. Federal pension accounts, on the other hand, have tended to purchase Treasury obligations only.

Trusteed Private Pension Funds

Nature and Scope

The importance of pension funds to the economy and to the capital markets is substantial and increasing. In December, 1978, the assets of all public and private pension and retirement funds totaled $555 billion. Although both public and private pension funds have made sizable gains since World War II, the greatest growth has been in the private sector. Private plans had reserves totaling $202 billion (at book value) at the end of December 1978. At the end of 1977 over 50 million workers were covered under private and public pension funds other than social security. About 38 million of these were covered under the private plans, although there is some duplication due to persons being covered by more than one plan.

Previously, private pension plans differed widely in a number of aspects, such as employees covered, service and age requirements for eligibility, retirement provisions, and vesting privileges. However, the Employee Retirement and Income Security Act of 1974 (ERISA) essentially eliminated several of the major differences and abuses. In later discussions our chief interest in ERISA, however, lies in its effect on the sources and uses of funds and its impact on capital markets.

For our purposes plans can be classified as follows: (1) total private pension and profit-sharing plans, including those of companies, unions, and nonprofit organizations; and (2) insured versus uninsured, or trusteed, corporate plans. The funds of insured corporate plans are invested in annuities and so are comingled with the other assets of life insurance companies.[1] Uninsured plans are usually administered by, or are at least in the custodianship of, bank trustees.

Table 6-1 shows the growth of total private plans since 1960. Their expansion reflects (1) growth in employment; (2) the increase in the number of persons approaching retirement age and needing protection; (3) the increase in number of plans, indicating acceptance by employers of responsibility for their employees' retirement years; (4) the use of retirement plans—both fixed and profit-sharing—as incentives to improve work quality and lower employee turnover; (5) the need for inflation protection for retirement income; (6) inclusion of pensions in labor union contracts; and (7) the tax advantages of company plans that meet the eligibility requirements of the Internal Revenue Code, under which contributions are tax-exempt to the company and to the employee until retirement.

Persons covered by private plans of all types in early 1978 amounted to 44 percent of wage and salary workers in private industry. Trusteed plans are more important than insured plans because they are larger, offer greater flexibility of investment policy, and hence are more involved in the capital markets.

Assets for all private noninsured funds, including those of nonprofit organiza-

---

[1] Under a ruling by the Securities and Exchange Commission, life insurance companies are exempt from its jurisdiction if they restrict annuity arrangements with employers to those involving fixed-income contracts. They may avoid SEC jurisdiction and still segregate the assets representing pension contracts and have their investment free from the usual restrictions on the acquisition of common stocks, provided that the risk of market fluctuations is borne by the employer and does not affect the dollar amount of the employees' annuities.

TABLE 6-1. Selected Data on All Private Retirement Plans,[a] at Year End, 1960-1978 (billions of dollars)

	1960	1965	1970	1975	1978 (est.)
Persons covered					
(number in 000's)	18,700	21,800	26,300	30,300	38,100
Contributions	$5.5	$7.4	$14.0	$27.6	$43.8
Benefit payments	$1.7	$3.5	$ 7.4	$14.8	$23.5
Reserves (book value)					
Insured plans	$18.8	$27.3	$ 40.1	$ 67.4	$113.5
Uninsured plans	33.1	59.2	97.0	145.2	202.2
Total reserves	$51.9	$86.5	$137.1	$212.6	315.7

[a]Includes multiemployer and union-administered plans and those of nonprofit organizations. Excludes the federal railroad retirement program.

Sources: Department of Commerce, Bureau of the Census, *Statistical Abstract of the United States;* Department of Health, Education and Welfare, Social Security Administration, *Social Security Bulletin;* Securities and Exchange Commission, *Statistical Bulletin;* Bankers Trust Company, *Credit and Capital Markets* (annual).

tions, multiemployer funds, and union-administered funds, totaled $315.7 billion (at book value) at the end of 1978. The reserves of insured plans aggregated $113.5 billion or slightly more than half the total of noninsured plans.

Sources of Funds: Private Plans

Private plans derive their funds from employer and employee contributions and from net investment earnings. In many cases, all contributions are made by employers in amounts based on wages and salaries, or company profits, or both. Excluding investment income, employers as a whole contribute more than 93 percent of the total yearly contributions to pension plans (Table 6-2).

As shown in Table 6-1, total contributions to all private plans increased from $5.5 billion in 1960 to $43.8 billion in 1978. From 1975 through 1978, the average annual input was over $30 billion. Investment income, exclusive of profit on sale of assets, has provided about 20 percent of total receipts.

Annual Sources of Funds of Noninsured Private Plans

Noninsured (trusteed) private plans exclude private plans administered by insurance companies but include nonprofit organization and labor unions. Funds available for investment consist of employer and employee contributions and investment income, net of benefits and expenses. The annual data from 1970 through 1978 in Table 6-2 reveal the steady growth of private plans, now at around $17 billion per year, or double the 1970 rate. Because the coverage of most plans is growing and will continue to do so for several years, receipts will be well in excess of expenditures and the excess will be invested primarily in

TABLE 6-2. Receipts of Private Noninsured Pension Plans, 1970-1978 (billions of dollars)

	1970	1971	1972	1973	1974	1975	1976	1977	1978 (est.)
Employer contributions	$ 9.7	$11.3	$12.7	$14.4	$17.0	$19.8	$21.8	26.5	30.5
Employee contributions	1.1	1.1	1.2	1.3	1.5	1.6	1.7	1.8	1.9
Investment and other income[a]	4.0	4.1	4.3	4.8	6.0	6.7	7.0	7.2	7.6
Total receipts	$14.8	$16.5	$18.2	$20.5	$24.5	$28.1	$30.5	35.5	40.0
Benefit payments and expenses	6.2	7.2	8.4	9.5	11.0	12.6	14.8	16.5	18.2
Net receipts	$ 8.6	$ 9.3	$ 9.8	$11.0	$13.5	$15.6	$15.7	19.0	21.8

[a]Not including profit (or loss) on sale of securities.
Sources: Social Security Administration, *Social Security Bulletin*; Securities and Exchange Commission, *Statistical Bulletin*; Bankers Trust Company, *Credit and Capital Markets* (annual).

capital-market instruments. It should be noted, however, that even though net receipts have continued to increase, benefit payments and expenses exceeded investment income in 1978 by 10.6 billion.

Investment income in 1978 of $7.6 billion was about 19 percent of total receipts—a drop from 28 percent in 1965. This reflects the increased role of employer contributions in funding the pension plan and low dividend payouts on common stock holdings. Investment income, as we use the term here, excludes realized and unrealized profits or losses on assets. If we include realized net capital gains of $2.9 billion and relate investment income to book value, the rate of return was 5.2 percent in 1978. Excluding gains, the rate of return was 3.8 percent.

Deducting from the sources above the annual changes in cash and miscellaneous assets, we have the following sums available for capital-market investment (billions of dollars):

1970	1971	1972	1973	1974	1975	1976	1977	1978
$6.9	$7.4	$6.6	$7.8	$8.1	$13.8	$12.6	$15.6	$12.9

A major factor contributing to the sharp increases in flows in 1975 and later years over 1974 was the retirement law (ERISA) enacted in 1974 that substantially expanded coverage to a number of employees.

Uses of Funds: Investment Policy

The growing accumulation of private pension fund capital reflects the increase in the number of plans, the number of persons covered, and the increase in net receipts of established plans. The asset expansion of trusteed corporate plans in recent years is indicated in Table 6-3. Assets grew about $12 billion per year from 1965 through 1972, a yearly compounded growth rate of better than 10 percent, but dropped sharply in 1973 as stock values declined by more than 14 percent as total assets of uninsured private pension funds went from $154.3 billion in 1972 to $132.2 billion in 1973. The decline accelerated in 1974 but rose substantially thereafter through 1978 as stock market prices increased and funds were placed in other securities.

Similar to those of insurance companies, the combined figures hide the wide range in investment policy of individual funds. Some hold only federal bonds, others consist mostly of common stocks. At the end of 1973, common stocks constituted about 68 percent of total assets. Poor experience with common stock holdings in 1974-1976, coupled with the high yields at less risk available on other securities, caused many pension fund managers to moderate their commitments to common stock, such that at the end of 1978 less than 54 percent of pension assets were invested in common stock (at market value).

Trusteed funds are normally managed by bank trust departments or investment advisors and are invested within the framework of trust regulations. The trust agreement may allow complete freedom in choosing investments. Even in

TABLE 6-3. Market Value of Assets of Uninsured Private Pension Funds,[a] 1965–1978 (billions of dollars)

	1965		1970		1975		1978	
	Amount	Percent	Amount	Percent	Amount	Percent	Amount	Percent
Cash and deposits	$ 0.9	1.2	$ 1.8	1.7	$ 3.0	2.1	$ 8.1	4.0%
U.S. Treasury securities	2.5	3.4	2.1	2.0	11.1	7.4	17.8	8.8
Federal agency securities[b]	0.5	0.6	0.9	0.9	3.3	2.5	4.1	2.0
Corporate bonds	21.9	30.1	24.9	23.8	31.2	21.4	45.5	22.6
Preferred stock	0.8	1.1	1.6	1.5	0.9	0.6	1.2	0.6
Common stock	40.0	54.8	65.5	62.6	87.7	60.2	106.7	53.0
Own company	(4.4)	(6.0)	(6.0)	(5.6)	(7.0)	(4.8)	(11.2)[c]	(5.6)
Other companies	(35.6)	(48.8)	(59.4)	(56.9)	(80.7)	(55.4)	(95.5)[a]	(47.4)
Mortgages	3.4	4.7	3.5	3.4	2.1	1.4	2.5	1.2
Other assets	3.0	4.1	4.4	4.1	6.3	4.4	15.6	7.7
Total	$72.9	100 %	$104.7	100 %	$145.6	100 %	$201.5	100%

[a]Includes all corporate funds except those administered by insurance companies; includes nonprofit organization and multiemployer plans. (Some columns do not add to totals because of rounding.)
[b]Includes securities of sponsored and budget agencies.
[c]Estimated.
Sources: Social Security Administration, *Social Security Bulletin;* Securities and Exchange Commission, *Statistical Bulletin;* Federal Reserve *Flow-of-Funds Accounts.*

113

nondiscretionary funds, however, wide latitude is provided by the agreements and by the "prudent-man" rule. In general, investment policy permits sufficient flexibility to take into account changes in the markets and the business cycle. These factors are especially important to funds emphasizing common stocks; even in these the steady inflow of cash permits the use of dollar cost averaging. Some funds buy stocks every day. Others vary the proportions in cash, fixed-income securities, and equities according to a rough or an exact formula.

Investment policy is also affected by the sources of funds and by whether the benefits are to be fixed or variable. More risk can be taken with company-contributed funds and in plans whose benefits are not determined on an actuarial basis. If inflation hedging over the long term is an important goal, a substantial investment in common stocks has generally been considered appropriate (at least until 1974).

The high rate of inflation and the sharp increase in future pension benefits have, until recent years, caused pension administrations to focus more on common stocks in hopes of securing higher returns. A mere ¼ of 1 percent improvement in annual return enables a company to cut its contributions or increase benefits by 4 to 6 percent per year. As noted earlier, however, the market decline in 1973–1974 resulted in disillusionment with the belief that equities would provide this improvement and substantial shifting to high-yield, low-risk securities occurred.

Cash position   Funds differ greatly in the degree of liquidity maintained. Cash held (including commercial paper) affects the rate of return on the portfolio and for this reason represents less than 2 percent of total pension fund assets. In periods of continued weakness in the bond and stock market, cash balances usually increase as a percentage of assets.

United States government securities   Although holdings are still small, the proportion of total pension fund assets held in Federal securities increased in the late 1970s, so that they now represent about 11 percent of total assets. Nevertheless, the small holdings reflect recognition of three factors: (1) that growing funds need little liquidity as payouts lag far behind cash receipts and receipts and benefits are readily estimated, (2) that the rate of return on assets is important—the assets of the fund are expected to grow through compounding of income as well as through new contributions, and (3) that other securities with little change in risk may provide higher returns over the long run.

Corporate bonds   Fixed-income securities such as corporate bonds continue to occupy an important place in most portfolios. Their steady income and generous yields, plus cash from spacing of maturities, help to provide for current expenses and benefits. At the end of 1978, corporate bonds totaled $45 billion, or 23 percent of total pension fund assets.

The sharp decline in bond prices in 1969, 1974, and 1979, reflecting sharply increased yields, caused a new look at the safety of these securities in an inflationary economy; however, the high bond yields prevailing in 1974 and 1979 and the continued weakness in common stock prices made corporate bonds more attractive than previously.

Common stock   As noted earlier, pension funds have had their greatest impact in the area of common stocks, where they are the largest institutional holder, owning about 10 percent of the value of all domestic common stocks outstanding. Disenchantment with the stock market spread to pension funds in the 1970s as interest rates on competing securities made these attractive alternative investments. In 1972 70 percent of pension fund net receipts went into stocks; by 1978 this figure had dropped to 9 percent. Furthermore, the 1974 passage of ERISA mandated prudence in investment purchases by pension fund managers such that many financial advisors called into question the appropriateness of heavy commitments in common stock in pension plans that are essentially set up on the insurance principle of steady income at retirement.

Pension fund investment policies, characterized by a relatively slow portfolio turnover but large investment purchases, may have contributed to a thinning of the market for selected issues, to the sharp changes in stock prices, and to modest stock yields as funds prefer long-term capital gains and growth.

Some stock activity by pension funds will likely continue in the future despite the disillusionment with the market as a result of the need for high returns over time to pay for future retirement benefits and vesting privileges for employees. Moreover, large wage increases, expanded programs under ERISA, and rapid inflation will place a greater premium on growth since retirement benefits are usually tied to a percentage of an employee's earnings and there will likely be continued pressure for expanded benefits to cover the effects of inflation.

Other investments   Preferred stocks do not appeal to tax-exempt institutions and thus continue to be in relative disfavor due to market yields that are as low as those on many high-grade bonds. This is a result of the 85 percent tax exclusion feature on dividends paid to other corporate owners. For the same reason, low-yielding, tax-free municipal bonds are not attractive to the qualified fund, whose income is exempt under the Internal Revenue Code.

Types of investments that may have increasing emphasis are direct ownership of real estate and mortgages. Although the latter totaled only $2.5 billion, or about 1¼ percent of total trusteed funds, at the end of 1978, their long-term nature and some inflation protection make these worthwhile investments to consider. In large funds, the attractive yields on mortgages offset their higher costs of management and lack of good marketability. Also, mortgage servicing can be left with originating companies and a good secondary market exists for certain mortgages if liquidation becomes necessary.

Annual Uses of Funds

The data in Table 6-4 show the annual net flows of investable funds into capital-market assets from 1970 through 1978. The trends indicated previously are apparent: the moderating flow of funds into common stocks, the substantial variations in the flow of funds into corporate bonds, and the increase in investment in federal obligations.

Employees Retirement and Income Security Act of 1974

Pension fund managers face a complex of issues as a result of the ERISA that sharply increases the cost of pensions to corporations. All existing and new corporate pension plans must conform to the requirements of the Act. The major changes in the Act allowed for (1) earlier employee coverage under a plan, (2) a more uniform accrual of pension credits, (3) a guaranteed pension or vesting rights, (4) increased funding of past service liabilities, (5) insured pension benefits, and (6) increased retirement allowances for self-employed. It should be noted, however, that the new law does not require a firm to have a pension plan and several have dropped their plans because of the cost and paperwork involved. Some of the more important aspects affecting pensions are discussed below.

In the past, new employees often had to wait several years before becoming eligible for pension plans. Under the new law, with few exceptions, any person who is at least 25 years old, and who has been with a company for one year, is automatically covered under a company plan, if it has one. If an employee commenced work several years before age 25, he must be given up to three years' credit for past service. Furthermore, the accumulation of pension credits must be done in an orderly and fair manner. The benefit credits to an employee in any one year cannot exceed $1\frac{1}{3}$ times the amount credited in any other year. This prevents a firm from accumulating few credits in early years and then sharply increasing credits after several years for the long-term employee. In this manner, a person leaving the employment of a firm receives a more proportional "vesting" of his retirement benefits.

The accumulation of these pension credits over time has often meant very little because in the past these credits were not "vested" with the individual. Since corporations at the end of 1978 were contributing more than 93 percent of all the private retirement funds, vesting (the right of the employee to claim the funds should he retire or quit the company) is important to the individual with many years of service. Previously, pension benefits contributed in an employee's name were often returned to the company if he left the firm before his earliest retirement date. Under the new Act, companies are given several options of ultimately vesting benefits with the employee. The plans allow for either partial vesting, immediately, or full vesting after as early as ten years or as late

TABLE 6-4. Annual Net Flow of Funds into Capital-Market Assets, Private Uninsured Pension Funds, at Year End, 1970–1978
(billions of dollars)

	1970	1971	1972	1973	1974	1975	1976	1977	1978
U.S. Treasury securities	$-0.1	$ —	$ 0.9	$ 0.2	$-0.2	$ 4.5	$ 3.7	$ 4.8	$ 0.4
Federal agency securities[a]	0.3	-0.3	0.1	0.6	1.3	0.7	0.3	0.6	2.0
Corporate bonds	2.1	-0.7	-0.8	2.1	4.7	2.8	1.3	5.3	8.2
Preferred stocks	—	0.4	—	-0.2	-0.1	0.2	0.2	0.4	} 1.7
Common stocks	4.6	8.5	7.3	5.5	2.4	5.6	7.1	4.1	
Home mortgages	—	-0.4	-0.4	-0.2	—	-0.1	-0.1	—	0.1
Other mortgages	—	-0.1	-0.5	-0.2	—	0.1	0.1	0.4	0.5
Total	$ 6.9	$ 7.4	$ 6.6	$ 7.8	$ 8.1	$13.8	$12.6	$15.6	$12.9

[a]Includes securities of federally sponsored and budget agencies.
Sources: Securities and Exchange Commission, *Statistical Bulletin*: Federal Reserve *Flow-of-Funds Accounts*. (Some columns do not add to totals because of rounding.)

117

as fifteen years, and full vesting—that is, a clam to all accrued credits in the employee's name—after age 45.

In the past, even if a plan had full vesting privileges from the start, there was no guarantee an employee would receive the benefits rightfully due him. Such a situation often resulted when a firm failed, or merged with another company, or merely dropped the plan. Since January 1, 1976, all plans must be funded on a current basis. Past service liabilities—obligations already accrued—must be amortized in an orderly and consistent fashion, and pension fund assets must be made independent of the firm itself. Accordingly, if a firm fails, the employees will not lose the benefits accumulated for them in the pension plan. In 1974, the Pension Benefit Guaranty Corporation was created to insure all vested benefits up to certain specified limits. The guarantee amounts to a maximum of $1,074 per month and up to 100 percent of the employee's wages in his five years of highest earnings. The insurance company has an automatic "draw" of up to $100 million from the Treasury, but the bulk of the funds come from annual premium assessments of $2.60 per employee for corporations.

The added burden to a corporation from earlier employee vesting privileges and eligibility under ERISA has caused concern as to the viability of some plans. Multiemployer plans (plans formed by several employers primarily in construction) are already experiencing problems, and the unfunded portion of vested benefits for the 100 largest U.S. companies alone amounted to more than $18.5 billion in 1976. From the new act the implication is clear: more funds and investment income will be needed to cover the added cost. Annual contributions in 1978, running at the rate of over $25 billion, need to be placed in investment securities, which necessarily means that the capital market will be one of the prime beneficiaries.

The Act also had a profound effect on the management of pension funds since it expressly stated that investments be made in a prudent manner. Given the vagaries of the stock market some have concluded that to invest in common stocks is questionable, and, if done at all, funds should be invested in the market portfolio only. In either case the implication is for closer scrutiny of common stock investments.

State and Local Government Retirement Plans

The wide attention given to corporate and other pension funds has obscured the fact that public retirement funds have also grown rapidly in the postwar period. Total assets of state and local employee retirement systems have increased from $5 billion in 1950 to $148 billion at the end of 1978. These resources are to provide retirement income to over 12 million persons.

State and municipal pension funds differ in scope of coverage, employee contributions, vesting provisions, actuarial assumptions, and many other factors. We, however, are concerned chiefly with investment policy.

Sources of Funds

Government and employee contributions and investment income provide the funds for these systems. The estimated annual sources of funds for calendar years 1970 through 1978 were as shown in Table 6-5. In comparison to private pension funds, where more than 93 percent of total contributions (excluding investment income) were paid by the employer, government contributions amounted to only 69 percent.

Although the net receipts (total receipts minus benefit payments) have been substantial (in 1976, 67 percent of total receipts were brought down to net), many plans are relatively mature, and in recent years the rate of asset growth has lagged behind that of corporate and other private pension funds. Nevertheless, the annual supply of funds to the capital markets is significant. Deducting the funds allocated to cash and miscellaneous assets, the figures are as follows (billions of dollars):

1970	1971	1972	1973	1974	1975	1976	1977	1978
$6.2	$6.5	$8.3	$9.1	$9.4	$11.6	$13.4	$12.9	$14.7

Uses of Funds: Investment Policy

In 1950, federal, state, and local bonds comprised more than 87 percent of total assets. The percentage of relative investment declined sharply after that time and in 1978 the two categories together represented about 15 percent of total assets (Table 6-6).

In the late 1970s, ownership of federal securities increased sharply as high yields and low risk made these securities among the favored investments. During this same period, the percentage of assets invested in corporate bonds—the major asset—rose from 11 percent in 1950 to over 50 percent in 1978. The shift to corporate bonds reflected a declining need for liquidity and the superior yields available on high-grade corporates. At the end of 1978, the funds owned about 20 percent of all corporate bonds outstanding. Federal agency bonds worth $6 billion constituted about 4 percent of their total assets. Although small in absolute amounts, federal agency securities have grown in interest because of the expanding number and variety of agency issues that offer favorable risk and return characteristics for retirement accounts.

State and local retirement funds still own nearly $4 billion of tax-free municipal securities, even though the tax-exempt feature is of no value since retirement funds pay no taxes. Political pressure and necessity often require investment in such securities in a number of jurisdictions, particularly when unsold municipal issues exist. However, except for political pressure, their influence in the municipal market will likely continue to decrease as fund managers aim for higher portfolio yields, and prudent management dictates a more responsible position.

TABLE 6-5. Annual Sources of Funds, State and Local Government Retirement Plans, 1970–1978 (billions of dollars)

	1970	1971	1972	1973	1974	1975	1976	1977	1978 (est.)
Government contributions	$ 4.9	$ 5.6	$ 6.0	$ 6.8	$ 8.2	$ 9.9	$11.6	$13.8	$16.0
Employee contributions	3.0	3.6	3.5	3.8	4.1	4.6	5.1	5.5	6.5
Investment income	2.7	3.4	3.8	4.2	5.2	6.1	7.7	9.1	11.0
Total receipts	$10.6	$12.6	$13.3	$14.8	$17.4	$20.6	$24.4	$28.4	$33.5
Benefit payments	3.9	5.6	5.1	5.9	6.9	8.1	9.2	10.4	12.3
Net receipts	$ 6.7	$ 7.1	$ 8.2	$ 8.9	$10.5	$12.5	$15.2	$18.0	$21.2

Sources: Bankers Trust Company, *Credit and Capital Markets* (annual). U.S. Department of Commerce, Bureau of the Census, *Government Finances*, and *Finances of Employee-Retirement Systems of State and Local Governments* (annual); Federal Reserve *Flow-of-Funds Accounts*. (Some columns do not add to totals because of rounding.)

TABLE 6-6. Book Value of Assets of State and Local Government Retirement Funds, Amounts and Percentages, Calendar Years 1965–1978 (billions of dollars)

	1965		1970		1975		1978	
	Amount	Percent	Amount	Percent	Amount	Percent	Amount	Percent
Cash	$ 0.3	0.9	$ 0.6	1.0	$ 1.4	1.3	$ 3.0	2.0
U.S. Treasury securities	7.1	21.4	5.1	8.8	2.5	2.4	10.0	6.8
Federal agency securities[a]	0.5	1.5	1.6	2.7	4.9	4.6	8.0	5.4
State and local government securities	2.6	7.8	2.0	3.4	1.9	1.8	4.1	2.8
Corporate bonds	16.6	50.0	33.1	57.0	61.7	58.2	81.3	55.0
Preferred stock	0.2	0.6	0.4	0.7	1.7	1.5	} 32.4	21.9
Common stock	1.4	4.2	7.6	13.1	22.6	21.0		
Mortgages	3.7	11.1	6.9	12.0	7.4	7.4	8.9	6.0
Other assets	0.8	2.5	0.8	1.3	1.4	1.8	–	–
Total	$33.2	100 %	$58.1	100 %	$106.0	100 %	$147.7	100 %

aIncludes federally sponsored and budget agencies.

Sources: U.S. Department of Commerce, Bureau of the Census, *Governmental Finances* (annual) and *Finances of Employee-Retirement Systems of State and Local Governments*; Securities and Exchange Commission, *Statistical Bulletin and Statistical Series*; Federal Reserve *Flow-of-Funds Accounts*.

TABLE 6-7. Annual Flows into Capital-Market Assets, State and Local Government Retirement Plans, 1970–1978
(billions of dollars)

	1970	1971	1972	1973	1974	1975	1976	1977	1978
U.S. Treasury securities	$-0.3	$-1.2	$-0.3	$-1.1	$-0.9	$ 1.0	$ 1.5	$ 2.4	$ 3.6
Federal agency securities	-0.1	0.1	0.6	0.9	1.0	1.1	0.1	1.0	1.8
State and local government securities	-0.3	0.1	-0.1	-0.4	-0.7	1.0	1.4	0.3	0.3
Corporate bonds	4.5	3.9	4.2	5.6	6.8	6.3	7.1	5.3	5.8
Corporate stocks	2.1	3.2	3.7	3.4	2.6	2.4	3.1	3.4	2.5
Mortgages	0.3	0.4	0.2	0.7	0.6	-0.2	0.2	0.5	0.7
Total	$ 6.2	$ 6.5	$ 8.3	$ 9.1	$ 9.4	$11.6	$13.4	$12.9	$14.7

Source: Federal Reserve Flow-of-Funds Accounts. (Some columns do not add to totals because of rounding.)

In more than 50 percent of the states, fund managers are permitted to invest in high-grade listed common stocks, reflecting the need for potential inflation protection and the minor importance of liquidity. Although experiencing generally poor investment results from common stock holdings in the 1970s, retirement funds still maintained significant commitments to the area by adding about $2 to $3 billion net annually of corporate stocks during the period. Since 1965, mortgages have shown some modest growth. Mortgages are likely to be more attractive in the future as the need for higher yields increases, legal barriers are removed, and fund managers become more familiar with mortgage instruments. Greater use of the services of mortgage correspondent and the expanding secondary mortgage market should also be an added inducement.

Annual Uses of Funds

Table 6-7 shows the net annual additions to capital-market assets from 1970 through 1978. The data show the generally declining investment in federal and municipal bonds and the steady accumulation of corporate bonds and stocks. Ownership of federal obligations, however, rose in 1975 and 1976 because of their higher rates relative to other securities. The increases in holdings in 1975-1976 of municipal securities—again surprising because of the tax-exempt feature, which is of no value to retirement funds—were primarily a result of the unsettled municipal market caused by New York and other cities that experienced financial problems. The generally poor financial condition of some municipalities caused interest rates to rise to abnormally high levels such that new issues at going market rates would exceed statutory ceilings. Consequently, in order to sell some unwanted bonds or to sell a municipal issue at the statutory limit but less than the going market rate, retirement accounts were a convenient repository.

The rate of growth of state and local government retirement funds has been exceeded only by that of private pension funds, credit unions, and savings and loan associations. Although there are signs of maturity, as government employment, salaries, and benefits continue to increase, these funds will also continue to grow. Their increasing interest in high-grade corporate bonds has already made them the most important buyer of publicly marketed securities of this type, especially in recent years. Their influence in the stock market will probably continue to increase as a result of the increased pressure for portfolio performance and growth. Moreover, as municipal finances receive closer scrutiny, there is growing evidence that cities and states are facing a major problem in unfunded pension debt. Efforts to correct the problem should mean that substantial funds will be available for capital-market investment.

Federal Retirement Funds

The federal government manages several trust funds that may be divided into two broad categories: retirement/disability funds and agency funds. Included as retirement funds are (1) Old Age and Survivors Insurance Trust Fund (OASI)–Social Security, (2) Disability and Insurance Trust Fund, (3) Civil Service Retirement and Disability Fund, and (4) Railroad Retirement Fund. The Railroad Retirement Fund is unique in that it is a private system administered by the federal government. The federal government manages a variety of other trust funds, acting as an agent in a fiduciary capacity. These include insurance funds, department trusts, and budgeted agency funds. Our concern in this chapter is with federal retirement funds. Of primary concern in this section is the Social Security Retirement Fund, the largest in terms of number of covered employees. It is interesting to note that despite numerous bills introduced in Congress that would merge the Social Security and the Federal Civil Service Retirement Funds, the legislation has never passed. (The federal retirement funds have larger balances on hand than the Social Security fund, but cover only about 10 percent of the number of employees eligible under Social Security.)

Combined Assets of Federal Retirement Funds

Federal retirement funds have grown substantially in the postwar period, reflecting the expanded benefits over time, the increasing number of employees covered by the retirement plans, and the growth in net receipts. Benefits have increased sharply as a result of competition from private pension funds, inflation, and political popularity.

Table 6–8 shows the asset sizes for federal retirement funds in representative years 1965 through 1978. The decline in assets of the Social Security fund is particularly noticeable. In total, federal retirement funds have not grown as rapidly as private pension plans or state and local retirement funds because of less concern about the fully funded status of the plans. Since the government has full taxing powers, there is a question on the necessity of a retirement plan such as Social Security being set up on an insurance basis, which was the initial intent. The burgeoning Social Security costs have almost made the insurance principle of the system a moot point and, in fact, some have proposed that the govern-

TABLE 6-8.   Assets of Federal Government Retirement Funds, 1965–1978
(billions of dollars)

	1965	1970	1975	1978
Old Age and Survivor's Insurance (Social Security)	$18.2	$32.5	$37.0	$27.5
Disability and Insurance	1.6	5.6	7.4	4.2
Civil Service Retirement and Disability	15.9	23.1	38.6	56.8
Railroad Retirement	3.9	4.4	3.1	2.9
Total	$39.6	$65.6	$86.1	$91.4

Sources: *Treasury Bulletin;* Securities and Exchange Commission, *Statistical Bulletin.*

ment fund the System from current operating revenues. Outlays for retirement programs currently account for more than 25 percent of the federal budget.

The assets of federal retirement funds include some marketable federal securities, but the bulk of their holdings consists of special nonmarketable securities issued by the federal government (see Chapter 8).

Social Security assets at the end of 1978 amounted to $27.5 billion. If placed on an insurance basis, astronomically more funds would be needed (and hence available for capital market investment). A fully funded program is now out of the question (there were about $2 trillion in unfunded liabilities at the end of 1978), but any increase in the asset base would most likely be invested in federal securities.

To avoid intergovernmental transaactions, changes in federal retirement trust holdings are excluded from the data on annual changes in the ownership of federal debt (p. 144) and from the master schedule of sources and uses of funds in Chapter 13. Federal trust fund and agency ownership of U.S. debt, however, is included in Table 8-5 (p. 147).

It is also important to distinguish the operations of these trust funds from Treasury management in a variety of federally sponsored agencies. The role of these agencies in supplying and using capital-market funds is discussed in Chapter 8, and their operations are included in the master data in Chapter 13.

```
77777777777777777777777777777777777777777777777777777777777777777777777777777777777777777
77777777777777777777777777777777777777777777777777777777777777777777777777777777777777777
777777777777777777777777777   77777777777   777   777   7777777777777777777777777777
777777777777777777777777777   777777777   7777   777   7777777777777777777777777777
777777777777777777777777777   77777777   77777   777   7777777777777777777777777777
7777777777777777777777777777   7777777   777777   777   7777777777777777777777777777
7777777777777777777777777777   77777   7777777   777   7777777777777777777777777777
77777777777777777777777777777   777   7777777   777   7777777777777777777777777777
777777777777777777777777777777   7   777777777   777   7777777777777777777777777777
7777777777777777777777777777777   777777777   777   7777777777777777777777777777
77777777777777777777777777777777   7777777777   777   7777777777777777777777777777
77777777777777777777777777777777   777777777   777   7777777777777777777777777777
77777777777777777777777777777777777777777777777777777777777777777777777777777777777777777
77777777777777777777777777777777777777777777777777777777777777777777777777777777777777777
```

Investment Companies
and Real Estate Trusts

THE rapid growth in investment company assets in the postwar period up to 1972 and the growth in real estate investment trust assets for the five years ending in 1972 were some of the outstanding successes among all financial intermediaries. Subsequently, poor performance, large losses, and investor disenchantment with both types of investment companies indicated one of the more distressing and surprising aspects of financial intermediaries in the middle and late 1970s. Equity investment companies—investing in common stock—were beset with redemption problems as the stock market fell and competition from higher rates on competing securities caused large liquidations of common stocks and investment company shares. Open-end investment companies, particularly, experienced heavy net withdrawals of funds during this period as well as their sharpest decline in assets ever.

The cliché that something is sold not bought, is frequently applied to mutual funds. Except for "money" and "tax exempt" funds this form of investment is not normally one that investors actively seek. To the industry's credit, however, new investment devices are always being devised to meet the needs of the investor. For example, since investors had been avoiding the traditional stock mutual funds in favor of higher-yielding fixed-income securities, several mutual funds stressing particular fixed-income securities were formed and offered to the public. The success of some of these funds such as municipal bond funds and Ginnie Mae unit trusts, has been phenomenal. During 1978 alone, these funds added more than $10 billion in gross new investment. By September of 1979 money market funds totaled more than $33 billion.

Real estate investment trusts (REITs), as the name suggests, specialize in real estate loans and ownership. At one time (early 1970s) they were the fifth largest institutional holder of real estate mortgages. The debacle in the real estate market in 1973-1974 and later, however, affected almost all REITs, as loan foreclosures and general investor dissatisfaction led to a precipitous decline in their market prices. If it were not for the banks and insurance companies rescuing the trusts that they directly or indirectly advised, wholesale bankruptcies on a much larger scale than actually reported would have occurred. Real estate investment trusts are discussed in greater detail at the conclusion of this chapter.

General Nature and Types

Investment companies pool the funds of investors, obtained through the sale of shares (and in some cases bonds), in a portfolio of securities. The portfolio is presumably managed to obtain for the shareholders the benefits of diversification, professional selection and supervision of securities, and skilled timing of purchases and sales that hopefully will lead to better performance than the shareholder could do on his own through direct investment.

For these companies, investment is the primary function. Funds are obtained and managed for this purpose in contrast to other financial institutions (such as banks and insurance companies), which invest funds in order to meet their obligations, or holding companies, which acquire stocks for purposes of control.

Investment companies differ widely in size, objectives (such as income versus appreciation), methods of operation, composition of portfolios (securities held and range of diversification), degree of risk undertaken, and relations with investors. A classification of main types from the standpoint of organization and financing is as follows:

1. Fixed. Here (using the trust form of organization) shares represent ownership of a portfolio over which management has little or no discretion.
2. Management. This group, to which our discussion will be confined, involves companies whose managements, within the limits of announced policy and legal regulation, adjust the portfolio to obtain superior results for shareholders. There are two major categories of managed funds:
   (a) Open-end, or "mutual" funds. Such organizations make a continuous offering of new shares at prices to net the issuer their net asset value. The share capitalization is "open" and shares are redeemable at net asset value on short notice. Such companies do not issue bonds or preferred stock. The investor in the shares of mutual funds acquires them from the company or from distributing dealers. There is no open-market trading. The market for their sale is the issuing company, through the redemption privilege.

(b) Closed-end. Such companies have a fixed capitalization. Funds are obtained originally from the sale of common stock and, in the case of "leverage" companies, bonds or preferred stock (or both) and bank loans. Shares are traded on the listed exchanges and over-the-counter markets.

In recent years a number of new types of investment companies, focusing on one particular segment or aspect of the securities markets, have been formed. This category would include such funds as specialized income funds (open- and closed-end), emphasizing short- and/or long-term, high-income securities; money-market funds, stressing short-term instruments; and funds specializing in government securities—both federal and municipal—such as federal and agency bonds and tax-exempt bonds.

The financial statements of open-end (mutual) and of most closed-end companies show their securities portfolio at market value. Changes in asset values of an individual fund thus represent (1) excess (or deficit) of shares issued, sold to existing and new shareholders, over shares redeemed; and (2) any change in the market value of the portfolio. The open-end company must engage in constant sales activity to prevent redemptions from shrinking the asset value of the fund. Dollar growth of a closed-end company reflects occasional new financing and the rising market value of portfolio assets.

A minor type of mutual fund sells face-amount certificates, designed to reach a set dollar amount at the maturity of the contract.

The degree of diversification, types of securities held, amount of risk assumed, and investment purposes of the company are interrelated and are all reflected in a funds securities portfolio. Closed-end companies are classifiable into two major types: (1) diversified, with portfolios consisting of a broad array of securities, mainly common stocks; and (2) those whose portfolios consist mostly of special situation investments.

Since the late 1960s a number of funds have been started that specialize in certain income or capital gain arrangements or else emphasize a particular type of asset. These funds may be of either the open-end or closed-end variety and would include dual funds, funds that invest in money market instruments, or funds that purchase tax exempt securities only.

A newer form of a closed-end fund, the dual fund, first appeared in 1967. These funds are capitalized at equal amounts of common stock (capital shares) which receive all the capital appreciation, and income shares which receive all net investment income and have a cumulative dividend requirement. The funds have a redemption date varying from ten to fifteen years after issue. A number of other closed-end funds were launched, mostly as income funds specializing in money-market instruments.

A unique characteristic of most closed-end funds in recent years is that they have been selling at sharp discounts—up to 30 percent—of their underlying asset values. Since the shares of the closed-end funds are traded and not redeemed—

| | Net Assets | |
Type	Amount	Percent
Common stock		
Aggressive growth	$ 2.3	5.1
Growth	11.4	25.3
Growth and income	15.2	33.8
Balanced	3.7	8.2
Income	4.6	10.2
Municipal bond	2.6	5.8
Specialized bond	4.7	10.5
Option income	0.5	1.1
	$45.0	100.0%

Source: Investment Company Institute. *1979 Mutual Fact Book*, Washington 1979, p. 64.

except upon "maturity" for dual funds—their prices can vary substantially from underlying per share asset values. Lackluster performance and low yields relative to returns on other competing securities are usually given as reasons for the sharp price discounts of closed-end shares.

Open-end (mutual) funds as a group have the greatest variety of investments. One classification of such companies, by general portfolio distribution at the end of 1978 is shown in Table 7-1.

Growth and Size

The number of all investment companies had grown from 366 at the end of 1945 to over 800 at the end of 1978, with total assets increasing from $3 billion to $61 billion. Although investment companies were in existence in the nineteenth century, almost all of their growth has occurred since 1945. A major factor in this growth have been open-end, or mutual, funds, with total assets of $45.0 billion at the end of 1978 excluding money-market funds. Including the latter, the total amounts to $55.9 billion.

Based on estimates by the Investment Company Institute, there were over 8.7 million individual and institutional investors holding investment company shares at the end of 1978, which was a drop of about 2 million from the peak in 1970.

The postwar expansion in investment companies up to 1973 reflects a number of factors: the general economic progress of the period, the growth in total savings, the rise in stock market values, the aggressive sales promotion of mutual fund shares, and their appeal for a variety of reasons, including the desire (through common stocks) to offset inflation. Other factors include the increase in the number and types of funds and the appeal of a growing number of conveniences and services, such as accumulation plans and dividend reinvestment arrangements. On the other hand, the decline in mutual fund popularity after 1973 paralleled the general disenchantment with stock market securities, and the increased criticism of poor mutual fund management and performance, especially after the "go-go" era of 1969–1970, and in the 1973–1974 period of sharply falling prices.

Basic Sources of Funds

Mutual funds can expand by selling more shares than they redeem. They stand ready to buy back shares at net asset value or sell shares at net asset value plus a commission. In every postwar year until 1972, mutual funds as a group sold more shares than were redeemed. Table 7–2 shows, however, that for conventional funds redemptions sharply exceeded sales in 1972 and 1973 and continued every year through 1976, and shows up again in 1978. The large number of redemptions in 1973, together with slumping stock market prices, produced a whopping $13.3 billion drop in mutual fund assets from the previous year, a decline of 17 percent. Since 1972 "money market" funds have somewhat offset the dismal sales performance of the conventional funds.

The data for 1974 through 1978 show separate figures for conventional and money-market funds. The divergence in the figures of the two basic funds was noteworthy in two respects: (1) based on money-market funds, individuals will buy fund shares that promise high yields; and (2) there was a strong dislike for common stock mutual funds in the late 1970s as exemplified by net redemptions of shares even in periods of rising market values, such as in 1975 and 1976. The asset changes in the last column of Table 7–2 show how risky investment in common stocks can be even with diversified portfolios. In five of the nine years from 1970 through 1978, mutual funds assets declined in value before adding net sales. It is the former figure that concerns existing mutual fund holders; therefore, the exodus from common stocks and mutual funds is not surprising. On the other hand, money-market funds grew to over $33 billion in 1979.

Annual Sources of Funds

Table 7–2 shows the excess of sales of capital shares over redemptions (investment income is all distributed in dividends) through 1978. A disconcerting trend for the mutual funds is the general decline since the late 1960s in the sale of new shares and the rise in redemptions. Even if mutual funds are able to reverse the trend, it will probably be some time before they enjoy anything close to the banner years of the late 1950s and early 1960s. Again, the relative decline in flows to mutual funds, even at a time when savings of individuals were at all-time highs as in 1971 through 1973, could be traced to (1) poor investment per-

TABLE 7-2. Net Assets and Net Sales, Open-End Investment Companies,
1955-1978 (millions of dollars)

	Total Change in Net Assets	Excess of Sales over Redemptions	Asset Change Attributable to Market
1955-1959 total	+$ 9,709	5,266	+$ 4,443
1960-1964 total	+ 13,298	7,105	+ 6,193
1965-1969 total	+ 19,175	13,026	+ 6,149
1970	- 673	1,638	- 2,311
1971	+ 7,427	397	+ 7,070
1972	+ 4,786	- 1,671	+ 6,457
1973	- 13,313	- 1,292	- 8,985
1974c[a]	- 12,456	- 290	- 12,166
m[b]	1,715	1,673	42
1975c[a]	8,117	- 379	- 7,738
m[b]	1,930	873	1,057
1976c[a]	5,358	- 2,441	7,799
m[b]	241	248	- 7
1977c[a]	- 2,488	374	- 2,862
m[b]	484	10	474
1978c[a]	70	- 527	597
m[b]	6,970	6,158	812

[a]Conventional funds.
[b]Money-market funds.
Sources: Wiesenberger Financial Services, *Investment Companies* (New York: Warren, Gorham Lamont, Inc.) (annual); Investment Company Institute, *Mutual Fund Fact Book* (annual); *Federal Reserve Balletin*.

formance, (2) high rates of return available on other securities, (3) public criticism of mutual funds, and (4) recent Securities and Exchange Commission rulings on sales of contractual plans that give the purchaser time to rescind the contract without penalty.

If we deduct changes in cash and other assets (net of liabilities) from yearly flows, the sources of funds available for capital market investment or disinvestment were (billions of dollars):

1970	1971	1972	1973	1974	1975	1976	1977	1978
$2.1	$0.7	$-1.5	$-3.2	$-0.4	$0.7	$-0.1	$-2.8	$-1.2

Uses of Funds

Historically, investment companies have operated mainly in the capital markets. With the exception of short-term bank borrowings of a few closed-end companies, and the new money-market funds, funds are generally raised from long-term sources (sale of securities) and are invested in the secondary securities markets in outstanding rather than in new issues. In contrast to other institutional groups—for example, savings and loan associations—investment companies differ very widely in objectives and portfolio composition. No generalizations as

131

TABLE 7-3. Combined Net Assets of Open-End Investment Companies,[a] Amounts and Percentages, at Year End, 1965–1978
(billions of dollars)

	1965 Amount	1965 Percent	1970 Amount	1970 Percent	1975 Amount	1975 Percent	1978 Amount	1978 Percent
Net cash[b]	$ 1.0	2.8%	$ 2.8	5.7%	$ 5.4	11.8%	$13.9	26.3%
U.S. Treasury securities	0.8	2.3	0.9	2.0	2.0	4.4	2.7	5.1
Corporate bonds	2.5	7.3	4.3	9.0	4.8	10.5	6.2	11.7
Preferred stocks	0.6	1.7	1.1	2.4	0.5	1.1	} 30.1	56.9
Common stocks	30.3	85.9	38.5	80.9	33.1	72.2		
Total	$35.2	100 %	$47.6	100 %	$45.8	100 %	$52.9	100 %

[a] Investment Company Institute members only. "Money-market" funds are included in 1975 and 1978.
[b] Cash and open-market paper less liabilities.
Sources: Investment Company Institute, *Mutual Fund Fact Book* (annual); Wiesenberger Financial Services *Investment Companies* (annual); Federal Reserve *Flow-of-Funds Accounts*.

TABLE 7-4. Annual Flow into Capital-Market Assets, Open-End Investment Companies,[a] 1970–1978 (billions of dollars)

	1970	1971	1972	1973	1974	1975	1976	1977	1978
U.S. Treasury securities	$ 0.2	$-0.3	$ 0.1	$ —	$ 0.5	$ 0.8	$ 0.2	$-0.1	$ 0.7
Corporate bonds	0.7	0.6	0.2	-0.9	-0.4	1.0	2.2	1.1	-0.3
Preferred stocks	-0.2	—	0.1	} -2.3	-0.5	-1.1	-2.5	-3.8	-1.6
Common stocks	1.4	0.4	-1.9						
Total	$ 2.1	$ 0.7	$-1.5	$-3.2	$-0.4	$ 0.7	$-0.1	$-2.8	$-1.2

[a] Include money-market funds.
Sources: Investment Company Institute. *Mutual Fund Fact Book*; Federal Reserve *Flow-of-Funds Accounts*. Data represent net flows and do not reflect changes in market value. (Some columns do not add to totals because of rounding.)

to the character of their assets are feasible, except to say that as a group the bulk of their money is still placed in common stocks, although many are now buying a number of marketable instruments that offer high yields. With their large and sometime volatile resources often committed to the investment media that seem popular at the time, mutual funds can be a major factor in the secondary securities market.

The combined balance sheets of mutual funds including "money-market funds" and their relative proportions at selected year ends are shown in Table 7-3. (Cash is shown net of all liabilities.) Until 1970, the burgeoning dollar growth of these funds showed up almost entirely in common stocks. Since then, other asset types have grown in importance so that in 1978 common stocks as a group comprised less than 60 percent of total mutual funds assets, down considerably from 86 percent in 1965. The proportion of cash and open-market securities in 1978, which stood at 26 percent of total assets, attests to the uncertainty surrounding the money and capital markets, and also to the fact that "money-market fund" assets were 25 percent of total mutual fund assets.

Annual Portfolio Changes

The data in Table 7-4 show the annual net accumulation of capital-market securities by mutual funds from 1970 through 1978. Government bond acquisitions have varied through the years, reflecting the need of the mutual funds for liquidity and their policy with respect to full investment and acquisitions by balanced funds that have bonds as an important part of their portfolio. In 1972, for the first time in the postwar era, mutual funds were net sellers of common stocks. (The figures in Table 7-4 represent net flows and not changes in market values.) This was caused by the large number of net redemptions, which induced mutual funds to sell securities in order to maintain liquidity. Corporate bonds have continued to gain favor, being attractive primarily for income. In 1978 a modest decline in stock prices caused many funds to increase their cash positions in expectation of later buying opportunities.

Influence in the Capital Market

The impact of investment companies in the secondary market for corporate stocks is primarily in those issues listed on the New York Stock Exchange. At the end of 1978, listed holdings of mutual companies totaled $30 billion, representing 6 percent of the value of all stocks listed on the New York Stock Exchange.

The contribution of mutual funds to stock-trading activity, however, is considerably greater than their stock holdings would indicate and has accelerated from the late 1960s. The activity rate of stock market trading by the mutual funds was the highest rate for all institutional investors in 1977—29 percent for the year. This rate, however, was the lowest turnover rate for mutual funds over the last decade.

The rise in trading until 1973 was caused by the emphasis on performance by fund managers, lower commission fees on stock transactions, and the rapidly changing fortunes of some companies that have precipitated wholesale acquisitions and liquidations of particular common stocks. Lower activity in 1977 and 1978 reflected the negative cash flows and cautious investment policy by most funds.

The influence of mutual investment companies on stock prices has been the subject of much debate. Some have claimed that they have contributed to stability, because in all periods of stock declines, until 1972 and 1973, investors purchased more mutual fund shares than they sold (thus contributing net capital for investment in common stocks), and the companies themselves, on balance, increased rather than decreased their portfolios. Other informants have been less positive and have concluded that it is difficult to say whether mutual funds have been a stabilizing or destabilizing influence because so many other factors are involved, although there is some evidence of a destabilizing influence in a price decline. In any event, the lack of new commitments in stock purchases and the liquidation of stocks by mutual funds to cover their redemptions in 1972 through 1978 has no doubt contributed to the poor market performance.

Closed-end companies (also called publicly traded investment companies), once established, grow relatively slowly as a group because of their fixed capitalizations. New funds, such as dual funds and unit trusts, have added to the assets of closed-end funds, but these developments are frequently offset by partial redemptions and liquidations or by a maturing of existing securities. Net assets of closed-end companies totaled about $7 billion at the end of 1978, an increase from less than $1 billion in 1945 but virtually unchanged from the end of 1973. Closed-end company funds have been generally placed in common stocks and bonds of all types.

Real Estate Investment Trusts

Background and Development

Real estate investment trusts (REITs), although in existence in one form or another since the nineteenth century, grew from less than $1 billion in assets in 1970 to over $21 billion (book value) by 1975 to become the fifth largest institutional holder of mortgages. The growth in the early 1970s was aided by the tremendous demand for mortgage money and by the lack of available funds from traditional mortgage lenders. The aggressiveness in marketing the REIT concept was also a contributing factor.

The Real Estate Investment Trust Act of 1960 gave the small investor an opportunity to participate and receive the returns from real estate investments without the concomitant management problems. Thus, the REIT investor was to enjoy essentially the same benefits as those enjoyed by mutual fund holders. It was not until after 1968, however, that REITs attracted any investor interest and became an important factor in the mortgage market (Table 7-5).

REIT companies are exempt from corporate income taxes if they meet the following qualifications: (1) They derive at least 75 percent of their gross income from rents, interest on mortgages, or capital gains on sales of property. Up to 15 percent of their income can come from regular security holdings, and not more than 30 percent of their gross profits can come from sale of securities held less than six months or real estate held less than four years. (2) At least 75 percent of their assets are in real estate, mortgages, cash, or government securities at the end of each quarter. (3) They distribute at least 90 percent of their income to shareholders, exclusive of capital gains.

REITs compare quite closely with closed-end investment companies in that investors hold the shares of the REIT and trade them on the exchanges and over the counter. Consequently, like closed-end funds, they may sell above or below their net asset values. The basic difference, of course, is that REITs are confined primarily to real estate investments, mortgages, and construction loans.

Although several types of real estate investment trusts are in existence, they can be classified as basically "equity" trusts or "mortgage" trusts. Equity trusts purchase real estate and receive the rents from the property. Mortgage trusts invest in mortgages and construction loans and do not own the property outright. Their income derives mainly from interest and loan fees charged the borrowers.

To increase profitability, mortgage trusts specializing in construction loans usually leverage themselves by borrowing short-term funds from banks or by issuing commercial paper in amounts up to two or three times their equity base, and lending at a higher rate to builders. This procedure worked well when short-term interest rates were relatively low in 1971 and 1972. As rates rose in 1973 and 1974, however, mortgage trusts found themselves squeezed as a result of (1) the decline in the spread between the short-term rates they paid on borrowed funds and previously committed rates to builders, and (2) defaults by builders on loans. These two factors caused the sharp drop in the market prices of REITs such that in 1978 most sold well below book value and most REITs have reported large losses at one time or another since 1974. The stronger trusts achieved an important recovery in 1979.

Investment Policy

Table 7-5, showing the combined assets of real estate investment trusts from 1970 through 1978, indicates a heavy emphasis on real estate mortgages, as expected. Since 1973, however, the real estate owned has increased significantly as properties previously mortgaged to REITs were foreclosed and held for dis-

TABLE 7-5. Combined Book Value of Assets of Real Estate Investment Trusts, 1970-1978 (billions of dollars)

	1970		1973		1975		1978	
	Amount	Percent	Amount	Percent	Amount	Percent	Amount	Percent
Home mortgages	$0.6	13%	$ 1.9	9%	$ 1.4	6%	$ 0.8	6%
Multifamily mortgages	1.3	28	6.6	30	4.8	23	2.0	14
Commercial mortgages[a]	2.0	42	7.5	39	7.0	33	3.2	22
Real estate and other assets	0.8	17	4.3	22	8.1	38	8.5	58
Total assets	$4.7	100%	$20.2	100%	$21.3	100%	$14.5	100%

[a]Mainly construction loans.
Source: Federal Reserve *Flow-of-Funds Accounts*.

TABLE 7-6. Annual Flow into Capital-Market Assets, Real Estate Investment Trusts, 1970-1978 (billions of dollars)

	1970	1971	1972	1973	1974	1975	1976	1977	1978
Home mortgages	$0.4	$0.2	$0.4	$0.7	$-0.2	$-0.5	$-0.2	$-0.2	$-0.1
Multifamily mortgages	0.8	0.9	2.0	2.4	0.2	-2.6	-1.7	-0.8	-0.3
Commercial mortgages[a]	0.7	1.2	1.7	2.5	0.2	-1.8	-1.8	-1.4	-0.6
Total	$1.9	$2.3	$4.2	$5.6	$ 0.2	$-4.8	$-3.8	$-2.4	$-1.0

[a]Mainly construction loans.
Source: Federal Reserve *Flow-of-Funds Accounts*. (Some columns do not add to totals because of rounding.)

posal. Within the mortgage category, the largest amount was committed to commercial mortgages, with multifamily properties also receiving considerable support.

Annual Uses of Funds

Table 7-6 shows the annual uses of funds by REITs from early 1970. The emphasis on commercial and multifamily mortgages is again noted, but the large liquidations of real estate and mortgage foreclosures occurring in the middle and late 1970s have resulted in net withdrawals of mortgage funds by real estate investment companies.

Sources of Funds

The annual sources of funds for capital market use for 1970 through 1978 are arrived at by deducting changes in miscellaneous assets such as cash and real estate. The growth in assets prior to 1968 was insignificant (billions of dollars):

1970	1971	1972	1973	1974	1975	1976	1977	1978
$1.9	$2.3	$4.2	$5.6	$0.2	$-4.8	$-3.8	$-2.4	$-1.0

The sharp increase in funds in 1972 and early 1973 reflected the availability of funds at moderate interest rates and the favorable response that investors accorded the REIT concept. This response was drastically curtailed in the latter part of the 1970s as liquidity problems faced most REITs due to "problem" loans and high interest rates.

In the early 1970s funds for real estate investment trusts came from three major areas: corporate securities (bonds and stocks), commercial paper, and bank loans. Table 7-7 traces the sources from 1970 through 1978. As noted earlier, corporate bonds, commercial paper, and bank loans were used mostly by the mortgage trusts to increase leverage and profitability, but when short-term rates were high, as in 1974, the effect of the short-term borrowings on REITs

TABLE 7.7   Annual Sources of Funds of Real Estate Investment Trusts, 1970–1978 (billions of dollars)

	1970	1972	1974	1976	1978
Open-market paper	$ –	$2.4	$-3.3	$-0.3	$-0.2
Bank loans	0.1	1.3	4.4	-1.9	-1.6
Bonds issued	0.5	0.4	0.2	-0.2	-0.2
Mortgages on					
properties owned	0.2	0.5	0.2	0.4	0.1
Equity issues	1.4	1.7	-0.9	-0.5	0.2
Total	$2.2	$6.3	$ 0.6	$-2.5	$-1.7

Source: Federal Reserve *Flow-of-Funds Accounts.*

and on ultimate borrowers became devastating. The increase in outstanding mortgage liabilities (Table 7-7) was a result of mortgages on properties owned primarily by equity trusts. The REIT collapse eliminated any further tapping of the commercial paper market and resulted in very sharp reductions in bank loans. The sharp rise in bank loans in 1974 was largely a response by banks to bail out or postpone the eventual demise of many REITs. The net decline in equity issues was a result of the bankruptcies or recapitalization of REITs as many tried to salvage their declining operations.

The strategy used by REITs to expand their operations in 1970-1973 is a prime example of institutions' speculating on differences in the maturity structure of their assets and liabilities (Chapter 2). By borrowing short-term through issuing commercial paper and through bank loans, and by lending longer term in construction loans and permanent mortgages, these institutions were in a highly unhedged position regarding their asset and liability structure. When borrowing rates were low and longer term lending rates were high they did exceedingly well. In high-interest-rate periods, such as 1973-1974, when short-term money was above 12 percent they faced a dilemma: they could lend the money at a high rate, but builders faced large losses at such high rates. On the other hand, they could not reduce their short-term debt because of the longer-term commitments and the inability of builders to repay their REIT loans on time. The net result was large losses for builders and REITs together, and a badly tarnished reputation for real estate investment institutions.

In order to try to salvage something from their operations and to cut losses, many mortgage lending REITs made application to shed their trust status and become operating companies. In this manner, they would not have to dispose of their foreclosed properties, could manage the properties for the trust's future benefit, and thus gain more freedom to operate. In addition, although it would mean loss of tax exemption on earnings, it would be an opportunity to carry forward losses to future earnings.

```
8888888888888888888888888888888888888888888888888888888888888888888888888888888888888888888
8888888888888888888888888888888888888888888888888888888888888888888888888888888888888888888
8888888888888888888888888     8888888888888     888     888     888     8888888888888888888888888
8888888888888888888888888     8888888888     8888     888     888     8888888888888888888888888
8888888888888888888888888     8888888     88888     888     888     8888888888888888888888888
8888888888888888888888888     8888888     888888     888     888     8888888888888888888888888
8888888888888888888888888     88888     8888888     888     888     8888888888888888888888888
8888888888888888888888888     888     88888888     888     888     8888888888888888888888888
8888888888888888888888888     8     888888888     888     888     8888888888888888888888888
8888888888888888888888888     8888888888     888     888     8888888888888888888888888
8888888888888888888888888888     88888888888     888     888     8888888888888888888888888
8888888888888888888888888888888888888888888888888888888888888888888888888888888888888888888
8888888888888888888888888888888888888888888888888888888888888888888888888888888888888888888
```

The Federal Securities Market

Our discussion of the federal securities market in this chapter emphasizes the obligations of the United States Treasury. Also discussed are the securities of federally sponsored agencies and those of the "buget" agencies. Federally sponsored agencies can be classified as financial intermediaries in most cases except that they often form a "second tier" of financial institutions that deal primarily with other financial institutions in providing depth and breadth to the capital markets. Budget agencies perform governmental services and their securities are distinguished from those of the U.S. Treasury proper. ·

United States Obligations

The subject of federal financing and debt management and its interrelations with monetary policy is complex. This discussion includes only a summary of federal borrowing policy, along with the demand, ownership, and yield aspects of the federal securities market.

Much of the Treasury debt is intermediate- or long-term in maturity. Yet it is difficult to consider this portion separately from short-term instruments, since maturities of all lengths are held by institutions for income and liquidity. Where possible, however, our discussion focuses on the capital-market or long-term aspects of the federal securities market.

Types and Trends of Total Federal Debt

The direct debt of the federal Treasury at the end of selected years is shown in Table 8-1. There are three major types of marketable federal securities:

	1960	1965	1970	1975	1978
Marketable					
Bills	$ 39.5	$ 60.2	$ 87.9	$157.5	$161.7
Certificates	18.4	–	–	–	–
Notes	51.3	50.2	101.2	167.1	265.8
Bonds	79.8	104.2	58.6	38.6	60.0
Total	$189.0	$214.6	$247.7	$363.2	$487.5
Nonmarketable					
Savings bonds and notes	$ 47.2	$ 50.3	$ 52.5	$ 67.5	$ 80.5
Convertible bonds (investment series)	6.2	2.8	2.4	2.3	2.2
Foreign series issues	–	2.4	5.7	21.6	29.6
Government account series[a]	44.3	46.3	78.1	119.4	157.5
State and local government series	0.1	0.1	0.9	1.2	25.0
Total	$ 97.8	$101.9	$139.6	$212.5	$294.8
Non-interest-bearing debt	3.4	4.4	1.9	0.9	6.9
	$290.2	$320.9	$389.2	$576.6	$789.2

[a]Before 1970 consisted of "special issues."
Source: *Treasury Bulletin.*

Treasury bills, notes, and bonds. Certificates of indebtedness have not been issued since 1963 and their range of maturity (around 1 year) has been covered by bills and notes.

Treasury bills are issued on a discount basis and are sold for cash at auction through the Federal Reserve Banks. Their maturity ranges from three months to one year. One-year bills were first issued in 1959 in an effort to lengthen the maturity of the federal debt, and compete for investors' savings.

Treasury notes are available in bearer or registered form with maturities of from one to ten years. Treasury bonds have original maturities ranging from five to twenty-six years. Both are issued for cash and for refinancing. Bonds are often callable five years before maturity.

Only the fully marketable issues are eligible for purchase by all investors, but there are minimum purchase amounts on some issues that effectively limit certain marketable federal securities to dealers and large institutions.

The remaining Treasury obligations are nonmarketable (nonnegotiable), so their supply has only an indirect effect on market yields. Savings bonds currently issued under Series EE replaced the old Series E in 1980. Under the Series EE program, bonds are sold for half the face amount and mature in eleven years and nine months. The interest rate is 6½ percent if held for five years or more. The bonds are redeemable after six months but at a lower effective interest rate. Also, effective January 1980, the Treasury eliminated the Series H bond and replaced it with the HH bonds. These bonds are sold at face value and pay interest at 6½ percent compounded semiannually and mature in ten years. Interest payments on the Series HH are a level 6½ percent interest rather than the previous graduated scale. Treasury convertible bonds or "investment series" are sold to large institutional investors and are convertible into marketable Treasury notes. Foreign series are issued to foreign governments and monetary authorities. Government account issues are sold directly to various agencies and government trust funds. State and local government series are issued primarily to state and local retirement funds and for short-term purposes.

Growth of Direct Treasury Federal Debt

The direct Treasury federal debt rose from $43 billion in June 1940 to its wartime peak of $278 billion in fiscal 1945-1946 as a result of wartime deficit financing. Peace brought a temporary decline in debt to $253 billion at the end of 1948, but this was followed by increases in all except four years through 1978. Since 1948, debt has increased by $536 billion to a total of $789 billion at the end of 1978. The debt ratio, as a percentage of gross national product, however, has declined from about 80 percent in 1948 to 36 percent at the end of 1978. The rapid rise in debt since 1968 was caused by (1) the Viet Nam war; (2) expanded programs in health, education, and welfare; (3) rising interest rates on federal debt; and (4) deficit financing.

At the end of 1978, marketable securities constituted $488 billion of the total debt of $789 billion. After deducting the $13 billion of marketable debt held by federal agencies and trust funds (in addition to their holdings of special issues), the debt involved in the money and capital markets, including holdings by the Federal Reserve banks, totaled $475 billion; of this amount, $229 billion had a maturity of less than one year and the remaining capital-market debt totaled $246 billion.

Table 1-2 (p. 9) shows that in the postwar period the federal debt has not increased at the same rate as other categories. This has facilitated the direction of institutional investment funds into municipal and private capital markets. The federal government has generally avoided competing for funds in the long-term market in order to aid corporate investment and to minimize the interest costs on the total debt as short-term rates are usually less than long-term rates.

Shifts in Types and Maturities

The variations in total federal debt have not been accompanied by similar changes in marketable debt or its various maturity classes. The data in Table 8-2 show the composition of public marketable debt from 1960 to 1978. From 1955 to 1965, marketable debt rose significantly while total nonmarketable debt fell as the federal government found the marketable approach to financing debt

TABLE 8-2. Composition of Federal Marketable Debt, at Year End, 1960–1978 (billions of dollars)

	1960	1965	1970	1975	1978
Within a year	$ 73.8	$ 93.4	$123.4	$199.7	$228.5
1–5 years	72.3	60.6	82.3	112.3	162.9
5–10 years	18.7	35.0	22.6	26.4	50.4
10–20 years	13.2	8.5	8.6	14.3	19.8
Over 20 years	11.0	17.1	10.7	10.5	25.9
	$189.0	$214.6	$247.7	$363.2	$487.5
Less debt held by federal agencies and trust funds	8.1	13.4	17.1	19.3	12.7
Total "public marketable" debt	$180.9	$201.2	$230.6	$343.9	$474.8

Sources: *Treasury Bulletin; Federal Reserve Bulletin.* Data are classified by final maturity. It should be noted that these data show the maturity classifications outstanding, not those at time of issue. A bond issued over nineteen years ago with a maturity of twenty years would be included in the "within-a-year" category.

easier and more preferable. With the advent of sharply higher interest rates and the already strained capital markets in the late 1960s and early 1970s, the federal government tapped the funds available in the several trust funds that it manages and issued special nonmarketable issues, which more than doubled from 1970 through 1978. Savings bonds, the other major nonmarketable category, have also grown and, at the end of 1978, were 50 percent higher than in 1970.

The shifting internal composition of the debt can have an important impact on yields. Yields on government bonds generally reflect changes in marketable debt outstanding rather than in total debt. Funds are more likely to move into other savings media or into capital-market securities, and the holding of special issues in government trust funds are in effect impounded. The data in Tables 8-1 and 8-2 reveal the increasing importance of debt with maturity of five years or less. Large amounts of marketable Treasury bonds, whose original maturity is over 5 years, have not been issued in large quantities because of a desire to minimize interest costs and not compete with private firms and state and local governments in the overburdened, long-term bond markets. At the end of 1978, debt due in ten years or more constituted less than 10 percent of the total, compared with 20 percent in 1955. Short maturities have been emphasized during periods of economic expansion when long-term rates have been kept relatively low to aid long-term investment. On other occasions, short-term maturities have been emphasized when interest rates are high, to avoid being "locked into" high long-term rates.

Medium maturities have been of more importance during periods of monetary ease such as 1967, 1971, and 1975 in order to maintain a position of maximum neutrality in the money and capital markets.

Movements in Treasury financing to add or subtract from the supply of different classes have reflected an attempt to balance the debt structure to minimize the total interest bill, aid our balance of payments, long-term investment, and so on. The cyclical debt management policy of the Treasury with respect to maturities, although exerting now and then an upward and a downward pressure on long-term yields, has in general followed the climate of the market.

Organization of the Primary Market

The Federal Reserve Banks serve as agents of the Treasury in issuing and redeeming government securities. Each new issue is announced by press statements of the Secretary of the Treasury, and the Federal Reserve Banks send out descriptive circulars to commercial banks, dealers, and other possible buyers. About twenty-five dealers account for the major activity in the government securities market—eleven commercial banks and fourteen nonbank securities firms.

New issues of Treasury bills are offered at auction regularly through the Federal Reserve Banks and their branches. The Secretary of the Treasury invites tenders for purchase on a discount basis below par and accepts bids from the highest price down until the approximate amount of funds stated in the offering circular is obtained. Federal Reserve Banks themselves may make bids to the limit of the maturing bills they hold.

Other marketable issues are sold at par at a specified rate of interest determined after analysis of the market and consultation with banks and other institutions. The government enters the market in competition with other users of capital and must pay the market yield, although this yield can be influenced by Treasury debt management and Federal Reserve open-market policy. The Federal Reserve Banks receive the applications of dealers, banks, and others, and make allotments in accordance with instructions from the Treasury. They also receive payments for the securities and deposit the proceeds to Treasury accounts.

Volume and Buyers of New Federal Government Securities

Each year the Treasury undertakes sufficient financing to cover deficits and refunding and to keep its cash balances satisfactory. In most years, the total volume of financing substantially exceeds that of the combined state and local governments, and in some years, that of corporations. The net increases (or decreases) in outstanding debt (after refunding) do not correspond with Treasury budget surpluses and deficits, because these in turn do not correspond with changes in Treasury cash balances. The balances reflect public and intragovernmental cash transactions, including transactions with government trust funds.

Table 8-3 (line 1) shows the change in direct federal debt. By deducting

TABLE 8-3. Annual Changes in Publicly Held U.S. Government Securities, 1970-1978 (billions of dollars)

	1970	1971	1972	1973	1974	1975	1976	1977	1978
Change in gross debt	$20.9	$35.0	$25.2	$19.8	$23.6	$83.9	$76.9	$65.4	$70.3
Less change in U.S. government trust agencies and trust accounts	8.1	8.9	10.9	12.7	14.8	7.1	4.3	5.2	15.2
Change in U.S. government securities not in Treasury agencies and trusts[a]	$12.9	$26.0	$14.3	$ 7.1	$ 8.8	$85.8	$72.6	$60.2	$55.1

[a]Figures may not add to totals because of rounding.
Sources: *Federal Reserve Bulletin; Treasury Bulletin.*

144

changes in government investment fund holdings (mostly special issues), the net annual changes in publicly held securities, including, for this purpose, those held by sponsored federal agencies and by the Federal Reserve Banks, are derived. Deficit spending in a peacetime economy, as evidenced by the substantial growth of the federal debt, especially since 1970, and in competition for funds with state and local governments, business, and individuals (for mortgages), has contributed to the high level of interest rates (see Figure 8-1). The drop in total gross debt in 1972 over 1971 (Table 8-3) was a result of increased treasury revenues from higher corporate profitability and personal income taxes and a smaller increase in governmental expenditures, particularly as the Viet Nam war wound down. The sharp change in gross debt in 1978 was caused by excessive government expenditures in an effort to stimulate the economy, especially through new programs, and generally increased operational costs due to high inflation.

The data in Table 8-4 show annual net acquisitions of government securities (excluding those of Treasury trust funds) and include the wide range of maturities, not just long-term maturities. Business corporations change their holdings (generally short maturities) in response to their changing needs for cash. Liquidation of government securities to meet expansion needs and to avoid high interest costs was apparent in 1973 and again in 1977-1978. In 1977 and 1978, when interest rates were rising, nonfinancial business corporations were net sellers of federal securities. Net additions were made in 1975 as corporate liquidity improved and temporary funds were available for security purchases.

Foreign and households acquisitions also show cyclical variations, although their purchases or sales are likely to be more influenced by interest rates available on alternative securities. In 1971, these groups made opposite investment decisions on their federal security holdings. Households and others were large net sellers ($9.3 billions), although foreign investors were large net purchasers ($26.3 billions). This reflected both the relatively higher rates available on other types of alternative domestic securities as well as the lower rates in some foreign markets and the weakness in other foreign currencies that forced some investors to hold federal securities. In 1977 and 1978, foreigners added substantial amounts of U.S. government securities and were easily the largest purchasers among all groups. Reasons for these substantial purchases were rising interest rates in the United States, international tensions that caused investors to seek safer investments, substantial funds available for temporary investment by the Arab countries and several foreign-currency-denominated bonds issued by the Treasury as a result of a declining dollar in international markets.

Among the institutional owners, commercial banks show acquisitions of the greatest volatility as funds move into and out of government securities with the changing cyclical demand for loans. In 1973 the net liquidation helped to meet the credit strain of that year (see Chapter 3). Large purchases of federal securities were made in 1975 and 1976 as time and savings inflows improved substantially and the period was one of monetary ease and weak loan demand.

TABLE 8-4. Annual Acquisitions of Publicly Held U.S. Treasury Securities, 1970-1978 (billions of dollars)

	1970	1971	1972	1973	1974	1975	1976	1977	1978
Commercial banks	$ 7.0	$ 3.2	$ 2.1	$-8.8	$-2.4	$28.7	$17.9	$ 0.9	$-5.8
Federal Reserve banks	5.0	8.1	-0.3	8.6	2.0	7.4	9.1	5.8	7.7
Mutual savings banks	-0.1	0.1	0.2	-0.5	-0.4	2.2	1.1	0.1	-0.9
Savings and loan associations	-1.3	-0.8	-0.5	-1.6	–	1.3	3.7	-1.3	-0.6
Life insurance companies	-0.1	-0.2	–	-0.4	-0.1	1.4	0.6	0.3	-0.6
Property and liability insurance companies	–	–	-0.1	-0.1	0.4	2.5	3.1	3.1	0.8 (est)
Private noninsured pension funds	-0.1	–	0.9	0.2	-0.2	4.5	3.7	4.8	0.4
State and local government retirement funds	-0.3	-1.2	-0.3	-1.1	-0.9	1.0	1.5	2.4	3.6
Mutual investment companies	0.2	-0.3	0.1	–	0.5	0.8	0.2	-0.1	0.7
Federal agencies	2.0	-1.3	-0.3	-0.8	–	0.3	1.7	-2.5	– (est)
Nonfinancial business corporations	0.6	2.8	-2.2	-4.9	0.9	9.9	4.0	-6.0	-7.2
State and local governments	0.9	-1.3	4.1	1.4	-1.9	-0.7	7.1	21.1	17.1
Foreign investors	9.3	26.3	8.4	0.2	4.1	7.7	11.6	31.5	27.5
Households and others	-10.2	-9.3	2.2	15.7	10.1	18.8	3.5	-2.5	12.4
Total	$12.9	$26.0	$14.3	$ 7.9	$12.0	$85.8	$69.1	$57.6	$55.1

Sources: Citations in schedules, Chapters 3 to 7; *Federal Reserve Bulletin*; Federal Reserve *Flow-of-Funds Accounts*. Bankers Trust Company, *Credit and Capital Markets*. (Some columns do not add to totals because of rounding.)

Federal securities were sold on balance in 1978 as monetary policy grew more restrictive and corporate loan demand increased modestly.

As noted earlier, life insurance companies, mutual savings banks, and pension funds normally have avoided federal securities. However, with sharply higher interest rates on these securities coupled with a large federal deficit and abundant funds held by these institutions that needed to be invested, federal securities became favored investments, particularly in 1975 and 1976. The variations in holdings by Federal Reserve Banks reflects the fluctuations of banks' reserve deposits and their influence on the money supply.

Ownership of the Federal Debt

At the end of 1978, the ownership of gross Treasury debt was as shown in Table 8-5. Almost three-fourths of the debt was held outside the commercial banking system. Although debt held by nonbank institutions is not demonetized in the technical sense, it is subject to only indirect fiscal influence. Nearly 35 percent of the total debt was held by federal investment accounts and individuals; the nonmarketable character of these holdings remove them from any impact on the market. The share of debt held by business corporations constitutes a volatile element and exerts a more than proportional influence on yields.

TABLE 8-5. Ownership of Direct Federal Securities, December 31, 1978
(billions of dollars)

	Amounts	Percent
Commercial banks	$ 97.4	12.3%
Federal Reserve banks	109.6	13.9
Mutual savings banks	5.0	0.6
Savings and loan associations	8.9	1.1
Life insurance companies	4.8	0.6
Property and liability insurance companies (est.)	14.0	1.8
Uninsured private pension plans	17.8	2.3
Federal agencies and trust funds	170.0	21.5
Investment companies (mutual)	2.7	0.3
Other corporations	20.6	2.6
State and local government retirement funds	10.0	1.3
State and local governments (general funds)	68.6	8.7
Households		
Saving bonds	80.7	10.2
Other	30.0	3.8
Foreign and international	137.8	17.6
Miscellaneous	11.3	1.4
Total	$789.2	100.0%

Sources: *Treasury Bulletin; Federal Reserve Bulletin;* adjusted from data in Chapters 3 to 7.

Foreign investors, for reasons noted earlier, have become significant owners of federal securities.

The changes in the ownership of Treasury obligations have resulted in interesting paterns. Foreign and international holdings represent mainly short-term obligations held for liquidity and as a hedge against fluctuating foreign currencies. The large percent owned by federal agencies and trust funds (mainly federal retirement and insurance funds) consists primarily of government account series bonds (see Table 8-1). State and local government holdings represent investment of miscellaneous trust funds and liquid assets. Together with retirement funds, their share is significant. Households owned $30 billion of debt in addition to $80.7 billion of savings bonds. The latter, yielding only 6 percent to maturity, have declined in attractiveness relative to competing savings and capital-market instruments. The federal insurance and pension funds own special nonmarketable issues for the reserves of the insurance and retirement plans managed by the Treasury.

Organization of the Secondary Market in Federal Securities

The secondary market in federal securities is largely a dealer market, both for short-term maturities, which are close substitutes for money, and for the longer-term issues. Yields vary with maturity, and the dealers arbitrage the yields on various maturities to produce spreads satisfactory to the buyers and sellers of the various issues. The market is the mechanism whereby the structure of interest rates affects the flow of savings according to the demands of borrowers and lenders.

Although federal obligations are listed on the New York Stock Exchange, most of the transactions in outstanding securities are made in the over-the-counter market through dealers and a limited number of banks. Operations are conducted by the telephone, teletype, and other electronic means. The Federal Reserve Bank of New York also operates a trading desk for open-market operations. Some dealers specialize in certain securities. Although active in the short-term market, the larger dealers and banks do most of the trading in long-term maturities. They keep in constant touch with the ownership of existing issues and with potential buyers, on a national basis. The smaller dealers tend to concentrate more in the New York market than elsewhere.

Dealers act mainly as principals for their own accounts, "making markets" for customers and other dealers by quoting firm prices or spreads at which they are willing to buy and sell. In large transactions in longer-maturity issues, the larger dealers also act as brokers. The broker function reflects the smaller size of longer-maturity issues and the frequency of Treasury refundings.

The Federal Reserve System provides important services. As we have seen, it auctions Treasury bills and acts as fiscal agent of the Treasury in the exchange of issues involved in refunding. The Federal Reserve Bank of New York is particularly active, serving as the medium for transactions of the Federal Reserve Open Market Committee with dealers. It also acts as agent for other buyers and sellers. The Federal Reserve banks also finance dealer positions through the use of repurchase agreements, which are, in effect, temporary loans.

Financial institutions, including commercial and Federal Reserve banks, are the dealers' major customers, although a growing volume of business in bills and certificates is done with corporations. The market for federal obligations is the largest security market in the country. In 1978, the dollar volume of transactions conducted by dealers reporting to the Federal Reserve Bank of New York averaged about $10 billion per day.[1]

Prices and Yields

The yields and prices of marketable government securities rise and fall with general changes in short- and long-term interest rates, which in turn reflect the demand of and supply for funds. Because these yields represent the price of riskless money, they are close to being pure interest rates. They are however, subject to two special influences: (1) changing Treasury debt policy with respect to the issue and redemption of different maturities, and its effects, through supply, on the yield pattern; and (2) Federal Reserve policy implemented through open-market operations, which affects both supply and demand and influences yields on different maturities through shifts in buying and selling between short- and long-term securities.

Figure 8-1 shows the market yields (averages of daily yields) of short-, medium-, and long-term Treasury obligations from 1965. Since 1951, after the Treasury–Federal Reserve Board accord where rates were "unpegged," yields have fluctuated in a pronounced pattern related to the general business cycle and to money- and capital-market conditions. After the Federal Reserve Open Market Committee abandoned its "bills only" policy in the 1950s, the actions of the Fed in influencing short- or long-term market rates became relatively neutral and interest rates were allowed to respond more naturally to market conditions. Particularly since 1965, interest rates have fluctuated considerably and have experienced an upward secular trend. Rates on all maturities rose steadily toward the all-time highs of 10 percent (bonds) to 13 percent (bills) reached in October 1979.

The substantial swings and high levels of interest rates can be attributed to (1) the high rate of inflation; (2) the development of international markets that are sensitive to interest rate levels, inflation, political disruptions, and other economic factors where the interest rate mechanism has been a primary tool in influencing balance of payments, trade deficits, and liquidity crises; (3) the demand for funds by government and business alike (see Chapters 3 to 6); (4) the

---

[1] *Federal Reserve Bulletin.*

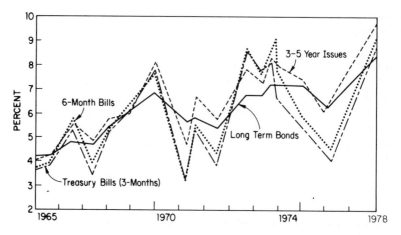

Figure 8-1. Market Yields of U.S. Government Securities, 1965-1978
Source: *Federal Reserve Bulletin.* For data, see Appendix, Table A-1.

gradual acceptance of higher interest rates by investors, borrowers and financial institutions; (5) the change in management philosophy and procedures by many financial institutions, emphasizing the free interplay of market rates without government interference; and (6) the formula-based methods of calculating prime rates that have tended to cause quick responses to rate changes.

Federal Agencies

The term *federal agency* covers a broad and changing group of often specialized organizations that serve many different purposes. The various agencies fall conveniently into three groups: (1) federally sponsored credit agencies, (2) budget agencies, and (3) other federally owned agencies.

Many of the federal agencies have had an important influence in the capital markets. On the supply side, they have made loans to member organizations that in turn acquired capital-market instruments. On the demand side, they have borrowed from or sold stock to the Treasury and have sold stock to and acquired deposits from member organizations and from the public at large. Some of the funds of the member organizations have also been diverted from direct employment in the capital markets.

"Budget" and Other Agencies

Budget agencies are owned by the U.S. government and are operated by various governmental departments. Most important in this group are the Federal Housing Administration, the Tennessee Valley Authority, the Government National Mortgage Association, and the Export-Import Bank of the United

States. These agencies' income and expenses are part of the U.S. government budget. All of the above, at one time or another, have issued their own securities. In our discussion we distinguish such debt from the direct Treasury debt-treated earlier in this chapter.

Table 8-6 lists the debt outstanding of budget and other agencies. Some of the debts are outstanding issues that are publicly traded and do not reflect the entire scope of an agency's operations or capital needs since the federal government supplies additional funds Also, an agency's role in the capital market may be much more pervasive than the figures indicate, largely because of federal guarantees that do not require funds unless default occurs. For example, the Government National Mortgage Association is heavily involved in the mortgage market and guarantees "pass through" securities of insured mortgages (see Chapter 12). At the end of 1978, almost $50 billion of these securities were outstanding which are not included in the figures in Table 8-6, to avoid double counting with mortgage debt outstanding (Chapter 12).

Other special "agencies" are owned by the federal government but with few exceptions have not issued securities to the public. Some of their operations may be a part of the budget or their obligations guaranteed by the federal government. Their funds come from appropriations by Congress and/or from fees that they charge for their services. Included would be such agencies as the Commoditiy Credit Corporation, the Small Business Administration, the Farmers Home Administration, and Federal Deposit Insurance Corporation, the Federal Savings and Loan Insurance Corporation, the Postal Service, and the U.S. Railway Association.

Recognizing the problems associated with the burgeoning number of agencies

TABLE 8-6. Budget and Other Agencies Debt Outstanding, 1970–1978
(billions of dollars)[a]

	1970	1975	1976	1977	1978
Export-Import Bank[b]	$ 1.9	$ 7.2	$ 7.8	$ 8.7	$ 8.7
Federal Housing Administration[c]	0.5	0.6	0.6	0.6	0.6
Government National Mortgage Assn.[d]	7.4	4.2	4.1	3.7	3.1
Postal Service	–	1.8	3.0	2.4	2.4
Tennessee Valley Authority[e]	0.9	3.9	5.2	6.0	7.5
Other[f]	0.2	1.0	1.2	1.3	1.2
Total	$10.9	$19.0	$21.9	$22.7	$23.5

[a]Includes short-term and long-term debt; includes share of FFB debt.
[b]Participation certificates, notes, and debentures.
[c]Debentures.
[d]Participation certificates.
[e]Priority revenue bonds and notes.
[f]Consists of assumed mortgages by Defense Department and U.S. Railway Association issues.
Source: *Federal Reserve Bulletin.*

	1975	1976	1977	1978
Export-Import Bank	$ 4.6	$ 5.2	$ 5.8	$ 6.9
Postal Service	1.5	2.7	2.2	2.1
Student Loan Marketing Association	0.3	0.4	0.5	0.9
Tennessee Valley Authority	1.8	3.1	4.2	5.6
United States Railway Association	0.2	0.1	0.3	0.4
Farmers Home Administration	7.0	10.8	16.1	23.8
Rural Electrification Administration	0.6	1.4	2.7	4.6
Other	1.1	5.0	6.8	7.0
Total FFM Lending	$17.1	$28.7	$38.6	$51.3

Source: *Federal Reserve Bulletin.*

and agency issues, the Federal Financing Bank was created by Congress in 1974. The purpose of the FFB is to raise its own funds in the capital markets and borrow from the Treasury, if necessary, and to relend these funds, in turn, to the various agencies eligible for participation in the FFB. The benefit from the bank is twofold: (1) it is able to borrow at a lower interest rate than any agency could obtain independently, and (2) it should make the capital market more orderly and efficient by reducing the number of separate issues.

The agencies currently participating in FFB lending operations are shown in Table 8-7. Many agencies are eligible for FFB financing, including one federally sponsored agency—the Student Loan Marketing Association—but other federally sponsored credit agencies handle their own financing in the capital markets. The table shows that the Farmers Home Administration (FmHA) has been the largest borrower of FFB funds. Most of the funds used by the FmHA have been employed in rural housing programs.

To avoid direct competition with the federally sponsored credit agencies and other institutions—particularly savings and loan associations—in the credit markets, the FFB security issues are designed primarily for large investors and, accordingly, have minimum denominations of $10,000.

Federally Sponsored Credit Agencies

Federally sponsored credit agencies are not owned by the U.S. government, but were initially authorized under its auspices. These *privatized* agencies are not included in the federal budget or in the U.S. government debt totals. Their shares are owned either (1) by the institutions that the agency is designed to directly benefit, such as Federal Home Loan Banks shares owned by savings and loan associations; (2) by the investing public, such as the Federal National Mortgage Association (FNMA), whose shares are traded on the New York Stock Exchange; or (3) by another agency, as in the case of the Federal Home Loan

TABLE 8-8. Outstanding Debt Securities of Federally Sponsored Credit Agencies,
1960-1978 (billions of dollars)

	1960	1965	1970	1975	1978
Banks for Cooperatives	$0.4	$ 0.8	$ 1.8	$ 3.7	$ 4.8
Federal Home Loan Banks	1.3	5.2	10.2	18.9	27.6
Federal Intermediate Credit Banks	1.5	2.3	4.8	9.3	11.5
Federal Land Banks	2.2	3.7	6.4	15.0	20.4
Federal National Mortgage Association	2.5	1.9	15.2	29.9	41.1
Federal Home Loan Mortgage Corporation	–	–	–	1.6	2.3
Student Loan Marketing Association[a]	–	–	–	0.3	0.9
	$7.9	$14.1	$38.4	$78.7	$108.5

[a]Includes loans from Federal Financing Bank.
Sources: *Federal Reserve Bulletin; Moody's Government Manual; Treasury Bulletin.*

Mortgage Corporation, whose shares are owned by Federal Home Loan Banks. The seven current agencies, as listed in Table 8-8, are the concern of this chapter. They supply funds to the capital market by acquiring federal obligations, mortgages, municipal bonds, and, to a certain extent, notes and securities of businesses, and obtain funds from the market by selling their own obligations to individual and institutional investors.

Public Borrowing

The direct debentures and notes of the federally sponsored credit agencies outstanding at the end of selected years are shown in Table 8-8.

The public debt of these agencies rises and falls with the needs of the individuals and institutions they serve. Although financing through 1960 was rather small, federally-sponsored agency debt since that time has increased measurably such that in recent years annual financing on occasion has exceeded that of many other major institutions. The primary cause for their rapid growth in the 1970s has been a result of the difficulty that the individuals and institutions they serve have encountered in securing funds from other sources—especially mortgage money by individuals and savings by savings and loan associations. These latter groups, particularly in periods of tight money and high interest rates, have been seeking more and more support directly or indirectly from the appropriate credit agency. In addition to their direct debt, three agencies— GNMA, FHLMC, and FmHA—have issued participation certificates backed by pools of mortgages. Holdings by these pools have become very significant, totaling $16.5 billions at the end of 1978 (Chapter 12).

Federally sponsored credit agencies direct funds to the capital markets mainly through loans and mortgages of different types. With the exception of the Federal National Mortgage Association, much of the influence of the federal credit agencies in the mortgage market has been indirect, through member organizations. The chief assets of the sponsored credit agencies are shown in Table 8-9. As shown in Table 8-10, the annual acquisitions of capital market assets by the federal agencies (sponsored and budget) were (billions of dollars):

1970	1971	1972	1973	1974	1975	1976	1977	1978
$8.0	$2.3	$3.1	$5.8	$14.7	$11.5	$4.3	$1.5	$12.5

Banks for Cooperatives make loans to farmers' cooperatives to finance the handling and packing of farm commodities. The twelve Federal Home Land Banks advance funds to member savings and loan associations (all federal- and state-chartered associations that choose to join) for mortgage loan purposes (see Chapter 4). The Federal National Mortgage Association (now privately owned) acquires FHA-guaranteed and conventional mortgages in both the primary and secondary markets (see Chapter 12). The twelve Federal Intermediate Credit Banks lend on farm notes pledged by member production credit associations. The twelve Federal Land Banks provide long-term mortgage credit through local member farm credit associations. The Federal Home Loan Mortgage Corporation sells investment securities and uses the funds to buy residential mortgages from federally insured savings associations.

The annual changes in the investments of federally sponsored credit agencies in major capital-market assets from 1965 through 1973 are displayed in Table 8-10. The data in Tables 8-9 and 8-10 show that most of the funds received

TABLE 8-9. Principal Assets of Major Federally Sponsored Credit Agencies, 1960-1977 (billions of dollars)

	1960	1965	1970	1975	1977
Banks for Cooperatives— loans to coops	$0.6	$1.1	$ 2.0	$ 4.0	6.0
Federal Home Loan Banks Advances to members	2.0	6.0	10.6	16.0	20.2
Investments	1.2	1.6	3.9	5.7	3.7
Federal Intermediate Credit Banks—loans	1.5	2.5	5.0	10.0	12.4
Federal Land Banks—mortgages (net)	2.6	4.3	7.2	17.0	22.8
Federal National Mortgage Association—mortgages (net)	2.8	2.5	15.5	30.8	33.2
Federal Home Loan Mortgage Corporation—loans, participations	–	–	–	4.9	3.2

Sources: *Federal Reserve Bulletin; Treasury Bulletin. Moody's Manual of Governments.* Federal National Mortgage Association (FNMA) data cover secondary market operations only.

TABLE 8-10. Annual Changes in Capital-Market Assets, Federally Sponsored Credit Agencies, 1970–1978 (billions of dollars)

	1970	1971	1972	1973	1974	1975	1976	1977	1978
U.S. government securities	$2.0	$-1.3	$-0.3	$-0.8	$ –	$-0.3	$1.7	$-2.5	$ –
Mortgages	5.7	3.6	3.3	6.5	14.4	11.5	2.1	3.5	11.9
Term loans (Banks for Cooperatives)	0.3	–	0.1	0.1	0.3	0.3	0.5	0.5	0.6
Total	$8.0	$ 2.3	$ 3.1	$ 5.8	$14.7	$11.5	$4.3	$ 1.5	$12.5

Sources: *Treasury Bulletin*; Federal Reserve *Flow-of-Funds Accounts*; Bankers Trust Company, *Credit and Capital Markets* (annual).

TABLE 8-11. Acquisitions of Federally Sponsored Credit and Budget Agency Securities, 1970-1978 (billions of dollars)

	1970	1971	1972	1973	1974	1975	1976	1977	1978
Commercial banks	$ 3.8	$ 4.0	$ 3.9	$ 7.5	$ 3.6	$ 1.6	$ 1.4	$ 0.9	$ 6.2
Federal Reserve Banks	–	0.4	0.6	0.7	3.2	1.0	0.9	1.4	-0.4
Mutual savings banks	0.4	0.8	1.1	0.1	0.2	1.7	3.3	2.6	1.8
Savings and loan associations[a]	1.9	3.0	2.4	2.3	1.2	4.1	0.7	4.9	5.6
Life insurance companies	0.1	0.2	0.1	–	0.2	0.4	0.9	1.6	2.3
Property and liability insurance companies	0.1	-0.2	-0.1		0.3	0.2	0.3	0.3	0.2 (est)
Private, noninsured pension funds	0.3	-0.3	0.1	0.6	1.3	0.7	0.3	0.6	2.0
State and local government retirement funds	-0.1	0.1	0.6	0.9	1.0	1.1	0.1	1.0	1.8
Nonfinancial corporations	-0.5	-0.3	0.1	1.5	1.4	-0.8	–	-0.4	0.7
State and local governments (general funds)	-2.1	-1.8	2.6	4.4	2.7	–	3.7	4.4	4.1
Foreign investors	0.3	–	0.1	0.6	0.4	-0.1	0.6	2.7	– (est)
Individuals and others	4.3	-4.0	-6.2	-1.6	1.2	-7.9	-8.0	-13.5	-2.8
Total	$ 8.5	$ 1.9	$ 5.3	$17.0	$16.7	$ 2.0	$ 3.4	$ 6.5	$21.5

[a]Savings and loan figures include GNMA mortgage-backed securities.
Sources: Federal Reserve Bulletin and Treasury Bulletin. Federal Reserve Flow-of-Funds Accounts; Bankers Trust Company, Credit and Capital Markets (annual). (Some columns do not add to totals because of rounding.)

by credit agencies and disbursed by them directly or indirectly have gone to support those institutions or individuals in the mortgage market.

Annual Changes in Ownership of Federal Agency Securities

Table 8-11, shows the annual changes in ownership from 1970 to 1978 of securities of both federally-sponsored agencies and budget agencies. Individual and consolidated issues of the sponsored credit agencies have virtually the same market as federal obligations. Because short-term issues generally have higher yields than federal securities, yet comparatively low risk, commercial banks have been their chief buyers; longer-term issues are acquired by a variety of owners.

Savings and loan associations, mutual savings banks, and other institutions increased their purchases of sponsored credit agency securities because of their high yields and low risk. Many of these were insured and mortgage-backed securities. For the same reasons, individuals find these securities appealing, especially in years of sharp declines in common stock prices.

Yields

Yields of sponsored agency securities follow closely those of other high-grade obligations and have usually been slightly above those of government bonds and slightly below those of high-grade corporate bonds. Temporary changes in supply and demand produce changes in the differentials. On occasion, as in 1971, 1973, and 1978, the yields paid on credit agency securities exceeded the rates the agencies charted the institutions they lent money to or otherwise supported. This phenomenon has been most often associated with mortgage-oriented institutions such as savings and loan associations. For instance, in 1974, the Federal Home Loan Bank issued bonds that carried a coupon rate of 9½ percent, yet the loans to savings associations and mortgage rates at the time were less than 9 percent.

Similarly, yields of budget agency securities are only very slightly higher than those of direct Treasury obligations with the same maturities.

```
9999999999999999999999999999999999999999999999999999999999999999999999999999999999
9999999999999999999999999999999999999999999999999999999999999999999999999999999999
99999999999999999999999999999999     999   99999    99999999999999999999999999999999
99999999999999999999999999999999     9999   999     99999999999999999999999999999999
99999999999999999999999999999999     99999   9      99999999999999999999999999999999
99999999999999999999999999999999     999999         99999999999999999999999999999999
99999999999999999999999999999999     9999999        99999999999999999999999999999999
99999999999999999999999999999999     999999         99999999999999999999999999999999
99999999999999999999999999999999     99999   9      99999999999999999999999999999999
99999999999999999999999999999999     9999   999     99999999999999999999999999999999
99999999999999999999999999999999     999   99999    99999999999999999999999999999999
9999999999999999999999999999999999999999999999999999999999999999999999999999999999
9999999999999999999999999999999999999999999999999999999999999999999999999999999999
```

The Market for State and Local
Government Bonds

STATE and local governments utilize three main types of debt: bonds, anticipation notes, and loans from the federal government. Tax, revenue, and bond anticipation notes—known as TANs, RANs, and BANs,—are the tax-exempt market's version of commercial paper. They are issued in expectation of monies coming in. Local governments also rely heavily on state and federal grants. Because bonds are the major source of security financing, we are concerned mainly with this category. Bonds are typically issued in serial maturities with designated par amounts due in successive years to final maturity. Investors have a wide choice among short-, intermediate-, and long-term maturities.

The maturities of state and local government bonds have tended to increase in recent years. Many issues of larger units run as long as thirty years and even longer when based on the revenue from specific projects. Such a trend parallels that of other long-term instruments whose buyers are also finding longer maturities acceptable.

With the exception of revenue bonds, the obligations of state and local governments are supported by the "full faith and credit" of the taxing jurisdictions. They all (including revenue bonds) enjoy exemption of interest from federal income taxation.[1] Tax exemption gives them a special appeal to many

---

[1] An exception is the limitation on firms issuing their own debt with interest payments that are tax-deductible and using the proceeds to invest in tax-exempt securities, and in cases where minimum tax laws apply. Municipal interest payments are also generally exempt from state and local income taxation in the jurisdictions of issue.

investors, although their yields, of course, are influenced by the general supply and demand for funds in the capital market.

The legal history of federal income tax exemption and the arguments pro and con is not discussed here.[2] The tax-exempt status, however, has had an enormous effect on the ability of state and local governments to attract low-cost funds to finance their enormous expenditures for schools, highways, and other projects.

Classification of Bonds

A convenient classification of bonds combines the issuer and the degree of tax support or other means of payment:

1. General ("full faith and credit") obligations secured by the general taxing power of governmental units
   (a) Regular:
       States
       Counties and parishes
       Cities, towns, boroughs, and townships
   (b) Special tax districts:
       School districts
       Water districts
       Others
2. Revenue bonds (nonguaranteed) secured only by special income
   (a) Municipal utilities and similar departments
   (b) Quasimunicipal authorities and commissions
   (c) Regular governmental units supporting the issue from special taxes only or from project income
3. Housing authority issues further supported by state or federal guarantee of principal and interest (a special type of revenue bond)

Bonds can also be classified as to quality. Security-rating services rate full faith and credit obligations of states from *Aaa* to *B*; local government bonds and revenue bonds show a range from *Aaa* to those in default. The ratings are a function of the (1) ratio of total debt to assessed valuation, (2) prior debt outstanding, (3) intended use of the funds, and (4) economic base of the taxing authority. Some local municipal issues have higher ratings than their state governments.

Regular government units possess broad general powers of taxation, limited only by statute with respect to types of taxes, total general debt in relation to property value, and limitations on the property tax rate. They ordinarily pledge their general credit but may also pledge specific revenues. Special districts, organized to operate a specific activity such as schools, also have the power to tax the property within their borders. Revenue bonds are issued by states,

---

[2] See D. J. Ott and A. H. Meltzer, *Federal Tax Treatment of State and Local Securities* (Washington, D.C.: The Brookings Institution, 1963).

counties, and local units payable from some specific source, and by departments and statutory authorities (quasipublic corporations without the power to tax) organized to operate revenue-producing projects.

Growth and Types of State and Local Debt

In the postwar period, the rate of growth of state and local government debt has outstripped that of the federal government. This growth reflects the expansion of governmental services, the growth of population, and the steady process of urbanization. The growth of state and local debt in relation to federal debt is also revealed by figures of year-end per capita debt:[3]

	1965	1970	1975	1978
Gross Federal Treasury debt (per capita)	$1,631	$1,816	$2,553	$3,588
State and local gross debt (per capita)	513	706	1,038	1,369

The figures show that since 1965 per capita Treasury debt has increased at an average annual rate of 9 percent compared to 13 percent for state and local. Moreover, if it were not for significant federal grants-in-aid, which in 1977 accounted for 23 percent of state and local revenues, the difference would have been even greater assuming that some municipal debt financing would have taken place in lieu of reduction in federal grants.

Table 9–1 shows the composition of state and local debt by major types for selected years (as of June 30). Net debt is after deductions for sinking fund. Revenue (nonguaranteed) bonds increased more than general obligation bonds in absolute amounts in the late 1960s and in the 1970s as industrial and pollution control facilities along with special commissions and authorities to operate utility toll-road and other ventures grew substantially. Another cause for the relative shift in emphasis has occurred as a result of municipal authorities avoiding general obligation bonds—and issuing revenue bonds instead—because these

TABLE 9-1. Outstanding Debt of State and Local Governments, 1965–1977, as of June 30 (billions of dollars)

	1965	1970	1975	1977
Long-term debt				
Full gaith and credit	$56.4	$ 75.3	$115.6	$137.7
Nonguaranteed	37.8	56.1	85.8	106.4
	$94.2	$131.4	$201.4	$244.1
Short-term debt	5.3	12.2	19.8	13.4
Total debt	$99.5	$143.6	$221.2	$257.5
Net long-term debt	$86.0	$121.7	$183.4	$212.3

Source: Department of Commerce, Bureau of the Census, *Governmental Finances* (annual).

---

[3]Department of Commerce, Bureau of the Census, *Statistical Abstract of the United States* and *Governmental Finances* (annual).

TABLE 9-2. Long-Term State and Local Debt, 1977 (billions of dollars)

	Full Faith and Credit	Nonguaranteed	Total
States	$ 42.9	$ 44.3	$ 87.2
Counties	15.2	6.2	21.4
Municipalities (cities)	38.6	28.3	66.9
Townships	3.2	0.2	3.4
School districts	27.7	–	27.7
Special districts	10.1	27.4	37.5
Total	$137.7	$106.4	$244.1

Source: Department of Commerce, Bureau of the Census, *Governmental Finances in 1976-1977.*

bonds were difficult to get passed by the general populace while revenue bonds seldom require voter approval. As of June 30, 1977 nonguaranteed bonds constituted about 44 percent of total "municipal" long-term bonds outstanding.

In addition, use of revenue rather than direct borrowing avoids certain statutory limits on "full faith and credit" debt, interest rate ceilings, and the legal restrictions on purposes for which tax revenues can be employed. The outstanding longer-term debt as of June 30, 1977, by governmental unit, is shown in Table 9-2.

Purposes of Borrowing

Long-term debt is issued to meet special operating expenses, to finance capital construction projects not borne by current revenues or grants from the federal and other governments, and to refund maturing obligations. Although there is no exact relationship between the amount of debt financing and capital expenditures, most of the debt bears part of the capital cost of projects involving fixed assets.[4]

In recent years, the annual increase in long-term debt has been about one-third of total capital outlay expenditures and an even smaller proportion of actual construction costs. Much capital construction by governments is financed from general and special tax revenues—for example, the use of gasoline taxes for highway construction. Revenue bond financing of self-supporting departments and authorities tends to follow more precisely the capital costs of these enterprises.

Organization of the Primary Market

The first step in the issuance of a new state or local government bond issue is its authorization by the governmental unit under the terms of the prevailing

---

[4]In recent years, federal funds have financed about 23 percent of state and local public construction through loans and grants.

statute. The financial officer then prescribes the terms of the issue—denominations, interest rate, serial maturities, and so forth—and, in most states, advertises it for sale under competitive bidding, ordinarily in the *Bond Buyer*. The chief buyers are large investment banking firms, some of which specialize in such securities, and commercial banks, which are authorized to act as underwriters of municipal issues (normally general obligations only).[5] Less than sixty banks are active in the market for large new issues. Some banks, even large ones, confine their holdings to bonds of issuers within their state. Smaller issues tend to be purchased by local banks.

In most states, individual underwriters or syndicates acquire general obligations by competitive bidding. Competitive bidding is expected to produce lower yields than negotiation; it does, however, deprive the issuer of the initial advice and continuous services of the investment banker. Revenue bonds are frequently sold on a negotiated basis; their more specialized nature and generally lower quality make the aid of a banker in consultation and tailoring of features more important.

Buying syndicates are managed by firms that invite other banks and dealers to participate in the underwriting. The larger underwritings are managed by a limited number of banks or firms, and underwriters often specialize in issues from a particular area or in certain types of obligations.

Bidding for municipal bonds (and their later resale) is on a yield basis on bids of par value or more. The syndicate determines the yields at which the various serial maturities will be absorbed, adds a gross spread to cover buying risk and distribution expense, and arrives at an overall net interest cost. Some invitations to bid require that all maturities bear the same coupon rate; in other cases the coupon may vary with maturity. Under the former arrangement, the offering price is adjusted above par for the different serial blocks because the market ordinarily requires that yields rise with length to maturity. Where the coupon varies with maturity, the rate may be set very high on early maturities, and these may be resold at substantial premiums.

The gross underwriting spread, or difference between cost and offering price, is the margin within which the successful bidder must be prepared to work. It ranges from less than 1 to 1.5 percent (with the average around 1 percent) and is a function of type, size, quality, marketability, and maturity.

The successful individual bidder or syndicate may retain the issue for its own inventory (as banks do for investment), retail it to its own customers, or reoffer it to dealers at a modest concession from the public offering price. Both in the original bidding and in later trading, the prices of the various maturities are indicated in terms of yield rather than in dollars.

---

[5] Housing Assistance Administration bonds are the exception.

In recent years, a fairly steady increase in municipal financing has resulted from the expansion of governmental services and the favorable market for tax-exempt securities. The data in Table 9-3 show the gross proceeds (at time of sale of new long-term issues, including those issues purchased by state and local government retirement funds. These proceeds are reduced to the net annual increase by deducting the cost of refinancing and retirements. Increases in loans from the federal government are added to produce the annual volume of total new debt.

The data reveal a secular increase in financing with some cyclical variations. In periods of tight money such as 1973-1974, characterized by rising yields and lower bond prices, a considerable amount of planned financing was withdrawn or postponed, some of this caused by the maximum-interest-rate ceilings on issued debt. The relatively small incremental amounts of state and local financing in 1975 and 1976 despite lower overall interest-rate levels was caused by (1) sharply higher federal grants to help combat unemployment and a recession, and (2) the reverberations in the municipal market caused by the financial problems of New York City. Publicity highlighting the financing problems and poor financial reporting requirements of most municipalities help to cause interest rates in the sector to be abnormally high. In 1977 and 1978, more normal municipal markets and increasing interest rates, leading to fewer new issues in the corporate bond market helped to expand new issues in the municipal market.

New issues are absorbed primarily by taxed institutions, especially property and liability companies, and commercial banks, which not only underwrite but also invest (except, in general, for revenue bonds) for their own account. Some bonds are placed with savings associations, and a modest amount with state and local governments proper and business corporations. Individuals seeking tax relief account for most of the balance. The data in Table 9-4 show the annual net changes in ownership since 1970.

Variations in annual net acquisitions by investors are only partly explained by changes in their available funds. Individuals, and especially institutions, switch in and out of municipals as the relative yields on competitive investments rise and fall. Bank acquisitions show the greatest variations in a loose cyclical pattern as banks may use these securities for their liquidity requirements. Changes in their reserve position and in the demand for loans, which banks prefer, determine their holdings and purchases of these securities. This situation is well illustrated by the drop in acquisition of municipals in 1969 and by the rebound in acquisitions to record levels in 1970 and 1971. Banks restricted purchases of municipal securities in 1975 and 1976 due to the unsettled market conditions as noted earlier.

Property and liability insurance companies demand for municipal bonds was stimulated by the comparatively high interest rates and increased income tax

TABLE 9-3. Long-Term Borrowing by State and Local Governments, 1970–1978 (billions of dollars)

	1970	1971	1972	1973	1974	1975	1976	1977	1978
New capital issues	$17.8	$25.0	$23.7	$24.0	$24.3	$30.6	$35.3	$46.8	$48.6
Less refunding and refinancing	8.9	10.1	9.6	11.4	12.2	17.4	17.9	22.0	22.3
	8.9	14.9	14.1	12.6	12.1	13.2	17.4	24.8	26.3
Federal loans	0.1	0.4	0.3	0.3	-0.6	-0.2	2.0	0.2	-1.5
Increase in debt	$ 9.0	$15.3	$14.4	$12.9	$11.5	$13.0	$19.4	$25.0	$24.8

Sources: *Federal Reserve Bulletin*; Federal Reserve *Flow-of-Funds Accounts*.

TABLE 9-4. Annual Acquisitions of State and Local Government Bonds, 1970–1978 (billions of dollars)

	1970	1971	1972	1973	1974	1975	1976	1977	1978
Commercial banks	$10.5	$12.8	$ 7.1	$ 5.6	$ 5.2	$ 1.6	$ 2.6	$ 9.2	$ 8.3
Mutual savings banks	–	0.2	0.5	–	–	0.6	0.9	0.4	0.5
Savings and loan associations	–	–	–	–	0.3	0.6	0.1	0.1	-0.1
Life insurance companies	0.1	–	0.1	0.1	0.3	0.8	1.1	0.5	0.2
Property and liability insurance companies	1.3	3.5	4.4	3.3	1.9	2.4	5.1	10.2	13.8 (est)
State and local government retirement funds	-0.3	0.1	-0.1	-0.4	-0.7	1.0	1.4	0.3	0.3
Business corporations	-0.6	1.0	1.0	-0.1	0.6	-0.2	-1.1	–	0.2
State and local governments	0.1	-0.3	-0.3	0.2	0.5	2.4	2.7	0.2	1.1
Households and other (residual)	-2.1	-2.0	1.7	4.2	3.7	3.8	6.6	4.1	0.5
Total	$ 9.0	$15.3	$14.4	$12.9	$11.5	$13.0	$19.4	$25.0	$24.8

Sources: See citations in schedules, Chapters 3 to 7; Federal Reserve *Flow-of-Funds Accounts*. Bankers Trust Company, *Credit and Capital Markets* (annual). (Some columns do not add to totals because of rounding.)

TABLE 9-5. Ownership of State and Local Government Debt, 1978
(billions of dollars)

	Amount	Percent
Commercial banks	$123.2	40.9%
Mutual savings banks	3.3	1.1
Life insurance companies	4.5	1.5
Property and liability insurance companies (est.)	55.0	18.2
State and local government retirement funds	4.1	1.4
State and local government general funds	8.4	2.8
Business and financial corporations (est.)	8.2	2.7
Individuals and others (residual)[a]	94.3	31.4
Total	$301.4	100 %

[a]Includes savings and loan associations.

Sources: Secretary of the Treasury, *Annual Report,* adjusted to year end and for data cited in Chapters 3 to 7. See also *Federal Reserve Bulletin,* annual Flow-of-Funds Accounts.

rates (Chapter 5). Life insurance companies and pension and retirement funds, because of lower or no income taxes, do not often find these securities appealing.

Variations in acquisitions by business corporations, individuals, and others are more difficult to analyze. Some countercyclical pattern in net purchases is evident, explained by variations in total savings and by the fact that in years of rapidly rising prices of common stocks, the latter become relatively unattractive for future capital gains. The higher the income tax bracket, of course, the more favorable is the after-tax rate from municipals.

Ownership of State and Local Government Bonds

At the end of 1978, the ownership schedule was as shown in Table 9-5. The last category, individuals and others, includes partnerships, bank trust accounts, savings and loan associations, dealers and brokers, and foreign owners. Individual ownership, direct and through trusts, accounts for close to 90 percent of that figure. Again the data show that those institutions (banks and property and liability insurance companies) and individuals who have the most to gain by holding tax-exempt issues are the prime holders.

Organization of the Secondary Market

Individual and institutional investors in tax-exempt bonds require a reasonably good secondary market, particularly when liquidations of holdings are necessary. Many municipal securities have limited markets and the purchasers generally hold to maturity. The secondary market is usually established by the original underwriting firms, banks, and dealers who specialize in these securities in the over-the-counter market. The secondary and primary marketing organizations consist largely of the same types of firms. The daily *Blue List of Current*

Municipal Offerings may list 2,500 to 3,000 available issues. Although no firm data are available, the interdealer volume of transactions is known to be substantial, but the total volume of trading is probably much lower than the volume of new offerings.

In order to increase the marketability and reduce interest costs, insurance organizations such as the Municipal Bond Insurance Association have been formed to unconditionally guarantee the principal and interest of municipal issues. The insurance is particularly helpful to small municipalities, which otherwise could not get acceptable ratings for their bonds and hence favorable interest rates. In another development to ensure better marketability, certain states are issuing their own obligations in behalf of small local governments and then lending the funds to the municipalities on a pro-rata basis.

Yields

The yields on state and local government bonds as a class are a function of (1) the level of interest rates in general, (2) the value to investors of the tax-exempt privilege, (3) the supply of new and outstanding securities of this type, (4) the supply of funds available for purchase of such investments, (5) the appeal of alternative investments, and (6) the risk of the security issue. Yields on individual issues are further affected by their size, quality, maturity, and marketability. Tax-exempt yields have fluctuated in a wider range than have other high-grade yields, mainly because of changes in supply in relation to that of federal bonds, in bank demand, and in market risk. Additionally, the market for tax-exempt bonds is more restricted than that of federal and corporate debt and is consequently more erratic. Figure 9-1 shows the annual average yields for Moody's U.S. Treasury long-term bond series compared with Moody's *Aaa* and *Baa* state and local government bonds series. The annual averages disguise the interim variations but are suitable for our purpose. Although all yields rose and fell in a common pattern, the spread between the yield on long-term Treasury bonds and the *Aaa* state and local government series has shown considerable variation. In general, in periods of prosperity yield spreads tend to narrow as risk factors become less of a consideration. Spreads also tend to narrow when overall market rates decline.

Modest increases in yields on Treasury bonds beginning in 1962 were accompanied by smaller increases in yields on high-grade municipals, so that by 1964 and 1965 the yield spread had widened to over 100 basis points (1%). In 1966, the "credit crunch" forced yields to record levels. Pressure for loan funds reduced bank investment in municipals in early 1966, but as the rise in yields continued, banks became aggressive buyers of municipals in later 1966 and 1967. Yields continued to rise throughout the intervening years and, in November 1969, the 6.3 percent yield on the composite group far surpassed previous levels. The high-interest-rate level posed a problem in many states as statutory limits were exceeded. Therefore, much new long-term financing was virtually stopped or postponed in 1969.

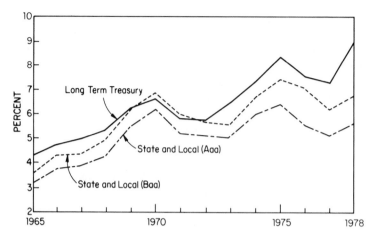

Figure 9-1. Average Annual Yields on U S. Government and Municipal Bonds, 1965-1978

Sources: *Federal Reserve Bulletin; Moody's Bond Survey.* For data, see Appendix, Table A-2.

Rates moderated from late 1969 through 1973 as available savings funds reduced demand by governments, and generally easier monetary policy relieved pressure on the long-term bond market. This process was again reversed in 1974 and 1975, however, as stringent monetary policy, questionable municipal finances and high inflation caused rates to rise along a broad front. Lower-grade municipals were especially affected as investors avoided these issues during unsettled market conditions. In 1977 and early 1978, the markets returned to more traditional levels but then rose sharply in late 1978 in response to higher inflation rates, restrictive monetary policy, and continued high demand for government funds. Rates on AAA bonds rose to a record 7 percent in October 1979.

The yield curve for state and local bonds has not been shaped like, nor has it necessarily followed, that for Treasury obligations (see Chapter 8). Longer maturities produce substantially higher rates, and the typical term structure of interest rates normally prevails. For example, early in June 1979, *Aaa*-rated 20-year general obligations bore an average yield of 5.90 percent, while five-year maturities sold to yield 5.0 percent and one-year maturities 4.9 percent. In the same month, yields on Treasury obligations of similar maturities were 9.06, 9.01, and 9.88 percent, respectively. Commercial banks generally prefer short- and intermediate-term obligations, while the longer-term bonds are most appealing to individual investors.

Yields on individual municipal issues are usually a function of quality, size, and marketability. Quality tends to correlate roughly with size—the big name issues finding the best market. Recent data reveal that the differential of *Baa* over *Aaa* yields has been increasing steadily in recent years, as concern over market risk caused investors to demand a larger premium on lesser-grade issues.

The Market for Long-Term Corporate Debt

Definitions and Reasons for Use

THE definition of the capital markets as a market for funds of over one year in maturity suggests a rather broad definition. It technically includes longer-term trade payables, mortgages, term loans, corporate one- to five-year notes sold in the open market, and corporate bonds. Precise data on some of these categories are lacking and because we are interested mainly in debt whose yields are determined in open competition, attention is confined to corporate term loans and bonds.

Term loans are business debts with more than one year maturity, negotiated directly with banks and insurance companies and ordinarily amortized on a serial basis. They are used to finance both working capital and fixed-asset requirements, and the repayment schedule is related to the future cash flow of the borrower. The latest available data on the volume of bank term lending are shown in Table 3–5. Insurance companies class their term loans as "industrial and miscellaneous" bonds, or as mortgages, and do not report separate figures for this investment.

Corporate debt finance rose in the late 1960s and 1970s as the stock market declined and low stock prices made stock sales an impractical and unpopular source of financing for most industrial firms. The heavy debt financing came at a time when inflation escalated, causing interest rates to climb to all-time highs and construction costs for new plant and equipment to burgeon, thereby compounding the need for new funds. All of this developed against a backdrop of

169

stagnant to declining corporate profitability from 1969 to 1972. Although corporate profitability improved in 1973, except for 1975-1978, the energy crisis and general uncertainty continued to undermine stock market prices.

Historically speaking, corporate bonds have been issued for a variety of reasons. The most important of these are to reduce the cost of financing and to increase the rate of return on equity capital through leverage. The after-tax cost of long-term debt, assuming a judicious use of debt, is lower than that of equity capital because of its preferred risk position and the fact that interest payments are tax-deductible. Bond financing also avoids possible dilution of control.

As many managers found out in 1969 and 1974, however, debt financing has many disadvantages. The contractual payments and the restrictions on working capital and retained earnings contained in the indenture agreement are among the factors inhibiting corporate flexibility and diminishing the appeal of debt financing. Management temperament is also a major factor determining the pattern of business financing. There is often a resistance to borrowing that may be based on rational risk avoidance or simply on innate conservatism. In regulated industries, limits to borrowing are imposed by the controlling commissions. For all companies, investors' standards with respect to appropriate debt burden have, of course, a powerful influence. Finally, high interest rates in 1973, 1974, and 1978-1979 tended to reduce corporate profitability and discourage borrowing.

General Corporate Financing

Sources of corporate funds from 1970 through 1978 are presented in Table 10-1. The data summarize the net financing after eliminating trade payables in order to avoid double counting of nonfarm, nonfinancial business corporations. (The data do not represent the total volume of actual capital-market activity in that they exclude refinancing and redemptions.)

Internal sources of funds exceeded external sources for every year except 1974, and customarily account for about 60 percent of all financing. Although internal funds are invested directly in corporate assets, they nevertheless affect the capital markets. To the extent that corporations can finance their needs in this manner, the need for securities and other outside financing is lessened.

Although the rise from $80.8 billion in total internal sources in 1972 to $141.9 billion in 1978 appears substantial, it barely kept pace with the rise in inflation. If internal sources are adjusted for price changes using the consumer price index, an entirely different picture of the true, real sources (in 1970 dollars) is revealed. The data at the bottom of Table 10-1 show that from 1970 through 1978 total real internal sources changed little during this period. If a construction index was used, rather than the CPI, to more closely reflect the probable cost of plant and equipment expenditures, a decline in real internal sources would have occurred.

The net result was that most corporations were starved for capital during the

TABLE 10-1. Sources of Funds, Nonfarm, Nonfinancial Corporations, 1970–1978 (billions of dollars)

	1970	1971	1972	1973	1974	1975	1976	1977	1978
Internal sources									
Retained profits[a]	$ 9.7	$ 15.3	$ 22.5	$ 32.5	$ 39.1	$ 35.1	$ 47.9	$ 50.5	$ 58.6
Depreciation and depletion	54.3	58.4	64.9	69.9	77.0	84.0	91.4	99.7	107.5
Inventory valuation	-5.1	-5.0	-6.6	-18.6	-40.4	-12.4	-14.5	-14.9	-24.3
	$58.9	$ 68.6	$ 80.8	$ 83.8	$ 75.7	$106.7	$124.7	$135.3	$141.9
External sources									
Bonds	$19.8	$ 18.9	$ 12.7	$ 11.0	$ 21.3	$ 29.8	$ 25.3	$ 24.5	$ 23.3
Bank term loans (est.)	2.0	2.0	6.4	8.4	11.0	1.3	-1.1	5.2	10.5
Mortgages	6.7	10.2	17.0	18.2	13.7	9.5	12.9	19.0	23.2
Stocks	5.7	11.4	10.9	7.9	4.1	9.4	10.5	2.7	2.6
Bank and other debt (mainly short-term)	6.6	2.0	11.3	27.2	31.6	-13.5	10.6	27.3	29.9
	$40.8	$ 44.5	$ 58.3	$ 72.7	$ 81.7	$ 37.0	$ 58.2	$ 78.7	$ 89.5
Total sources	$99.7	$113.1	$139.1	$156.5	$157.4	$143.7	$182.9	$214.0	$231.4
Total sources adjusted for price increases (1970 = 100 CPI)	$99.7	$108.6	$129.2	$136.8	$124.2	$103.6	$124.8	$137.2	$138.0
Internal sources adjusted for price increases (1970 = 100 CPI)	$58.9	$ 65.4	$ 75.0	$ 73.3	$ 59.6	$ 77.1	$ 85.0	$ 87.0	$ 85.1

[a]Includes foreign branch profits.

Sources: *Survey of Current Business*; Federal Reserve *Flow-of-Funds Accounts*; term loan data from Bankers Trust Company, *Credit and Capital Markets* (annual).

171

1970s and had to seek substantial external funds, which placed an added burden on the capital markets. Most of the external funds have come from borrowing rather than from equity markets. The large growth in external funds is evident from the data, as they about doubled in the seven-year period ended in 1978 for a compounded growth rate of about 10 percent.

Faced with declining profits, yet a desire to keep a stable dividend, retained earnings dropped sharply in 1970 and 1975 before recovering nicely in 1978. Given a need to finance plant and equipment and other asset expenditures in an inflated economy, firms were forced to seek funds from almost any available source. Thus, in addition to issuing bonds and current debt, firms tapped other infrequent sources, such as mortgages and common stocks (Table 10-1). Stock offerings rose in 1975 and 1976 as rising prices made financing cheaper.

The stock figure, although up sharply in 1971-1972 and 1975-1976 is somewhat illusory in that about 50 percent of this total financing was accounted for by utilities, which by law have to maintain a representative balance between debt and equity. Nevertheless, rising markets generally afford corporations an opportunity to sell stock and retire loans made in earlier years. A weak stock market in 1973, 1974, 1977, and 1978 substantially restricted additional equity financing for most firms.

Bank loans continued to be important sources of funds. In some cases, the rise in mortgages was more a result of lenders "reaching for security" than business corporations revealing a preference for this type of financing (see Chapter 12).

Outstanding Long-Term Corporate Debt

The high level of bond issues (a high of $29.8 billion in 1975) in the early 1970s reflected the pace of economic growth in the postwar period, the rise in prices, and the growing willingness of corporations to borrow to save on income taxes. The sharp drop in this form of financing and the corresponding sharp increase in bank borrowing in 1973 indicated that firms were borrowing short-term in hopes of refinancing in the long-term market when yields declined. In addition, fluctuations reflect variations in the pattern of corporate expenditures, mainly for fixed assets, as well as capital cost conditions in the competitive capital markets. The dominance of bond financing relative to stock financing is somewhat overstated in that convertible bonds are counted as debt when first issued; nevertheless, the total debt of nonfinancial corporations totaled $318.2 at the end of 1978, more than double the amount outstanding in 1969 (see Table 10-2). Financial corporations, including banks, showed a similar growth pattern in corporate bond liabilities outstanding.

Corporate borrowing is somewhat understated in that many corporations are making use of industrial revenue (and pollution control) bonds issued by state and local governments (Chapter 9). Here facilities are constructed using government funds and then leased by corporations with the lease payments used to amortize the debt.

TABLE 10-2. Corporate Bonds Outstanding at Year End, 1960–1978
(billions of dollars)

	1960	1965	1970	1975	1978
Nonfinancial corporations	$75.3	$ 97.8	$167.3	$254.3	$318.2
Financial corporations and banks	9.1	15.1	19.9	37.3	59.3
Total	$84.4	$112.9	$187.2	$291.6	$377.5

Source: Federal Reserve *Flow-of-Funds Accounts.*

Public Distribution of Bonds in the Primary Market

Public issues of corporate bonds are distributed through investment banking houses that underwrite bond issues for resale to institutions and individual investors. The investment banker provides the issuer with advice on the form, timing, and pricing of bond financing and with continuing counsel after the issue is floated. The banker's check on the financial condition of the issuer, the form and terms of the financing, and the maintenance of a continuous market, and his general investment information and advice are valuable to the investor. By screening issues and influencing their timing and yields, the investment banker plays a major role in the primary bond market.

Formerly called "bond houses," the larger investment banking firms engage in a variety of ancillary activities. Some serve as securities brokers and dealers and as underwriters of stock issues. In the flotation of new issues, some investment bankers are wholesalers, doing the original underwriting and then selling to retail dealers for wider distribution. Others serve also as distributors to the general investment public. Some are national in their operations; others are local. Although about fifty firms originate and manage the major issues of securities, hundreds of others are involved in the final sale of the larger flotations.

Investment banking firms acquire new corporate bond issues by either negotiated or competitive bidding. Direct negotiation between issuer and underwriter (acting alone or as the manager of a syndicate) ends in a purchase contract whereby the banker, or a purchase syndicate in the case of larger flotations, acquires the issue at a net price and yield determined by bargaining. Such underwriting is largely confined to industrial and financial offerings. Competitive bidding, in which the issuer invites sealed bids of price or yield or both on an issue whose terms are already determined, is ordinarily required by federal or state statute in the case of public utility and railroad issues. Regardless of the process of acquisition, the final purchase takes the form of a firm commitment.

Two other arrangements sometimes used do not involve total underwriting: (1) "best efforts," or agency selling, whereby the underwriter(s) agrees simply to merchandise the securities at the issuer's risk; this arrangement is used primarily in common stock rather than in bond offerings; and (2) "standby" underwriting of convertible bonds; this method involves the guarantee of funds to the issuer from an offering of such bonds by the corporation by privileged subscription to existing stockholders; here the underwriter agrees to take up only the securities not bought through the exercise of rights.

The public offering of corporate bonds in interstate commerce or through the mails is subject to the registration and prospectus requirements of the Securities Act of 1933, save for railroad issues, which are controlled by the Interstate Commerce Commission. State "blue sky" laws apply to intrastate offerings.

Direct, or Private, Placement of Bonds

A notable development in the postwar period has been the substantial growth of private placement of bonds with institutions, mostly life insurance companies (see Chapter 5) but also commercial banks, pension funds, and investment companies. Industrial bonds predominate in such direct sales because railroad and many utility bonds must be sold through competitive bidding. Direct placements avoid the investment banking machinery save for those cases in which investment bankers act as finders or agents at a modest fee (0.25–0.50 percent). Corporate bond offerings for cash (for both new money and refinancing) from 1960 through 1978 were as shown in Table 10-3. Private placements have increased in recent years as a percentage of total offerings, rising from a low of only 16 percent in 1970 to 43 percent of total offerings in 1978. Public offerings have continued at a high plateau as large financing needs by utilities and rails that normally use competitive bids accounted for about 50 percent of the total. Life insurance companies, which provide the chief demand for corporate

TABLE 10-3. Publicly and Privately Offered Corporate Bonds, 1960–1978 (billions of dollars)

	Publicly Offered	Privately Placed	Total	Privately Placed (%)
1965	$ 5.6	$ 8.1	$13.7	60%
1966	8.0	7.5	15.5	48
1967	15.0	7.0	22.0	32
1968	10.7	6.7	17.4	38
1969	12.7	5.6	18.3	31
1970	25.4	4.9	30.3	16
1971	24.8	7.2	32.0	21
1972	17.4	8.7	26.1	33
1973	13.2	7.8	21.0	37
1974	25.9	6.2	32.1	19
1975	32.6	10.2	42.8	24
1976	26.5	15.9	42.4	38
1977	24.2	18.0	42.2	43
1978	19.9	15.2	35.2	43

Sources: Securities and Exchange Commission, *Annual Reports; Federal Reserve Bulletin.*

debt, tend to alter their commitments to corporate bonds depending upon yields available on alternative investment—especially mortgages—and on available funds. Although policy loans increased in 1970s, thereby restricting investment resources cash flows at insurance companies, coupled with lower mortgage commitments, have resulted in sharply higher private bond placements by these institutions from 1976 through 1978.

Private placements offer several advantages to the corporation and to the lender. They reduce the risk of delay involved in registered public offerings, save on costs of flotation (except for any finder's fee), make the funds available sooner, and permit the tailoring of each loan indenture to the particular situation. Smaller corporations find such financing a substitute for bond issues they would have difficulty selling in the open market. Institutions prefer private placements because they can get comparatively higher yields and place a large amount of funds at one time with less paperwork.

Acquisitions of Corporate Bonds

The *net* change in outstanding corporate bonds is shown in Table 10-4. Annual variations in demand for bonds by investors reflect conditions and policies discussed in Chapers 3 to 7. Briefly, life insurance companies, state and local government retirement funds, and individuals have been traditional heavy purchasers of corporate bonds as interest rates on these latter securities made them favored investments. More recently, private pension funds and foreign investors have purchased corporate bonds in substantial amounts for the same reason.

Ownership of Corporate Bonds

The holdings of corporate bonds at the end of 1978 are shown in Table 10-5. The same institutions and individuals that have been heavy acquisitors of bonds in recent years are, likewise, large holders of these instruments. As noted earlier, in Chapter 5, life insurance holdings dominate all others—they find bonds with their definite yield and long-term maturities attractive investments as their chief investment obligation from the standpoint of income, is to earn at least the assumed rate at which reserves are compounded. Corporate pension fund investment in bonds remains significant, although these instruments have constituted a steadily declining proportion of their total assets because of the greater relative emphasis on common stocks (Chapter 6).

Secondary market activity in corporate bonds, especially high-grade corporate bonds, is somewhat limited because of the large institutional ownership, which tends to hold these bonds to maturity. The recent fluctuating interest rates that cause sharp drops or rises in bond prices, however, may result in a more active market in the future.

TABLE 10-4. Annual Net Acquisitions of Corporate and Foreign Bonds, at Year End, 1970-1978 (billions of dollars)

	1970	1971	1972	1973	1974	1975	1976	1977	1978
Commercial banks	$ 0.8	$ 1.2	$ 1.4	$ 0.4	$ 1.0	$ 1.8	$-0.7	$-0.2	$-0.3
Mutual savings banks	1.2	3.9	2.1	-1.1	0.9	3.5	2.8	1.2	0.3
Life insurance companies	1.8	5.6	7.7	6.2	4.5	10.2	15.7	18.3	17.4
Property and liability insurance companies	1.5	0.3	-0.7	-0.2	2.0	2.1	3.8	3.4	2.5 (est)
Private, noninsured pension funds	2.1	-0.7	-0.8	2.1	4.7	2.8	1.3	5.3	8.2
State and local government retirement funds	4.5	3.9	4.2	5.6	6.8	6.3	7.1	5.3	5.8
Investment companies (mutual)	0.7	0.6	0.2	-0.9	-0.4	1.0	2.2	1.1	-0.3
Foreign investors	0.3	0.2	-0.1	—	0.5	0.7	0.3	1.0	0.8 (est)
Households and others	10.4	8.5	4.4	1.5	3.9	8.0	4.7	0.7	-2.3
Total	$23.3	$23.5	$18.4	$13.6	$23.9	$36.4	$37.2	$36.1	$32.1

Sources: See citations in schedules, Chapters 3 to 7; Federal Reserve *Flow-of-Funds Accounts*; Securities and Exchange Commission, *Statistical Bulletin*; Bankers Trust Company, *Credit and Capital Markets* (annual). (Some columns do not add to totals because of rounding.)

TABLE 10-5. Ownership of Corporate Bonds, 1978 (billions of dollars)[a]

	Amount	Percent
Commercial banks	$ 6.6	1.7%
Mutual savings banks	21.6	5.7
Life insurance companies	156.0	41.3
Property and liability insurance companies (est)	16.5	4.8
Private noninsured pension funds	53.8	14.3
State and local government retirement funds	81.3	21.5
Mutual investment companies	6.2	1.6
Individuals and other	35.5	9.5
Total	$377.5	100 %

[a]Includes bonds of foreign corporations.
Sources: Federal Reserve *Flow-of-Funds Accounts* and data on institutional investments, Chapters 3–7.

Most trading occurs in the over-the-counter market. The New York Stock Exchange constitutes virtually the entire listed market. The market value of the 2,478 domestic corporate bonds listed on the Big Board was $159 billion; bonds of foreign governments, companies, and banks amounted to $155 billion, and U.S. government bonds added another $305 billion.[1] Of the thousands of unlisted corporate bond issues, probably fewer than 500 are traded on the over-the-counter market in a typical day, since the majority are only occasionally transferred. Even so, about 80 percent of corporate bond resales take place in the "off board" rather than on the organized exchanges. The transactions are handled by broker-dealers, mainly the members of the National Association of Securities Dealers. A high concentration of resales are in the New York market, with only a handful of houses making a continuous market.

At the end of 1977, 2,478 bond issues of American corporations were listed on the New York Stock Exchange. Of this total, fewer than 100 were actively traded. The sales of listed bonds in 1977 totaled $4.6 billion.

Data on changes in corporate bonds outstanding, listings on exchanges, and trading are increasingly influenced by the growing volume of convertible bonds. These securities, although bonds in name, are convertible into common shares at predetermined ratios and are, in effect, calls on common stock at a fixed price. The volume issued and traded is in part a function of the course of the stock market. In 1977, 25 of the 50 most actively traded bonds on the New York Stock Exchange were convertibles.[2]

---

[1]New York Stock Exchange, *Fact Book*, 1978.
[2]Ibid.

Yields

The factors determining interest rates in the capital markets and the inter-relations among rates on different instruments are discussed in greater detail in Chapter 13. Comment here is restricted to the historical pattern of corporate bond yields.

Bond yields change through time as long-term interest rates rise and fall. The spread between yields on straight corporate bonds and on Treasury bonds of like maturities represents the margin required by investors to compensate for the risk of default. It also reflects the relatively poor marketability of corporate bonds.

Figure 10-1 graphs the average annual yields of long-term Treasury bonds, and *Aaa* and *Baa* corporate bonds. The data reveal that the three series rose and fell together, but not to the same degree. The differential between *Aaa and Baa* bond yields and between *Aaa* corporate and long-term Treasury bond yields was by no means uniform through time, reflecting the differences in demand for and supply of securities of different quality.

As yields in general rise, the premium for risk and poorer liquidity tends to increase, although this relationship has been by no means uniform. Also, the risk premium tends to vary with the economy. When the economy is booming, yield spreads tend to narrow—and increase when the opposite obtains.

A most significant development in recent years has been the large spread between the yields on long-term Treasury bonds and *Aaa* corporate bonds. This

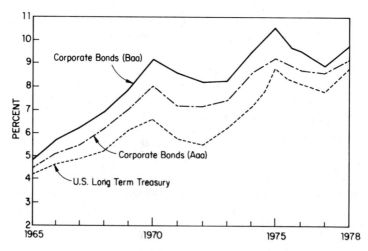

Figure 10-1. Average Annual Yields on Corporate and Treasury Bonds, 1965–1978

Sources: *Federal Reserve Bulletin: Moody's Bond Survey.* For data, see Appendix, Table A-3.

has been as low as 20 basis points in 1978 and as high as 165 basis points in 1971.[3] This was attributable in part to the heavy debt financing by large corporations—causing corporate bond rates to rise—and to the emphasis by the Treasury on sales of short-term securities, thereby reducing the supply of long-term Treasury bonds—which led to a drop in rates on these issues.

In years of recession, such as 1971 and 1975, investors require higher compensation for lesser quality, as indicated by the larger spreads among the Treasury, *Aaa,* and *Baa* groups. In years of sharply rising interest rates, it is normal for the lower quality bonds to suffer most from the credit squeeze and spreads therefore widen. This general rule does not always hold, however, as witnessed in the 1970–1974 period. Yield spreads in 1971 and 1972 were among the greatest for any period, yet these years were years of relative monetary ease. In 1974, a year characterized by very high rates and tight money, the spread dropped between corporate bonds and rose only moderately compared to long-term treasuries. Although difficult to measure, some of the rise in *Aaa* interest rates in 1974 was attributed to the operating difficulties experienced by many *Aaa* firms—mostly utilities—caused by high interest rates and an inflationary economy.

In 1978, long-term rates increased due to restrictive monetary policy and inflation, although there were differential impacts compared to earlier years. For example, in 1975 the yield spread between corporate *Baa* bonds and long-term treasuries was 363 basis points (3.63 percent). At the end of 1978, the yield spread had been reduced to 156 basis points. This reflected some significant changes. First, many investors worried over the viability of *Baa* firms in 1974 given the energy crisis such that rates were driven abnormally high. Second, the same *Baa* firms worked hard in the intervening years 1975–1977 to reduce their debt exposure. Third, the sharply higher federal deficits caused considerably more Treasury financing and a relative rise in interest rates.

Within a given rating, such as *Aaa,* rates can vary from issue to issue. During the 1970s, of the same rated issues telephone bonds tended to sell at lower yields than electrical or gas utilities because of the uncertainties associated with gas and electric supplies and costs. Also, even though they have somewhat higher-risk than utilities, corporate bonds have generally sold at lower yields than the same-rated utility bonds because of the shorter average maturity of the former and the larger number of offerings of new utility issues.

In October 1979, interest rates rose to all-time highs. AAA-rated corporate bonds yielded over 10 percent, and Baa bonds yielded nearly 13 percent. These spectacular yields reflected continued inflation and Federal Reserve attempts to control it.

---

[3] A basis point is one one-hundredth of a percentage point. Thus, 100 basis points are 1 percent, and a rise of 165 basis points is 1.65 percent.

```
111111111111111111111111111111111111111111111111111111111111111111111111111111111111111111
111111111111111111111111111111111111111111111111111111111111111111111111111111111111111111
1111111111111111111111111111111111    11111    111    111111111111111111111111111111111111
1111111111111111111111111111111111    111    1111    111111111111111111111111111111111111
111111111111111111111111111111111    1    11111    111111111111111111111111111111111111
1111111111111111111111111111111111    111111    111111111111111111111111111111111111111
11111111111111111111111111111111111    1111111    11111111111111111111111111111111111111
11111111111111111111111111111111111    111111    11111111111111111111111111111111111111
1111111111111111111111111111111111    1    11111    111111111111111111111111111111111111
1111111111111111111111111111111111    111    1111    111111111111111111111111111111111111
1111111111111111111111111111111111    11111    111    111111111111111111111111111111111111
111111111111111111111111111111111111111111111111111111111111111111111111111111111111111111
111111111111111111111111111111111111111111111111111111111111111111111111111111!11111111111
```

The Corporate Stock Market

Definitions and Concepts

No attempt is made in this book to describe all the legal and financial characteristics of stocks or their role in corporate financial policy. Our concern is with
the nature and scope of their primary and secondary markets. A few reminders
of their basic features are, however, appropriate.

Corporate stock in the form of transferable certificates represents the equity
interest in the company. The owners of the certificates presumably enjoy the
basic rights of proprietorship, some of which, however, are delegated to directors
and officers or are limited by the corporate charter. As the residual equity in a
company, common stock owners participate in the net assets at liquidation and
in net earnings (when declared in dividends) after all claims of creditors and the
dividends on any preferred stock have been met. The net assets and earnings, and
therefore the prices of common stocks, are volatile, but the possibility of very
high returns gives these instruments unusual investment and speculative appeal.

Preferred stock ranks above the common in preference to assets and dividends.
Participation in assets in liquidation is generally limited to par or a stated preference value; dividends are usually set in the charter at a maximum rate that
must be paid before any dividends go to the common. Preferred dividends are
ordinarily cumulative; that is, all past-due preferred dividends must be paid before
any can be paid to the common. Because of their preferences and limitations,
preferred stocks possess some of the attributes of bonds. Indeed, the very
strongest preferreds rival bonds in strength and yield. Weak preferreds are akin

to common stocks in that their dividend prospects are contingent on sufficient earnings.

Convertible preferred stocks (or bonds) have a dual appeal. They offer the owner the option of exchange into common stock at a predetermined ratio, so their prices and yields often reflect the prospects of the common itself. The conversion feature, however, has little or no value if the market value of the preferred is well above that of the common shares into which it is convertible. The preferred then sells close to its "straight" value. When the market price of the common approaches or exceeds the conversion price, the value of the preferred equals (or exceeds) that of the number of shares of common for which it may be exchanged.

The market value of common stock is mainly a function of its projected future earnings and dividends. Asset (book) value may have some influence, particularly in certain industries, as will marketability or a good volume of trading. The price-earnings multiplier reflects opinion on the future stability and growth of earnings and dividends. The dividend yields of common stocks are a function of their present and estimated future dividend rates.

Common and preferred stock do not normally have maturity dates. Principal can ordinarily be recovered only through resale. However, two standard provisions of preferred stock give it some of the maturity features of bonds: (1) the right of the issuer to call in the stock at a value set by the charter—the call price forms a plateau or peg through which the market price is unlikely to break unless the stock is convertible or unless a call is very unlikely; (2) many preferreds, especially of industrial companies, have a sinking fund or repurchase clause that requires the issuer regularly to retire shares at either a fixed rate or one contingent on earnings. Steady retirement for sinking fund has a supporting influence on market price.

Outstanding Corporate Stock

The year-end market value of all corporate stock of different categories in the United States as estimated by the Securities and Exchange Commission is shown in Table 11-1. The value of total publicly held domestic stock is found by deducting the value of investment company shares (to eliminate double counting), shares of foreign companies, and intercorporate holdings. The data reveal both the volatility (1972-1978) and the modest secular rise in net domestic stock. Although corporate stock values as a group have not fared well since 1968, the chief factor causing the long-term growth has been appreciation in price rather than substantial increases in the number of issues traded.

The Primary Market for New Stock Issues

New corporate stocks are sold to investors both directly by the issuers and indirectly through investment bankers and dealers. Direct selling may be em-

TABLE 11-1. Estimated Value of Traded and Closely Held Domestic Corporate Stocks, 1970-1978 (billions of dollars)

	1970	1971	1972	1973	1974	1975	1976	1977	1978
Listed stocks	$ 681	$ 796	$ 933	$ 764	$537	$ 719	$ 898	$ 838	$ 866
Traded over the counter	203	241	256	196	167	208	244	243	262
Closely held	153	179	205	166	122	160	198	187	195
	$1,037	$1,216	$1,394	$1,126	$826	$1,087	$1,340	$1,268	$1,323
Less stock of investment and foreign companies	114	130	135	127	117	145	163	162	166
Less intercorporate holdings	77	97	131	108	76	102	127	119	125
Net domestic stock	$ 846	$ 989	$1,128	$ 891	$633	$ 840	$1,050	$ 987	$1,032

Source: Securities and Exchange Commission, *Statistical Bulletin.*

ployed by new, weak, and speculative concerns that cannot obtain or afford the services of an investment banker, or more recently under dividend reinvestment plans established by many firms. Sale of securities to employees and executives in connection with savings, stock purchase, and stock option incentives is also direct. A few stock issues are privately placed with institutional buyers; these are chiefly higher-grade preferred stocks of public utility companies.

Excluding dividend reinvestment plans, the chief means of direct sale of common stocks are through the issuance of rights to existing stockholders entitling them to buy new shares (and convertible bonds and preferreds) in proportion to existing holdings. Such "privileged subscriptions" allow the purchase of stock at a discount from current market price. The value of the right itself is determined by the difference between market and subscription price, adjusted for the increase in the number of shares. In some states, the "preemptive right" is required; in others it is optional. In the latter states the corporate charter may require it. Where optional, management assesses the advantages of this method of financing in comparison with either public offering of stock or some other means of financing. The investment broker often participates in the offering of stock through rights by entering into a standby agreement where, for a fee, the banker (or a syndicate) agrees to take up any shares not subscribed by stockholders.

A rough approximation of the amount of securities sold by privileged subscription, or dividend reinvestment for the twelve months ending June 30, 1977, regardless of whether the sale was accompanied by standby underwriting, is indicated by the size of the "to securityholders" figure (Table 11-2) within the total of securities offered for immediate cash sale and registered with the Securities and Exchange Commission. The data exclude private placements, categories such as railroad securities that need not be registered, and exempt small issues. A very small percentage of bond and preferred stock total was sold directly to security holders. About 10 percent of the new common stock was offered through privileged subscription.

Where stock is sold to the public, the use of investment bankers and syndicates depends on the size and quality of the issue and on the range of services needed by the issuers and for which they are willing to pay.

TABLE 11-2.   Registered Corporate Securities Offered for Immediate Cash Sale,
Year Ended June 30, 1977 (millions of dollars)

	Bonds	Preferred	Common	Total
To the general public	$23,613	$2,320	$5,962	$31,895
To securityholders	9	96	717	822
Total	$23,623	$2,416	$6,679	$32,717

Source: Securities and Exchange Commission; *43rd Annual Report* (1977), p. 319. (Some figures do not add to totals because of rounding.)

It is convenient at this point to summarize the various methods of sale of new bond and stock issues:

1. Direct sale without investment banker assistance:
   (a) Small, new, and weaker issues (bonds and stocks)
   (b) Employee and executive purchase plans (stocks)
   (c) Privileged subscriptions without standby underwriting (convertible bonds and preferred stock, common stock)
   (d) Dividend reinvestment plans
2. Direct sale with some investment banking services:
   (a) Privileged subscriptions with standby underwriting
   (b) Private sale to institutions, the banker acting as finder (bonds, preferred stock)
3. Sale through investment bankers:
   (a) On an agency or best-efforts basis (mainly stocks)
   (b) Full commitment underwriting (all types of securities)

Volume and Buyers of New Common Stock Issues

The use of common and preferred stocks in business financing and their importance relative to bonds is indicated by the data in Table 11-3, which cover the gross proceeds of all new corporate securities sold for cash in the United States for both new money and refinancing from 1970 through 1978. The figures include all public and private sales including registered and unregistered issues.

The volume of bond financing has far outstripped that of stock financing over the last two decades. Common stock financing in 1975-1978 has increased sharply compared to 1974 as funds have been needed from all sources for corporate expansion, but even so the figures pale by comparison to bond financing. Preferred stock—often convertible preferred issues—expanded modestly during the same period. As discussed in Chapter 10, declining corporate profitability and high inflation have combined in recent years to compound the need for external funds.

The bond figures for the various years are somewhat illusory in that almost

TABLE 11-3. Types of New Corporate Securities Sold for Cash, 1970-1978
(billions of dollars)

	1970	1974	1975	1976	1977	1978
Bonds, notes, and debentures	$29.0	$31.5	$41.7	$41.2	$39.9	$36.0
Preferred stock	1.4	2.2	3.4	2.8	3.9	2.8
Common stock	7.0	4.0	7.4	8.3	8.0	8.0
Total	$37.4	$37.7	$52.5	$52.3	$51.8	$46.8

Sources: Securities and Exchange Commission, *Statistical Bulletin; Federal Reserve Bulletin.*

15 percent of the total bond volume consisted of convertible bonds. The latter issues have their greatest appeal when stock markets are rising as in 1975 and 1976. Also, convertible issues have expanded recently because of their usefulness in merger financing and as a method for reducing the coupon payment during high-interest-rate periods. Typically, new issue convertible bonds have coupon yields that are from 1½ percent to 3 percent lower than straight debt issues.

The drop in external financing in 1973 compared to 1971 and 1972 was a result of improved corporate profitability and liquidity along with a declining stock market that made stock financing less attractive. The sharp jump in common stock financing in 1975 and 1976 occurred for the opposite reasons—a rising stock market, the need for greater corporate liquidity, and the desire to convert short-term bank loans to long-term securities.

Data in Chapter 10 show that the major sources of corporate funds have been internal—retained profits and depreciation allowances. The small volume of new common stock financing relative to the amount of total stock outstanding attests to the minor importance of the primary stock market as a source of funds. The $8.0 billion of new corporate stock issued in 1978 amounted to less than 1 percent of total stock outstanding. This contrasted with bond financing of $36.0 billion in 1978, which represented almost 10 percent of total corporate bonds outstanding. This difference tends to be accentuated in periods of falling stock prices as most firms shun common stock financing.

Public utility and communication companies with their tremendous need for capital have been the chief issuers of corporate bonds and stocks. In recent years they have accounted for approximately 60 percent of total yearly issues of corporate security issues.

Acquisitions of Corporate Stock

Table 11-4 shows the annual net acquisitions of corporate stock for 1970 through 1978. To avoid double counting, the figures exclude issues of investment companies. The "individuals and others" group includes bank-administered trust funds, foundations and other nonprofit organizations, and minor institutions. The data represent only the net increases in stock outstanding after deducting issues sold for refinancing and those retired from earnings. Hence, they do not show the full activity of the various institutions in the primary market for stocks.

The growing importance of an institutional market for new stock issues is revealed by the data. From 1970 through 1978 institutional holdings of stocks grew more than the net increase in total outstanding stocks. Most of the acquisitions were in the open market. Individuals and others, although acquiring many of the new issues, were net sellers on balance especially in 1971-1973 and 1977-1978. Pension funds and retirement funds together absorbed more than the total amount of all new financing. These increased holdings provided support for

TABLE 11-4. Annual Net Acquisitions of Corporate Stock, 1970-1978 (billions of dollars)

	1970	1971	1972	1973	1974	1975	1976	1977	1978
Mutual savings banks	$ 0.3	$ 0.5	$ 0.6	$ 0.4	$ 0.2	$ 0.2	$ 0.1	$ 0.4	$ 0.1
Life insurance companies	2.0	3.6	3.5	3.6	2.3	1.9	3.0	1.2	1.1
Property and liability insurance companies	1.1	2.5	3.0	2.8	-0.2	-1.3	0.1	2.3	2.5 (est)
Private, noninsured pension funds	4.6	8.9	7.3	5.3	2.3	5.8	7.3	4.5	1.7
State and local government retirement funds	2.1	3.2	3.7	3.4	2.6	2.4	3.1	3.4	2.5
Investment companies (mutual)	1.2	0.4	-1.8	-2.3	-0.5	-1.1	-2.5	-3.8	1.6
Foreign investors	0.6	0.7	2.2	2.8	0.5	4.7	2.8	2.7	2.2 (est)
Individuals and others (residual)	-1.4	-4.8	-5.2	-6.8	-3.5	-1.9	-2.0	-6.9	-8.6
Total	$10.5	$15.0	$13.3	$ 9.2	$ 3.7	$10.7	$11.9	$ 3.8	$ 3.1

Sources: Securities and Exchange Commission, *Annual Reports* and *Statistical Bulletin;* Federal Reserve *Flow-of-Funds Accounts.* Bankers Trust Company, *Credit and Capital Markets* (annual). See also sources cited in Chapters 3 to 7. (Certain columns do not add to totals because of rounding.)

stocks in a generally declining market, and contributed to a shift in ownership of the better stocks into institutional hands, resulting in the "two-tier" stock market in the middle 1970s.

"Individuals and others" have been net sellers of stocks throughout the 1960s and 1970s. A number of reasons have been advanced for this selling activity. First, individuals have been withdrawing from direct participation in the market in favor of indirect participation through institutions like pension funds and insurance companies. This parallels the general intermediation of funds by individuals noted earlier. Second, individuals, especially in recent years, have been disappointed in the general stock market performance. Third, the high rates of interest on alternative securities have drawn funds from the stock market. Fourth, individuals have not been encouraged to participate directly in the market because of higher commissions charged by brokers, generally high margin requirements, and minimum account balances. Nevertheless, it should be remembered that individuals are still the largest owners of corporate stocks, holding more than $770 billion in market value at the end of 1978. Consequently, in perspective, the net sales of around $4 billion annually could easily reflect the individual's preferences in securing a more favorable and balanced portfolio position among all types of securities.

The low figure for new stock acquisitions in 1974 reflected the poor market performance during this period, which caused corporations to postpone stock offerings. Also contributing to the decline in stock offerings throughout most of the 1970s were conglomerate firms that often purchased other firms by issuing debt or paying cash and retiring the stock. Other companies also retired their own shares through stock tender offers for cash or an exchange of senior securities. As a result, and as indicated in Table 10-1, companies have increasingly relied on internal sources of funds rather than on new stock financing in the 1970s as low stock prices, reflected in lower price–earnings ratios, have plagued most firms.

It may appear as measured by absolute figures that noninsured pension funds and state and local retirement funds are heavy purchasers of corporate stock. However, given their rapid growth in fund assets and hence monies available for investment, both institutions in 1977 and 1978 made a relative shift away from equity investments into higher-yielding fixed-income securities. Also, investment companies continued their more-or-less forced withdrawal of funds from corporate stock as net redemptions of investment company shares persisted.

The Secondary Market for Stocks

Securities markets aid in the mobilization of capital and in the transfer of savings by providing facilities for orderly trading. On the organized exchanges, listed securities are bought and sold on an auction basis through brokers. In the over-the-counter market, prices are determined mainly by negotiations between buyers and sellers through dealers acting as principals. Since 1975, commissions are no longer "fixed" on the organized exchanges.

The organized exchanges provide a continuous market for the exchange of outstanding issues that meet the listing requirements. But mere listing does not automatically guarantee good marketability. Large orders are often difficult to fill without a substantial price movement from the previous trade.

The New York Stock Exchange has the strictest listing requirements and serves as a prototype for the other exchanges. At the end of 1977, 2,177 stock and warrant stock issues of 1,575 different companies were listed on the exchange. The market value of these stocks totaled $771 billion and the value of trades during the year amounted to $187 billion, a turnover ratio of about 24 percent. The increase in the turnover rate from the early 1960s, which was approximately 14 percent, was caused in part by the expanding role of institutions in the stock market, lower commissions, and greater uncertainty in the market.

The American Stock Exchange (ASE), also located in New York, generally lists the securities of smaller, more unseasoned companies than those that qualify for the Big Board. Activity on the ASE has increased in the last decade and amounted to nearly 10 percent of the total number of shares traded on organized exchanges in 1978. As the ASE tends to list small firms, however, they accounted for less than 6 percent of the total market value of shares traded on the exchanges in 1978.

The regional exchanges provide trading facilities for stocks with a local interest, but the bulk of their activity is in Big Board issues that are also listed on the regionals ("multiple listing"). Given the duplication of listed firms, the SEC has pushed for legislation that would create a national market. Although delayed in operation and faced with strong opposition, a nationwide exchange should create a better market and additional operating efficiencies for the investor.

The increase in share ownership by the institutions has precipitated a number of new arrangements for buying and selling large blocks of stock. These new arrangements have resulted in an active market in listed securities "off the board" and in the over-the-counter market.

In response to this competition as well as to pressure from the SEC, commissions are now negotiated. This has not been accomplished without a great deal of turmoil among brokerage houses as several went bankrupt or were forced to seek a merger partner. Although these failures and other problems cannot be blamed entirely on negotiated commissions, it is true that the intense competition for institutional business, resulting in lower commission charges, has reduced brokerage revenues. However, the demise of some brokerage houses and the consolidation of others has not seriously affected the marketability of stocks.

A much larger number of securities are traded in the over-the-counter (or unlisted) market. This has been estimated at about 50,000 securities in all, with about 14,000 stocks and 3,500 bonds being actively traded. The total value and volume of bonds traded is much larger in the over-the-counter market than on listed exchanges; however, the opposite holds for trades in common stocks.

Transactions in federal securities are off-board, as are those of all but a few state and municipal bonds. Most corporate bonds are unlisted, as are all but a few bank, insurance, and mutual fund shares and a large number of industrial and utility shares. At the end of 1978, the value of stocks actively traded over the counter was estimated at $262 billion, about 30 percent of the aggregate of the market value traded on organized exchanges.

As noted earlier, trading in the over-the-counter market is not confined to unlisted securities. A number of listed securities are bought and sold in the "third market," which consists of dealers with an inventory of listed stocks. The volume of "third market" trading in stocks listed on the New York Stock Exchange is about 10 percent of the volume on the exchange.[1]

The "fourth market," where institutions interested in selling or buying securities deal directly with each other without the services of a broker or dealer, has not grown in importance. The methods and procedures already developed for handling large institutional orders efficiently and economically— including negotiated commissions—through brokers and dealers have been the main reasons for this lack of growth in the fourth market.

Ownership of Corporate Stock

At the end of 1978, over 22 million individuals owned stock of publicly held corporations.[2] This represents a drop from the 1972 high of about 32 million as many investors indicated their dissatisfaction with stocks and their preference for the higher yields available on bonds and savings deposits.

Table 11-5 shows the institutional ownership of corporate stocks held by institutions from 1960 through 1978.[3] In addition to the institutions we have

---

[1] Securities and Exchange Commission, *Statistical Bulletin*, May, 1978.

[2] Source: New York Stock Exchange, *Fact Book*, 1979.

[3] Data on the distribution of all outstanding stocks, especially institutional holdings, are incomplete or inconsistent. The list of institutions holding stocks also differs from source to source. The Securities and Exchange Commission totals for institutional holdings at the end of a given year differ considerably from that calculated in the Federal Reserve flow-of-funds data as the former includes bank personal trust funds, which are nominal but not actual owners of shares.

Assets held by bank trust departments are omitted from the table because these are not owned, but are managed by the banks for the benefit of others. At the end of 1977, common stocks held totaled $252 billion, of which $205 billion were in trust accounts and $47 billion in agency accounts. Deducting the value of stocks on employee benefit funds managed by the banks, so as to avoid duplication with the pension fund figures in the table, produces the still formidable figure of $136 billion in stocks under bank management for personal trusts and estates. (Federal Deposit Insurance Corporation, *Trust Assets of Insured Commercial Banks*, 1977.)

TABLE 11-5. Ownership of Corporate Stock by Major Institutions, 1960–1978
(billions of dollars)

	1960	1965	1970	1975	1978
Mutual savings banks					
Preferred	$ 0.3	$ 0.4	$ 0.7	$ 2.9 ⎱	$ 4.9
Common	0.4	1.0	1.8	1.5 ⎰	
Life insurance companies					
Preferred	1.8	2.9	3.5	7.8	10.5
Common	3.2	6.2	11.9	20.3	25.0
Property and liability insurance companies[a]					
Preferred	0.8	1.1	1.6	3.0	4.2
Common	8.6	14.1	16.0	20.2	15.2
Private, noninsured pension funds					
Preferred	0.7	0.8	1.6	0.9	1.2
Common	15.8	40.0	65.5	87.7	106.7
State and local government retirement funds					
Preferred	–	0.2	0.4	1.7 ⎱	32.4
Common	0.4	1.4	7.6	22.6 ⎰	
Investment companies[b]					
Preferred	0.7	0.6	1.1	0.5 ⎱	30.1
Common	14.1	30.3	38.5	33.1 ⎰	
Foundations					
Preferred	0.4	0.4	0.4	0.4	0.5
Common	13.1	19.1	21.6	22.7	26.5
Educational Endowments					
Preferred	0.2	0.1	0.1	0.1	0.1
Common	3.8	6.9	7.7	8.7	10.1
Total	$ 64.3	$125.5	$180.0	$233.7	267.4
Market value of traded stocks	$388	$753	$844	$927	$1,128
Percentage held by major institutions	17%	17%	21%	25%	24%

[a]Excludes holdings of stock in insurance companies.
[b]Includes open-end companies only.
Sources: Securities and Exchange Commission, *Statistical Bulletin,* and sources cited in Chapters 3 to 7.

studied, the table also includes closed end investment companies, foundations, and educational endowments. At the end of 1978, all institutions together held 24 percent of the value of stocks outstanding. If holdings of personal and common trust funds (generally under control of banks) are added, the percentage rises to 30 percent.

Private noninsured pension funds continue to be the largest, although perhaps a reluctant institutional holder of common stocks. At the end of 1978, their holdings constituted more than 39 percent of the holdings of all institutions. Investment companies, normally heavy purchasers of stocks, were slowed in the

1970s because of the large number of redemptions. The drop in the asset values of these two largest institutions in 1974 over 1972 also reflected the sharp market drop in 1974.

Perhaps the most significant change revealed in the table is the substantial funds committed to corporate stocks by insurance companies—both life and property—and state and local retirement funds in the 1970s. This again reflects the relaxation of laws regarding investment by life companies in stocks and the general stress on performance and capital gains by insurance companies in their portfolio management policies.

The steady shift in stock ownership, as measured by dollar amount, to institutions reflects not only the growth of savings held by them, but also their interest in common stocks as investments in a growing and inflationary economy, although the experience in the 1970s caused many to question this emphasis. The relative decline in individuals' holdings has been accelerated by the big breaks in stock prices and the general market sluggishness since 1965 and especially in 1973 and 1974. As before, however, the net holdings of corporate stocks by individuals have continued to rise over the long run with the modest secular rise in stock prices.

The percentage of stocks held by the institutions we have studied (Table 11-5) was 20 percent at the end of 1978. Although the totals and percentage exclude bank-administered trusts, closed-end investment companies, nonprofit corporations, and minor institutions, the leveling in institutional ownership is apparent.

Stock Trading and Institutional Activity

The market value of stocks (preferred and common) traded on all registered exchanges totaled $250 billion in 1978, and the total number of shares traded during 1978 rose to $9.4 billion from $7.0 billion in 1977.

According to the Securities and Exchange Commission, purchases and sales of four institutional groups—private noninsured pension funds, open-end investment companies, life insurance companies, and property and casualty companies—reached all-time record levels, totaling $99.7 billion in 1972, but declining to $51.5 billion in 1974 and to $70.6 billion in 1977. The 1977 total was equal to nearly 36 percent of the volume of trading on all registered exchanges.[4]

The New York Stock Exchange has measured the role played by institutions in stock market activity for several short test periods. The broad list covers all major and minor institutions, including nonmember broker-dealers. In the last test period institutions accounted for 54.7 percent of all trading activity on the Big Board.[5]

---

[4] Securities and Exchange Commission, *Statistical Bulletin*. Not all trades were in listed stocks.

[5] New York Stock Exchange, *Fact Book*, 1978.

Combining the ownership of securities with the trading activity produces the portfolio turnover ratio for institutions.[6] The turnover rate has moderated in recent years for all institutions. Turnover reached 45 percent for mutual funds in 1972, declining to 32 percent in 1977. The rate for private pension funds in 1977 was 17 percent, life insurance companies 20 percent, and property and casualty insurance companies 22 percent, in contrast to the rate for all New York Stock Exchange stocks of 25 percent.[7] The turnover rate for pension funds and insurance companies should be relatively low because of their long-term commitments for their liabilities and assets.

Yields and Rates of Return on Stocks

Preferred Stock

The yields on preferred stocks as a whole rise and fall with the general level of interest rates. The return on individual issues reflects the market estimate of their quality and marketability and any special features such as convertibility.

Dividends on preferred stocks are a distribution of profits and are contingent upon earnings and declaration of the dividend. Preferred dividends may not be paid in a given year even though earnings are sufficient to cover them. On other occasions, preferred dividends have been paid when the firm is operating at a loss. As most investors tend to view a preferred dividend as an implied contractual agreement, failure by the firm to declare and pay preferred dividends, when due, generally implies that the firm is in serious financial condition.

The yields on high-grade bonds and preferred stocks are shown in Figure 11-1. As revealed by the data, the yields on long-term bonds have exceeded those on preferred stocks since 1963. Preferred rates have risen since the 1960s to more or less match the higher interest rates. The negative spreads reflect the shortage of new preferred issues, the increase in the safety of preferreds, the conversion feature on several preferred issues, and, most important, the special demand by institutional investors subject to income taxation who enjoy an exemption of 85 percent of the dividend received. Other things equal, the after-tax return on the dividend received by a corporation is greater than the same interest received on a high-grade taxable bond. In fact, some high-grade preferred stocks have yields lower than the yields on the bonds of the same company. In this case, it would not be advisable for an individual to hold the preferred stock rather than the bond unless the preferred has a conversion feature, or the probabilities of calling the preferred at a substantial premium are high.

---

[6]The activity rate is the average of purchases and sales divided by the average value of stock portfolio for the period.

[7]Securities and Exchange Commission, *Statistical Bulletin* (April, 1978).

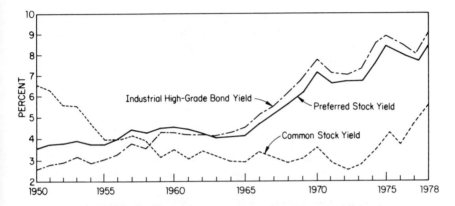

Figure 11-1. Interest and Dividend Yields on High-Grade Industrial
Bonds, Preferred Stocks, and Common Stocks, 1950-1978
Sources: *Moody's Bond Survey, Stock Survey,* and *Moody's Industrials.* For data, see
Appendix, Table A-4.

The figure shows the stability in yields and interest rates from 1955 through
1965. Since then, rates have generally risen to historic levels, with preferred and
corporate bonds yielding above 9 and 10 percent, respectively, in October 1979
in response to inflation and Federal Reserve policy.

Common Stock

The returns on common stocks are different from contractual-type securities
like bonds and preferreds in that their return is theoretically unlimited. The
common shareholder receives not only the dividend declared from residual earnings, if any, but also enjoys potential capital appreciation in the value of the
stock as a result of favorable reinvestment of funds that were obtained either
from borrowed sources or from retained earnings. As common stock ownership
is riskier than bonds or preferred stocks, its expected and realized return, including dividend plus capital appreciation, should be higher than senior security
instruments offering a more certain return.

Historically, *total* rates of return on common stocks have been around 9 to
10 percent per year, with about 60 percent representing dividend yield and 40
percent coming from capital appreciation. The famous study by Lorie and
Fisher, for instance, showed that ignoring taxes and assuming dividend reinvestment, the average rate of return on all stocks listed on the NYSE from January
1926 through December 1965 was 9.3 percent compounded annually.[8] Other
evidence has corroborated the long-run average return on common stocks of

---

[8] J. Lorie and L. Fisher, "Rates of Return on Common Stocks," *Journal of Business,*
January 1964.

about 9 percent annually.[9] Moreover, since stock price levels have risen little or in some cases have declined from 1965 through 1978, long-term rates calculated including these years would be considerably less than the 9.3 percent noted above. Thus, it is not surprising that, with little capital appreciation, the investor is demanding a higher dividend return which comes with declining prices and increasing dividend payments, as in 1974 and 1978.

The return on corporate stocks for any given year, however, can be large and highly variable. Yearly increases in average stock prices exceeding 20 percent are not uncommon when stocks are on the rebound from previous lows; a drop of 15 to 20 percent in a bear market is also quite possible. Nevertheless, as stocks should be considered long-term investments, it is the overall long-term rate that is of prime concern.

Lorie also noted that longer-term rates (ten to fifteen years) were abnormally high after World War II, when the average rate of return on stocks was 12.6 percent.[10] The abnormally high yield in the postwar period was achieved at a time when many foreign countries lacked productive capacity, inflation was low, raw materials were plentiful, and domestic demand was strong—a combination of factors not often duplicated. In any event, total rates of return on common stock over long periods have been around 9 percent annually, and a total return of over 12 percent for an extended time period would be abnormally high.

Conversely, the average total rate of return on common stocks, including both dividend and price appreciation (which was nonexistent), since the early 1960s has been slightly more than 4 percent per year. By any standard of comparison with past performance, this return has to be considered abnormally low. Just how devastating the stock price performance has been is revealed in Figure 11-2. The figure shows the general decline for the Dow Jones average of 30 industrial stocks, since 1965.[11] If the "normal" appreciation in stock prices of about 4 percent per year had continued through 1978, assuming 1965 to be normal, the Dow Jones Industrial average would have been close to 1,575 instead of the actual 815 in October 1979.

Furthermore, the poor performance in stock prices in the 1970s was unusual in light of improved corporate earnings. Stocks sold at their lowest price–earnings ratios in twenty years—many as low as 3 or 4 to 1—throughout much of this period and in mid-1979, despite some improvement in stock market prices, the Dow Jones 30 Industrials still stood at less than eight times current earnings. Thus, in the 1970s amid high inflation, common stocks had lost their value as an inflation hedge, except possibly over the very long run.

Reasons for the general weakness in stock prices in the 1970s include

---

[9] J. Lorie and M. Hamilton, *The Stock Market: Theories and Evidence* (Homewood, Ill.: Richard D. Irwin, Inc. 1973), p. 31.

[10] Ibid., p. 36.

[11] The authors are indebted to Arnold Bernhard and Company Incorporated, publishers of *The Value Line Investment Survey* for preparing the chart.

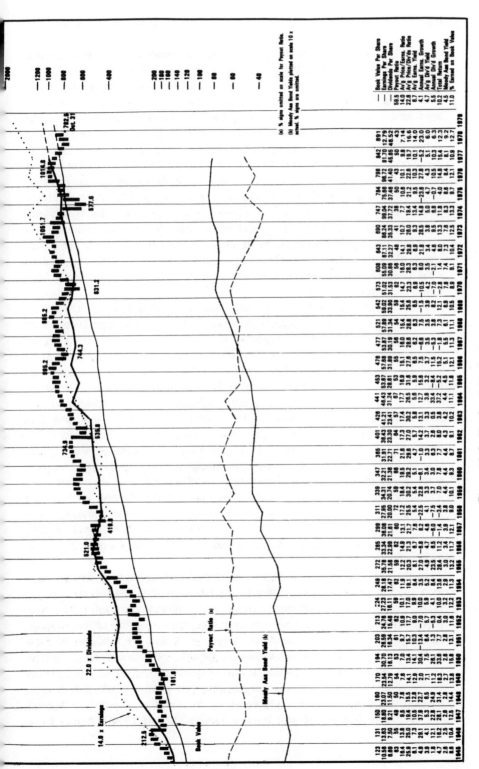

Figure 11–2. The Stock Market Record

continuing inflation, the oil-energy crisis, the high yields available on competing fixed-income investments, the expectations of corporate earnings, particularly during the economic recessions, and the weakness of the dollar in world markets.

The data in Figures 11-1 and 11-2 show that the dividend payout ratio has been generally less than 50 percent in the 1970s and the yield on common stocks was more than 4 percentage points below the yields on high-grade bonds in late 1978. This inverse gap implied that the expected capital appreciation on the average common stock had to be considerably above 4 percent per year to make common stock investment preferred over bonds for the average investor. Since the average spread between the total return on common stock and high-grade bonds has been on the order of about 5 percentage points; that is, dividend yield plus price appreciation amounting to about 9.3 percent annually has exceeded long-term, high-grade bond yields of around 4.3 percent, and with high-grade bonds yielding (1978) 9.5 percent, stocks should be expected to yield near 13 percent for historic differentials to hold—an abnormally high return for common stocks.

Another rule frequently used is that, because of risk differences, the overall rate of return on common stock should be twice the rate on high-grade corporate bonds, which would place the expected annual yield on corporate stocks in the high teens—an unlikely prospect. Nevertheless, the conclusion follows that, if the historical differential (at 5 percent) in total return on common stocks over bonds is to be maintained at present levels of interest, stocks should show abnormally high returns as a result of either substantial capital appreciation or a high dividend yield. Otherwise, if this prospect is doubtful, then investors should prefer high-yielding bonds and other investments. In the period 1965–1978, there was little secular capital appreciation in common stock prices (Figure 11-2). It follows that if common stocks are to equal the yield on high-grade bonds plus an additional increment to offset inflation, they must offer unusually high dividend yields. Although many stocks of good quality were yielding 7 to 8 percent or more in 1978, the average yield on all common stocks was less than 5½ percent, and hence it would be difficult to conclude that, based on returns available on competing instruments, common stocks are grossly undervalued.

In the 1970s, several other factors developed that do not bode well for common stock investment. First, three of the fastest-growing institutions—pension funds, state and local retirement funds, and insurance companies—who have previously invested in stocks are now examining the advisability of this stragegy. Although the long-term value of corporate stock and the liabilities of these institutions make common stocks natural acquisitions from a hedging concept, the more important consideration is one of stable income. Given the volatility of common stock returns, it is questionable that pension fund or retirement monies should be placed in anything where the return is so uncertain. Second, the Employee Retirement and Income Security Act of 1974 (Chapter 6) required prudence in investments and many have interpreted this to mean fewer—not more—holdings in common stocks, because the goal of retirement funds should be a high but stable income, which can be better achieved through investment in bonds and mortgages of all types. Third, the contractural nature of debt, and the tax deductibility of interest payments, make these securities the preferred issues by buyers and sellers alike. Furthermore, some view new debt issues as being "priced to sell," in that the interest rate is set high enough to ensure investor acceptance.

Finally, the double taxation of dividends, the capital gains tax, flotation costs, and delays in approval of a stock issue cause investors and management to currently favor other forms of supplying (or obtaining) funds. The indexing of capital gains for changes in inflation or elimination of the capital gains tax (Japan, France, and Germany have no capital gains tax) could help renew investor interest in common stocks.

```
12121212121212121212121212121212121212121212121212121212121212121212121212121212
12121212121212121212121212121212121212121212121212121212121212121212121212121212
1212121212121212121212121212121    12121     121     121     1212121212121212121212121212
12121212121212121212121212121212     212     2121     121     1212121212121212121212121212
1212121212121212121212121212121    1     12121     121     1212121212121212121212121212
12121212121212121212121212121212         212121     121     1212121212121212121212121212
1212121212121212121212121212121    1212121     121     1212121212121212121212121212
12121212121212121212121212121212         212121     121     1212121212121212121212121212
1212121212121212121212121212121    1     12121     121     1212121212121212121212121212
12121212121212121212121212121212     212     2121     121     1212121212121212121212121212
1212121212121212121212121212121    12121     121     121     1212121212121212121212121212
12121212121212121212121212121212121212121212121212121212121212121212121212121212
12121212121212121212121212121212121212121212121212121212121212121212121212121212
```

The Mortgage Market

Basic Characteristics

A mortgage is a lien on real property to secure a loan. The mortgage and the actual note evidencing the debt are different instruments, but we shall use the term *mortgage* to represent the combination. Corporate bonds secured by pledge of fixed assets and chattel mortgages secured by personal property and business equipment are excluded from our discussion; however, some secured business loans are included in the commercial mortgage category. Mortgages are almost exclusively capital-market instruments in that their maturity may run from five to forty years. Consistent with the hedging principle, proceeds obtained from mortgage commitments are normally used to finance long-term capital assets.

Mortgages appeal to investors because the tangible assets that are pledged as security can be inspected and permanently attached to the land and are of substantial importance to the borrower. Furthermore, yields on mortgages are frequently higher than those on other fixed-income securities of similar maturity. This refelcts the specialized nature of mortgages, their lesser marketability compared with that of bonds and stocks, and the delays involved in foreclosure and final settlement in the event of failure.

Traditionally, most mortgages require the borrower to amortize the principal by remitting a uniform periodic sum covering principal and interest. The shift to amortized loans followed the adoption by the Home Owners' Loan Corporation and by savings and loan associations after the shortcomings of single-principal-payment loans became apparent in the depression of the 1930s. Amortization was also required by the Federal Housing Administration for insured loans (1934) and by the Veterans Administration for guaranteed loans (1944). In the 1970s, as construction costs and high interest rates made payments on amortized loans larger and more difficult for some, several older as well as new types of mortgage payment schemes grew in importance. Among these were (1) interest-only mortgages for a specified period before any principal reduction, (2) graduated payment mortgages where payments increase as ability to pay increases, and (3) reverse mortgages where monies are received by the owner and eventually paid off out of the equity of the home upon sale.

More recently, many financial institutions have been offering variable-rate mortgages where the interest rate is adjusted periodically, if necessary, to reflect existing interest-rate levels. Savings and loan associations favor these mortgages, since it places them in a much better hedged and lower-risk position. Moreover, variable rates allow S&Ls to pay higher rates on time deposits, as long as they can pass the cost to the consumer, and thus allow them to continue to attract funds during tight money periods.

Other characteristics of the modern mortgage are lower down payments, higher loan-to-value ratios, and lengthening of final maturity to more than forty years on some liens. Periodic repayment (often monthly), along with rising home values, provide a turnover of investors' funds and a steady growth in the owner's equity, reducing some of the loan risk from this combination of features. The modern mortgage has had a tremendous impact on the real estate market, especially on home ownership, and has been partly responsible for the diversion of savings into real estate financing through the expansion of institutions serving this market.

Types

In addition to differences in size, risk, geographical origin, and payment scheme, mortgages can be classified in a number of other ways.

1. By type of property pledged:
   Farms
   1-4-family residences
   Multifamily dwellings (apartments)
   Commercial and industrial property
2. By level of lien:
   First mortgages
   Junior mortgages (second, third)
3. By type of lien:
   Conventional
   Government-supported: FHA-insured, VA-guaranteed
4. By use of property:
   Owner-occupied: residential, commercial, industrial
   Rental: residential, commercial, industrial

5. By type of borrower:
   Consumers–Farmer
   Corporations
   Partnerships
   Single proprietorships
6. By purpose:
   New construction
   Acquisition of existing property
   General financing
7. By type of lender:
   Financial institutions
   Governmental agencies
   Individuals

Size and Growth

Table 1-2 showed that, of all debt instruments, mortgages have had the greatest expansion in the postwar period. Since 1970, the net annual increase in the amount outstanding—the flow of funds into mortgages—has averaged about $70 billion a year and at the end of 1978 was running at the rate of about $125 billion annually. Mortgages outstanding at the end of 1978 totaled $1,172 billion. With about 8 percent of total mortgage debt retired yearly, this means that the amount of new mortgage debt written was over $200 billion at an annual rate at the end of 1978.

Table 12-1 shows the mortgage debt outstanding at the end of selected years

TABLE 12-1. Mortgage Debt Outstanding, at Year End, 1965–1978
(billions of dollars)

	1965	1970	1975	1978
Farm	$ 21.2	$ 29.8	$ 50.9	$ 76.0
Residential				
1–4-family	220.5	297.7	490.8	761.9
Multifamily	38.2	60.1	100.6	122.0
	$258.7	$357.8	$591.4	$ 883.9
Commercial and industrial	55.5	85.5	159.3	212.6
Total	$335.3	$473.1	$801.5	$1,172.5
Conventional	$254.1	$363.9	$654.5	$ 996.1
FHA-insured	50.1	71.9	} 147.0	} 176.4
VA-guaranteed	31.1	37.3		
Total	$335.3	$473.1	$801.5	$1,172.5

Sources: *Federal Reserve Bulletin;* National Association of Mutual Savings Banks, *National Fact Book of Mutual Savings Banking* (New York, annual); Federal Reserve *Flow-of-Funds Accounts.*

in the postwar period, classified by major types of property pledged and by major types of liens.

Farm Mortgages

Farm mortgage debt grew somewhat less than total mortgages in the early 1970s. This was explained in part by (1) large amounts of personal property financing by farmers on equipment purchases in lieu of mortgage financing, (2) a tendency for farms to sell less often than single-family homes, (3) the general decline in farm population, (4) less-developed financial markets in rural areas, and (5) substantial down payments by farmers on large purchases as a result of good crop years in 1972 and 1973. In the late 1970s, farm mortgages increased substantially as poor crop years, new land purchases, and higher operating costs, including land, forced farmers to seek additional financing. Growth in financial institutions serving rural areas was also a contributing factor.

Farm mortgage debt is typically first-mortgage debt financed by conventional means. Only a small portion is FHA- or VA-supported; it is, however, often guaranteed or supplied by other special agencies. This debt is incurred mainly for financing property, although the proceeds are sometimes used for general purposes.

Commercial banks and life insurance companies historically have been the largest suppliers of farm mortgages; however, in recent years, there has been a steady drift toward financing by governmental agencies such as the Federal Land Banks, which make long-term loans through National Farm Loan Associations, and the Farmers Home Administration, which makes one- to five-year operating loans and farm-ownership loans (see Table 12-5). At the end of 1978, commercial banks and life insurance companies together held $19.4 billion, or 26 percent of all outstanding farm mortgages, down from 35 percent in 1968. On the other hand, federally sponsored credit agencies and Federal budget agencies together held $29.4 billion, or 39 percent, in 1978, which was up from 18 percent of the amount outstanding in 1968. Individuals and others, including real estate trusts, held $27.1 billion, or 36 percent of the total. Many of the holdings by individuals are a result of second contracts on sale of properties where the seller carried back some of the financing for the purchaser.

Home Loans

Home mortgages (on one- to four-family homes) constitute the largest single category of mortgages. Loans secured by one- to four-family dwellings amounted to 65 percent of total mortgages outstanding at the end of 1978. This was down from 70 percent in 1960 but up from 60 percent in 1973. The relative decline in home mortgages in the 1960s was a result of sharply increased financing of multifamily and commercial properties as well as the increased difficulty individuals experienced in securing mortgages at interest rates they were willing to pay and in sufficient amounts that they were qualified to handle. The rebound in single-family housing in the 1970s occurred as a result of decreased multifamily housing because of overbuilding, high costs, and the rapid increase in new family formations.

Net home mortgage financing (new financing less repayments) has increased every year since World War II and now averages about $100 billion a year, although the latter amount is quite variable from year to year.[1] This substantial growth reflects both the demand for housing and the availability of mortgage financing from institutions and the federal government. Populations, consumer incomes, and construction costs all rose during the postwar period, as did the supply of funds available to savings associations and other financial institutions. The result has been a tremendous overall increase in home construction and financing in the postwar era, even though the amount of construction often varies sharply from year to year as a function of interest rates, costs, and the state of the economy. As shown below, the major cause of increased mortgage debt has been the higher construction costs rather than a sharp increase in housing starts.

Housing Starts

The data in Table 12-2 reveal the dominance of single-family housing in residential construction, the variability in total starts from year to year, and the total dollar value of private residential construction activity. Housing starts rose to an all-time high in 1972 of 2,345,000 units as interest rates declined from previous highs in 1970 and mortgage funds were plentiful. Housing starts were only 1,160,000 units in 1975 as high interest rates, energy concerns, and a recession cut demand for new housing. They recovered nicely, however, in 1976-1977 and ended 1978 at over 2 million units for the first time in six years. Higher interest rates in 1979 again resulted in a decline in housing starts.

The wide fluctuations in housing starts from year to year are often caused by the double-barreled effect of monetary policy. When money is tight and interest rates are high, individuals resist paying the higher rates and cut demand. At the same time, savings associations are discouraging new loans as they are experiencing, or are at least fearful of, disintermediation. Consequently, people are not buying homes, and savings associations are not encouraging them to do so. The opposite effect occurs in periods of easy money.

Duplexes and attached single-family housing (condominiums), although still

---

[1]To show farm mortgage debt as separate from residential debt is not quite accurate, as the total of the former in Table 12-1 includes some mortgages incurred for residential purposes.

TABLE 12-2. Housing Starts and Residential Construction Activity, 1960-1978

	1960	1965	1970	1975	1978
Housing starts (000's)					
Private	1,252	1,473	1,434	1,160	2,019
Public	44	37	35	11	3
Total	1,296	1,510	1,469	1,171	2,022
Number of family units (000's)					
1-family	1,009	965	815	896	1,433
2-family and more	287	545	654	275	589
Total	1,296	1,510	1,469	1,171	2,022
Mobile home shipments (000's)	103	216	401	213	276
Private residential construction activity, excluding mobile homes (billions of dollars)	$22.5	$27.9	$31.9	$93.6	$92.7

Sources: *Federal Reserve Bulletin;* United States League of Savings Associations, *Savings and Loan Fact Book* (Chicago, annual); U.S. Department of Commerce, Bureau of the Census, *Construction Reports, Series C20, C30.*

accounting for a minority of total private housing starts, have recorded increases in recent years. This has been caused by (1) sharply higher land costs, making high-density housing more economically feasible; (2) demographic and life-style changes, revealing a preference for smaller families and recreation-type living; and (3) higher costs of home construction.

The figures for housing starts do not include mobile home shipments, as they are frequently considered personal property rather than real estate. If mobile home shipments are included, total units started (or shipped) would have amounted to 2,625,000 for 1973, with mobile homes accounting for 580,000 units, or 22 percent of the total. Since then, through 1978, annual mobile home shipments have been cut by almost 50 percent.

Types of Mortgage Liens

The three nonfarm basic home mortgage loans are conventional loans with or without insurance or guarantee, those insured by the Federal Housing Administration, and those guaranteed by the Veterans Administration. Table 12-1 shows the amounts outstanding at the end of selected years. Except in default cases, where insurance or guarantee funds are used to pay off the mortgage holder, and in a few isolated programs, the FHA and VA do not generally supply funds to the market. They only insure or guarantee the mortgages and supply funds in case of default. Hence, the figures for FHA and VA loans in Table 12-1 represent the amount of mortgages issued with the applicable guarantee.

Conventional loans have consistently been the most important category, approximating 85 percent of total new financing in recent years. This is up from

70 percent only a few years earlier as the influx of abundant private funds into the mortgage market and the general disenchantment with the loan procedures of FHA and VA insured loans pushed conventional mortgages to record levels.

Although representing only about 6 percent of the total mortgage debt financing, FHA-insured mortgage loans have increased steadily in the postwar period at a growth rate comparable to that of conventional financing. At the end of 1978, outstanding FHA guaranteed mortgages totaled about $100 billion.

Programs under FHA auspices receive different emphasis, depending upon political, economic factors, and an assessment of current housing needs.

Federal Government Housing Assistance

Since the National Housing Act of 1934 and as subsequently amended and added to, the federal government has been a significant force in the housing market. Although it is not the purpose of this book to cover in detail the multiplicity of programs, several of them deserve mention because of their size and activity.

Under the Housing and Community Development Act of 1974, the Community Development Block Grants program was formed. The "block" grants to local governments are a more flexible program and replace many of the previous programs that were separately funded, such as model cities, urban renewal, neighborhood development grants, rehabilitation loans, and urban beautification. The current program allows spending priorities to be determined at the local level within broad guidelines established by law and under the supervision of the Housing and Urban Development agency. The grants are to be used primarily to provide adequate housing and expanded job opportunities for lower-income groups and for rehabilitation of downtown areas.

Section 203 of the act provides insurance of mortgages to commercial lenders on loans to finance new and existing dwellings if they are first-mortgage amortized loans bearing a maximum nominal interest rate of 10 percent (July 1979), with the mortgagor paying an additional 0.5 percent to the FHA mutual insurance fund as an insurance premium. Maximum maturities range up to thirty years, with maximum loan-value ratios as high as 97 percent. Section 203 has been the standard financing arrangement for the one- to four-family program, which accounts for the bulk of FHA financing.

Section 207 provides for mortgage insurance for the construction and/or rehabilitation of multifamily units as well as for mobile home parks. Section 221 [especially 221(d)(4)] insures mortgages of multifamily projects designed for low- to moderate-income families. The foregoing programs are considered nonsubsidized in that the interest rate paid can be up to the maximum rate listed above and no special payments are otherwise made to tenants or owners.

There are also several subsidized housing programs established by the National Housing Act. Some of them include such benefits as rent supplement payments, interest-free loans to nonprofit corporations, and below-market interest rates (BMIR) for construction of multifamily housing projects. Two presently active programs are established under sections 235 and 236. Section 235 provides for an FHA interest subsidy to low-income families that essentially reduces the monthly payments of the mortgagor on a single-family home. Section 236 is the multifamily counterpart to section 235 and provides interest subsidy to the owner or investor who rents to low-income families at a reduced rate. Section 8 (Housing Act of 1937) provides for a rent subsidy to lower-income families. An eligible tenant need not pay any more than 25 percent of adjusted gross income for rent. HUD makes up the difference between what a tenant can afford and the fair market rental for the housing unit.

The Farmers Home Administration (FmHA), an agency of the Department of Agriculture, generally supplies credit, insures loans, and makes grants for rural housing programs. Under one program—similar to HUD's 235 program—borrowers/contractors may receive reduced interest rates to as low as 1 percent for rent reductions to qualified tenants. In another program FmHA provides insurance guarantees to lenders who make private mortgage funds available to farmers for housing.

The federal government has also directly and indirectly influenced the interest rate on mortgages. This has usually been accomplished through the setting of maximum rates on government-insured loans or through supplying funds to the market, especially in tight money periods. Historically, the FHA has set maximum rates that may be charged by lenders on nonsubsidized loans insured by the FHA. Typically, the maximum rate is below the going market rate, but it is raised occasionally, or lowered, depending upon the competitive position with respect to yields on conventional mortgages and long-term bonds (Table 12-6). In recent years, FHA-insured loans have been heavily discounted to reflect the going market rates. Thus, the homeowner, while receiving a lower interest rate through FHA financing, found that the lender was charging him a higher loan fee than on a conventional loan to make up the difference. The FHA has worked to eliminate these discount "points" by taking a more flexible position on interest-rate ceilings. Accordingly, recent legislation was introduced to remove all interest-rate ceilings on FHA and VA loans and let these rates move with market levels.

The nominal rate on FHA/VA single-family home loans was raised to a maximum of 11½ percent (11 percent on apartment loans) in October 1979, reflecting the high level of interest rates. But even then the rate failed to match market yields, which were 12 percent and higher, at that time.

Until 1969, FHA-insured loans could be purchased by qualified institutions only. Individual investors became eligible in that year, but their demand has not been substantial. The chief market for FHA-insured loans is the Federal National Mortgage Association (FNMA) and, more recently, the Federal Home Loan Mortgage Corporation (HLMC). In 1978, the association committed funds to their purchase at the annual rate of $18.9 billion, while the FHLMC committed $7.4 billion.

With their controlled appraisals, stated credit standards, and amortized terms, FHA loans have had an important impact on the standardization of lending practices. They have been chiefly responsible for the acceptance of high loan-to-value ratios and longer-term loans of up to forty years in some cases.

The Serviceman's Readjustment Act of 1944, commonly called the "GI Bill of Rights," as amended, provides for the guarantee by the Veterans Administration of institutional loans for the financing of veterans' homes, farms, and businesses. The maximum maturity of home loans is 30 years except for farm home loans, which is 40 years.

Yield rates on VA loans approximate those on FHA loans and therefore suffer the same consequences. VA loan rates were often unattractive to lenders relative to those on other mortgages and bonds, and consequently they sold at substantial discounts. VA loans with their 100 percent loan-to-value ratio and guarantee by the Veterans Administration (to $25,000 or 60 percent of the amount of the loan, whichever is less) are attractive to some institutions. The value of new recordings (Table 12-1) and the total amount of outstanding VA mortgages increased sharply in 1976-1978 as the number of eligible veterans and increased loan limits encouraged more applications.

Junior Mortgages

Much obscurity surrounds the amount and use of secondary financing arrangements, primarily because they are held by individuals and institutions that do not report these figures separately. Nevertheless, the amount of secondary financing is probably over $50 billion at the end of 1978. The revival of secondary financing is an interesting feature of the mortgage market and reflects the great postwar demand for housing and commercial properties that have required many buyers to request, and sellers to accept, a junior lien to bridge the gap between the existing balance on a conventional first mortgage plus the equity down payment and the selling price of the property. High interest rates on new loans make it even more important for a purchaser to secure some secondary financing and assume the first mortgage if it has a low interest rate and is assumable.

The use of junior mortgage financing (known as "equity loans") for home purchases has also increased in recent years as purchasers assume existing mortgages to minimize closing costs as well as to receive a lower interest rate than the current market level. Many mortgages written with institutions, however, now contain provisions that any loan assumption must receive prior approval from the lender. At time of sale, the lender may raise the interest rate to the market level.

Second mortgage financing, called "gap" financing, has grown in importance in multifamily and commercial properties. When the down payment on the purchase of an apartment or other similar property is insufficient to clear the seller's equity—the difference between the sales price and the existing total mortgage balance—a "gap" exists. Some lenders specialize in providing this special second mortgage type of financing to fill the gap. This financing might take the form of a straight second mortgage or a "wraparound" mortgage, in which an institution writes a new loan for the entire amount of outstanding debt, including the first mortgage, with the institution making payment on the first mortgage. In any event the marginal interest rate on the gap financing is customarily around 13 to 15 percent and higher.

The modern second mortgage often requires rapid amortization of principal or matures ("balloons") over a period seldom longer than five years. Steady repayment of principal, along with that of the senior mortgage, builds an increasing equity. However, subordination to the first lien often requires a high yield, ranging from 11 to 15 percent.

The seller who is willing to accept a second or "equity" lien can retain it or, in some cases, sell it to a permanent holder through local mortgage brokers and dealers, who discount the principal balance anywhere from 10 to 40 percent, depending upon riskiness, time to maturity, amount, and interest rate on the loan. Such loans are likely to be used most frequently in periods of tight money (such as 1974, 1978, and 1979) when adequate senior financing is limited and expensive. They are also often used for general fund-raising purposes when the property already supports a first lien.

Because many large institutions are prohibited or dislike holding junior mortgages, individuals and specialized real estate firms are the chief investors in such loans. Banks, however, have recently entered the field in substantial amounts.

Multifamily (Apartment) Loans

Loans secured by multifamily dwellings grew substantially in the early 1970s but declined in later years and accounted for less than 15 percent of all residential loans outstanding in 1978. The rise in land values, high interest rates, low rents relative to costs, and an abundance of vacant units discouraged greater construction of apartments. The number of private nonfarm housing starts other than one-family residences decreased from 1,069,000 in 1972 to less than 600,000 in 1978.

In the late 1970s, construction of new apartments complexes was generally limited to particular groups, such as low-income or old-age, and where subsidy funds could be obtained from government sources. Also contributing to the general decline in apartment construction was the strong demand by individuals for single-family homes.

Multifamily loans are held primarily by savings and loan associations, mutual savings banks, life insurance companies, and commercial banks (Table 12–5). Many loans are obtained in the national market either by direct representatives of the investors or through the efforts of local mortgage correspondents. As in the case of commercial and industrial loans, institutional investors, especially life insurance companies, have developed a preference for large mortgages on income properties and those that provide some equity participation.

Commercial and Industrial Mortgages

Loans secured by business property (other than apartments) are highly specialized instruments, mainly in amortized conventional form, with final maturities ranging from ten to thirty years. Such mortgages constituted 18 percent of total mortgage debt outstanding at the end of 1978. They are incurred by builders and developers for construction purposes and by business firms for general financing. This latter category of commercial loans has been a prime factor in the rapid growth of commercial mortgages as firms have sought financing from all sources in a relatively tight money market coupled with high interest rates. In addition, many commercial mortgage loans are classed as term loans by banks and insurance companies and are excluded from the regular mortgage category, as are mortgage bond issues issued by corporations.

Industrial mortgages to finance the construction and acquisition of manufacturing properties are frequently amortized within a period as short as ten years because of their special risks. Recent years have seen longer amortization periods in order to reduce payments caused by increased interest rates.

Loans on retail shopping centers, department stores, and warehouses are often secured by property leased to large national tenants. Such mortgages are in effect two-name paper. Usually, leased properties must also be amortized within the initial lease period. Yields on the best of these approximate the yields on good-grade corporate bonds. Many residential construction loans that will eventually be refinanced on a permanent basis are classed as commercial until taken out by the original or ultimate investor. Thus, this category is not completely distinguishable from that of residential liens.

The Primary Mortgage Market

In Chapters 3 to 7, the role of the major institutions in supplying funds to the primary mortgage market was discussed. The primary mortgage market refers to the origination of mortgages, which involves the creation of the mortgage instruments and the funds for direct borrowers. In contrast, the secondary mortgage market pertains to the mechanism for transferring existing mortgages from one group to another.

The demand for mortgage financing follows the housing cycle, which has had in the postwar period a longer swing than the general business cycle. When peaks and valleys coincide either with the general cycle or with ease and tightness of capital (such as in 1969 and 1974), marked variations appear in housing starts, construction volume, and mortgage financing. A greater variation might have taken place except for the large use of long-term federally supported programs and loans, which are often used in a countercyclical fashion.

The data in Table 12-3 show the annual changes in the major categories of outstanding mortgage loans from 1970 through 1978. As noted previously, the volatility of the net flow of funds into mortgages results from variation in the amount of construction and capital-market conditions. The late 1960s were characterized by smaller increases in farm mortgages and by the gradual growth in nonfarm residential and commercial mortgages. The early 1970s witnessed continuing moderate farm mortgage financing, but sharply higher mortgage financing in nonfarm and commercial properties, which was almost double the average net additions in the 1965 to 1969 period. Again, the plentiful funds from all institutions, federal programs, a large number of new household formations, and tax benefits from real estate ownership all contributed to the rapid growth in the 1970s. In the late 1970s and for reasons noted earlier, funds allocated to farm and single-family mortgages advanced sharply while those for multifamily and commercial, although increasing in absolute amounts, declined relative to the others.

Annual Changes in Owners' Shares

Table 12-4 shows the annual amounts of funds supplied to the market by the major investors from 1970 through 1978. The factors influencing the annual flows were discussed in Chapters 3 to 7, and are briefly summarized here.

The large increases in funds placed in mortgages in 1971-1973 by commercial banks, mutual savings banks, and savings and loan associations were a direct result of the large savings inflows experienced by these institutions during the same period. Commercial bank lending in real estate was primarily in short-term construction loans. The total flow of funds, largely into savings accounts, is an important determinant in the availability of mortgage funds. Hence, during tight money periods, as in 1973, 1974, and 1979, net mortgage loans are likely to diminish or only modestly increase as higher rates on competing investments are favored investments. The unprecedented flows of funds to depository institutions of all types in the late 1970s resulted in substantial commitments to the mortgage market. Foremost among the institutions were savings and loan associations, which placed most of their funds into single-family homes and commercial banks, which divided their funds between commercial properties and single-family housing.

Although mortgages represent the primary investments for mutual savings banks and savings and loan associations, they are relatively less important to commercial banks. Furthermore, commercial banks may add to mortgage hold-

TABLE 12-3. Annual Changes in Mortgages, 1970–1978 (billions of dollars)

	1970	1971	1972	1973	1974	1975	1976	1977	1978
Farm	$ 0.8	$ 2.4	$ 3.6	$ 5.5	$ 5.0	$ 4.6	$ 6.1	$ 8.8	$ 10.3
1–4-family	15.0	30.6	43.8	44.9	33.3	41.4	65.4	99.5	102.3
Multifamily and commercial	14.1	19.6	29.6	29.5	22.0	11.2	15.6	25.7	33.3
Total	$29.9	$52.6	$77.0	$79.9	$60.2	$57.2	$87.1	$134.0	$145.9

Sources: *Federal Reserve Bulletin; Federal Reserve Flow-of-Funds Accounts.*

TABLE 12-4. Annual Acquisitions of Mortgages, 1970–1978 (billions of dollars)

	1970	1971	1972	1973	1974	1975	1976	1977	1978
Commercial banks	$ 2.0	$ 9.6	$16.8	$19.6	$12.3	$ 4.1	$13.9	$ 27.3	$ 34.6
Mutual savings banks	1.8	3.9	5.5	5.7	2.2	2.3	4.1	6.5	6.9
Savings and loan associations	9.8	23.8	32.0	26.5	17.6	29.5	45.0	58.2	51.8
Life insurance companies	2.3	1.1	1.5	4.4	4.9	2.9	2.4	5.2	8.2
Private (noninsured) pension funds	–	-0.5	-0.9	-0.4	–	–	–	0.4	0.6
State and local government retirement funds	0.3	0.4	0.2	0.7	0.6	-0.2	0.2	0.5	0.7
Federal agencies	5.7	3.6	3.3	6.5	14.4	11.5	2.1	3.5	11.9
State and local	0.8	1.1	1.4	1.7	2.5	1.6	1.3	0.6	1.0
Real estate investment trusts	1.9	2.3	4.2	5.6	0.2	-4.8	-3.8	-2.4	-1.0
Mortgage pools	1.6	4.8	4.9	3.6	5.8	10.3	15.7	20.5	16.5
Households and others	3.7	2.5	8.1	6.0	–	–	6.2	13.7	14.7
Total	$29.9	$52.6	$77.0	$79.9	$60.5	$57.2	$87.1	$134.0	$145.9

Sources: Citations in schedules, Chapters 3 to 7; Federal Reserve *Flow-of-Funds Accounts.*

ings as additional security for commercial-type loans, or to secure construction loans that have permanent financing elsewhere. Thus, rather than an overt search for mortgages, much of it has been "reaching for security." The fact that many banks sponsored real estate investments trusts that later had financial problems was a contributing factor in the "forced" increase in mortgage holdings.

The generally steady increase in mortgage acquisitions by savings associations was interrupted by the moderating of their fund flows in 1970, 1974, and 1979. However, record inflows in 1976–1978 caused the net increase in mortgages in those years to reach all-time highs. Multifamily mortgages accounted for a substantial part of this expansion in the early 1970s but declined sharply until 1978 (Table 4-9). The rise in interest rates in 1977 and 1978–79 was not accompanied by the usual disintermediation, as relaxed maximum rates under Regulation Q and new deposit instruments allowed savings institutions to compete effectively for consumer savings.

Mutual savings banks' mortgage experience has been similar to that of savings and loan associations, as the two are closely allied. As noted in Chapter 4, however, mutual savings banks have added relatively much more to their holdings of bonds and other nonmortgage instruments because of the favorable returns on these securities compared to mortgages. In 1978, mutual savings banks also experienced fewer deposit withdrawals despite rising interest rates, with the result that net additions to mortgages increased moderately during the year.

Federal agencies of all types have grown in importance in the mortgage market in the 1970s. The role of federal credit agencies has expanded considerably as the Federal National Mortgage Association, and the Federal Home Loan Mortgage Corporation all added significantly to their holdings of mortgages. These latter institutions deal primarily in the secondary market for mortgages (discussed later) and supply liquidity to the mortgage market in general.

Annual increases in holdings by mortgage pools sponsored by the credit agencies have been very significant, reaching over $20 billion in 1977 and more than $16 billion in 1978 (see Table 12–4).

Real estate investment trusts were the newest significant institution in the mortgage market. As noted in Chapter 7, their dramatic growth in the 1970–1973 period was a result of investor acceptance of REITs as a suitable investment, the demand for multifamily housing, and favorable tax benefits available in real estate investments that encouraged borrowing from REITs. Unfortunately, many of the operations of REITs turned out to be ill-conceived and poorly managed such that bankruptcy or sharply curtailed operations resulted. Consequently, investor confidence waned and REITs were forced to liquidate large amounts of mortgages to pay off bank loans or improve liquidity.

Other institutions have contributed minor amounts to mortgages in recent years. Life insurance investment shows the volatility discussed in Chapter 5. In recent years, high-yielding and more marketable corporate bonds have been attractive, and, as a result, mortgages have had less appeal. Table 12-4 indicates that pension funds have been insignificant factors in the mortgage market. However, they have been increasing their purchases of mortgage-backed securities, which are not included in the table to avoid double counting. The acquisitions of individuals in total mortgage holdings increased sharply in 1977 and 1978 due to purchase money mortgages and mortgage backed securities.

Ownership of Mortgages: 1978

Table 12-5 summarizes the ownership pattern of outstanding mortgage debt of all types at the end of 1978. Savings and loan associations held 37 percent of the total, reflecting their increasing share of single-family residential financing and their growing interest in multifamily instruments. Their preference for conventional loans is evident. "Individuals and others" held 13 percent of the total debt, predominantly of the conventional type. Along with Federal Land Banks, they form the chief market for farm loans.

The table shows a degree of specialization on certain types of mortgages for each institution. Life insurance companies, for instance, tend to invest in commercial and multifamily properties rather than single-family homes. This reflects their need to place very large amounts of funds with a minimum of paper work. The opposite holds for mutual savings banks and savings and loan associations, which have shown a preference one-to-four-family homes. Commercial banks have relatively large holdings in both single-family and commercial mortgages.

Federal credit agencies (primarily Federal National Mortgage Association), mutual savings banks, and individuals tend to have relatively large holdings of federally underwritten—FHA and VA—loans. Federally-sponsored mortgage pools are almost exclusively invested in one-to-four family mortgages in either insured or conventional form.

Mortgage Companies

We have previously referred to the special role of mortgage companies as correspondents in originating and servicing loans for institutional investors. They deserve special mention in a discussion of the primary market for mortgages.

Nature and Functions

The modern mortgage company is typically a closely held, private corporation whose principal activity is originating and servicing residential mortgage loans for institutional investors. It is subject to a minimum degree of federal or state supervision, has a comparatively small capital investment relative to its volume of business, and relies largely on commercial bank credit to finance its operations and mortgage inventory.

TABLE 12-5. Ownership of Mortgage Debt, December 31, 1978 (billions of dollars)

	Commercial Banks	Mutual Savings Banks	Savings and Loan Associations	Life Insurance Companies	Federal Agencies and Pools[a]	Individuals and Others	Total
Farm	$ 9.0	$ 0.1	$ –	$ 10.4	$ 29.4	$ 27.1	$ 76.0
Residential							
1–4-family	$127.0	$62.3	$356.2	$ 14.4	$118.4	$ 83.6	$ 761.9
Multifamily	10.9	16.5	36.0	19.0	17.4	22.2	122.0
	$137.9	$78.8	$392.2	$ 33.4	$135.8	$105.8	$ 883.9
Commercial and industrial	67.1	16.3	40.7	62.0	3.7	22.9	212.6
	$214.0	$95.2	$432.9	$105.8	$168.8	$155.8	$1,172.5
Conventional	}214.0	$69.2	$403.9	$ 96.5	}168.8	}155.8	996.1
FHA-insured		14.2	13.2	6.1			}176.4
VA-guaranteed		11.8	15.8	3.2			
	$214.0	$95.2	$432.9	$105.8	$168.8	$155.8	$1,172.5

[a]Total includes federal and related agencies, $82.1 billion; mortgage pools or trusts (mortgages backing securities insured or guaranteed by agencies) $86.7 billion.

Sources: *Federal Reserve Bulletin*; *Federal Home Loan Bank Board Journal*. See also sources cited for institutions, Chapters 3 to 7. (Some figures may not add to totals due to rounding).

Such inventory is usually held only for a short interim between closing mortgage loans and their delivery to ultimate investors.[2]

Although mortgage companies may hold permanent mortgages in their own name, they are primarily merchants of residential and commercial mortgages. They seek out loans, secure interim bank financing, resell the loans to institutions, and thereafter service the loans for the final owner.[3] They are not to be confused with mortgage brokers, who serve solely as intermediaries and maintain no continuous relationship with borrower or investor.[4]

Mortgage companies are similar to investment banking concerns in that they are involved mainly in the distribution of new instruments. They originate mortgages and collect an origination fee of from 1 to 2.5 percent from borrowers or, as is often the case for conventional loans, from the investor in the form of a premium of about 0.5 percent above par. However, in contrast to the investment banking firm, the mortgage company operates primarily on the basis of prior and continuing relationships with the institutions it serves as "correspondent." Typically, it derives at least one-half of its income from the administration or servicing fee charged for collecting and remitting interest and principal of monthly amortized loans and from representing the investor throughout the life of the mortgage. Other income is derived from interest on mortgages held in inventory and from insurance and other ancilliary activities.

By originating mortgage loans in areas needing financing and by placing them with institutions in areas enjoying surplus funds, the mortgage company has been very instrumental in the development of a national mortgage market. Its contribution was greatly accelerated by the advent of FHA-insured, VA-guaranteed loans, and privately insured loans.

Mortgage companies are in all states, with a concentration in the South and West, where local funds are often insufficient to meet the demand for mortgage loans. The correspondent system brings in funds from Eastern capital markets.

Role in the Mortgage Market

Mortgage companies perform their role of originators and servicers of mortgages through their relationships with three institutional investors. In 1977, 15 percent of their servicing volume was for life insurance companies; 5 percent, for mutual savings banks; and 13 percent, for the Federal National Mortgage

---

[2]B. Klaman, *The Postwar Rise of Mortgage Companies,* Occasional Paper 60 (New York: National Bureau of Economic Research, Inc., 1959), p. 1.

[3]Other activities include making construction loans, serving as mortgage dealers, and writing property insurance.

[4]Mortgage companies, as defined herein, are often known as "mortgage bankers." The latter term, however, may be appropriately applied to all institutions that engage in mortgage financing.

Association. They sell a growing volume (10 percent) to savings and loan associations, and service a modest amount (6 percent) for commercial banks. Mortgage companies are also the principal users of the FNMA as a secondary market and are major factors in GNMA mortgage pools which now take 42% of their loans originations.

Mortgage companies traditional role as originators of home mortgages has diminished as institutions diverted funds to other investments. Mortgage companies had to develop more loans on income properties and offer incentives such as varible yields, equity participations and other "kickers" to attract funds, especially from life insurance companies.

Large institutional investors are originating more of their own loans than before, and commercial banks are also entering the servicing field, so mortgage companies are broadening their activities to include mortgage pooling, holding more permanent inventories of mortgages, selling more to individual investors and to pension funds, and expanding related lines of business such as real estate brokerage and insurance. Such an expanded role will require further growth in the size and resources of the typical company.

Bank loans are used to carry two types of mortgages: (1) those for which investors have made advance commitments but which will be delivered later, and (2) those accumulated for later placement when the opportunity arises. An extensive "warehousing" operation requires a sufficient spread between the rate on bank loans and the mortgage rates. The operations of the mortgage company are therefore directly affected by changes in general credit policy.

As of the end of 1977, a sample of mortgage company members of the Mortgage Bankers Association of America showed bank notes payable representing 31 percent and commercial paper 42 percent of total assets, compared with 10 percent for net worth.[5]

Uses of Funds

In 1977, for all mortgage companies combined, it was estimated that the first mortgage loan inventory constituted about 47 percent and construction loans 20 percent of total assets. It is not surprising that FHA-insured and VA-guaranteed loans on one- to four-family houses predominated. The FHA insured mortgage (and later the VA-guaranteed mortgage) avoided state restrictions on loan-to-value ratios, overcame the diverse foreclosure requirements in the various states, and with its uniform property requirements and appraised procedures became an acceptable negotiable instrument. The conditions making for the development of a national market led to a broad geographical distribution in which the mortgage company played the leading role.

---

[5]Mortgage Bankers Association of America, *Mortgage Banking* 1977 (Washington, 1978), p. 7.

The Secondary Mortgage Market

Three basic transactions take place in the mortgage market: (1) originating and holding of mortgages by investors; (2) origination of mortgages by institutions and mortgage companies as agents with prior commitments to deliver them to other investors, who are in effect the principals and the ultimate permanent investors; and (3) transfer of outstanding mortgages from old owners to new owners. Secondary market activity involves the third operation. Within the secondary mortgage market, two types of transactions take place: (1) the buying and selling of individual mortgages, and (2) the formation of mortgage pools and the issuance of a covering security.

The secondary market was primarily local in scope until the advent of FHA-insured and VA-guaranteed loans in 1934 and 1944, respectively. As we have seen, the uniformity of standards and terms and the new features of government support gave these instruments homogeneity and thus made them readily transferable, and facilitated the flow of mortgage funds across geographical barriers. In recent years, conventional loans have been taking on common characteristics, but each one still represents a separate credit risk, although the beginning—in the late 1950s—of privately insured conventional mortgages helped reduce the objections to this latter mortgage form. Nevertheless, the secondary mortgage market did not become well developed until the last half of the 1960s with the rapid development of the "second tier" of mortgage lenders.

Measured in dollar amounts, individuals have not participated to any great extent in the secondary mortgage market. By and large the market is still dominated by financial institutions, which are on both the buying and selling end of each transactions. Recently, however, new instruments backed by mortgages have been devised with the intention of attracting individual investors who desire high yields and monthly returns.

Individual and institutional investors use the secondary market to acquire and sell mortgages—chiefly residential—either directly through their own contacts or through mortgage brokers.[6] Most of the latter are local concerns, although a few large firms in big cities operate on a national scale. Investors sell mortgages through brokers to switch funds into other assets or to acquire them for immediate delivery to round out portfolio requirements that have not been fulfilled by advance commitments.

Commercial banks make construction loans for later placement or resale. Savings banks only recently have made substantial use of the secondary market. Savings and loan associations originate virtually all of their mortgage holdings. Some of their construction loans may be transferred to others. Since 1970, they have turned more to the secondary market to satisfy their overall portfolio needs.

---

[6]These should not be confused with the mortgage banking companies described previously.

Insurance companies occasionally make construction loans but prefer to acquire permanent loans from others and seldom resell in the secondary market. As we have seen, mortgage companies are engaged mainly in originating loans for resale to others. Their activities in the secondary market have increased sharply with the advent of new mortgage instruments. Individuals and federal agencies deal primarily in the secondary market. The secondary market emphasis by the FNMA, GNMA, Federal Home Loan Mortgage Corporation (FHLMC), and private firms deserves separate discussion.

Federal Credit Agencies in the Secondary Market

Federal credit agencies participate in the secondary market by buying and selling mortgages. They also make loans to the primary lenders they support. FNMA, GNMA, and the FHLMC have no direct contact with the public but instead offer their securities through brokers, commercial banks, savings associations, and others.

When deposit flows are strong as in 1971 and 1972, federal (sponsored and other) agencies tend to reduce their support in the mortgage market and restrict their secondary operations. When opposite conditions hold, they increase their mortgage support.

The original purpose of the FNMA in 1938 was to provide a secondary market for FHA-insured residential mortgages. In 1948, FNMA operations were expanded to include VA-guaranteed mortgages. In 1954, its basic functions were redefined into three main areas of support: (1) management and liquidation of mortgages acquired from a variety of other government agencies, (2) special assistance programs for subsidized housing and other government home programs, and (3) secondary market operations in which FHA and VA mortgages were to be acquired from mortgage companies and institutions.

In 1968, under Title VIII of the Housing and Urban Redevelopment Act, the management, liquidation, and special assistance functions of the FNMA were transferred to a new agency, the Government National Mortgage Association (GNMA). (See later discussion of GNMA operations.) After the retirement of its preferred stock, FNMA became a separate and private corporation and its stock was listed on the New York Stock Exchange. Its secondary market operations, under which purchases had been determined by the volume of government-supported mortgages attracted at market yields, were shifted to a "free market" system. FNMA does not originate mortgages; it makes commitments for existing mortgages only.

Institutions, such as commercial banks and mutual savings banks, that have been approved as "sellers" enter into a selling agreement with FNMA that provides for the institution to be qualified to service the mortgage offered for sale and to own stock in FNMA.

In 1968, the Free Market System (FMS) was introduced and greatly facilitated the secondary market in mortgages. Previously, the FNMA unilaterally established the price it was willing to pay for FHA and VA mortgages on a take-it-or-leave-it basis. Under the FMS, FNMA holds preannounced purchase auctions, usually biweekly, and each week the association indicates the total volume of forward commitments it will make to purchase eligible mortgages within three months, six months—up to a maximum of eighteen months. The mortgages must be delivered to FNMA during the commitment period and must meet FNMA quality standards.

In 1970, FNMA was authorized to operate in the secondary market for conventional loans to provide an expanded mortgage portfolio and add depth to the conventional mortgage market. Since 1970, their mortgage holdings almost tripled, from $15½ billion at that time to over $43 billion in 1978.

In 1978 FNMA-held mortgages consisted of over 80 percent in FHA/VA loans and the remainder in conventional loans. The latter holdings have increased substantially in the late 1970s as a result of the relative decline of FHA/VA financing and FNMAs purchase plans for conventional mortgages, which have exceeded government-insured mortgage purchases in 1976–1978.

The rapid growth in outstanding mortgages held by FNMA have caused some criticism that this agency is not fulfilling its proper role in the secondary market, since buying commitments far exceed sales. Also, despite the activity, few purchases of mortgages written on ghetto or downtown urban areas were made prior to 1978. Recent agreements between Housing and Urban Development (HUD) and FNMA should facilitate purchases in these areas.

The Government National Mortgage Association (GNMA) was established in 1968 to take over several former FNMA operations that were left with the Department of Housing and Urban Development when FNMA became a quasi-private corporation. In addition to the special assistance function and the management and liquidations function, a third function, the mortgage-backed security program—called Ginnie Mae "pass through"—is offered. Under this last function, pools are formed and securities are issued by a GNMA-approved originator. The securities are typically marketed through a securities dealer and promise monthly principal and interest payments. Since these securities are backed by pools of mortgages guaranteed by the FHA, VA, or Farmers Home Administration, the Ginnie Mae securities are essentially backed by the full faith and credit of the federal government and thus are riskless securities.

In addition to mortgage-backed pool operations, GNMA engages in two other important functions: (1) buying and selling of mortgages in the secondary market, and (2) guaranteeing payment of principal and interest on mortgage-backed bonds issued by FNMA or the Federal Home Loan Mortgage Corporation (FHLMC). The buying and selling of mortgages is primarily to support the market but also to aid in housing for low-income families. The total direct holdings by GNMA were less than $4 billion at the end of 1978. The guaranteeing of FNMA and FHLMC mortgage-backed bonds allows these latter institutions to issue securities up to the full face (100 percent parity) amount of the bond issue.

In order to facilitate the operations of savings and loan associations in particular and the secondary mortgage market in general, the Federal Home Loan Mortgage Corporation, called "Freddy Mac," was created in 1970. The corporation's stock, $100 million, is held by the twelve regional Federal Home Loan Banks and is under the supervision of FHLB officials. Additional financing has come from issuing bonds and advances from the FHLB System.

The operations of these institutions in the secondary market are accomplished by purchasing mortgages originated by others and by creating mortgage pools. When money is tight, they provide liquidity by purchasing mortgages from institutions and reverse the process when mortgage funds are plentiful.

Since its inception in 1970, FHLMC holdings rose sharply and amounted to $3.5 billion at the end of August 1974, with more than half of this total in FHA or VA mortgages ($1.9 billion) and the remaining amount in conventional mortgages ($1.6 billion). From 1975 through 1978, the direct holdings of mortgages declined to less than $2.5 billion as funds remained generally available at thrift institutions for purchases from FHLMC. In contrast, mortgage pools sponsored by FHLMC rose from less than $1 billion in 1974 to more than $10 billion at the end of 1978. The FHLMC sponsors pools through two programs: participation certificates (PCs) and guaranteed mortgage certificates (GMCs). PCs represent shares in pools of mortgages originally purchased by the agency in the secondary market. Principal and interest payments are made monthly and are guaranteed by the FHLMC. GMCs also represent mortgage pools, but these instruments are similar to bonds in that interest is paid semiannually rather than monthly and minimum amounts of principal are paid off each year. (See page 153).

As seen by the data above, most of the mortgage activity by FNMA, GNMA, and FHLMC has been in FHA and VA Loans. Although all three institutions are allowed to purchase conventional loans, the preference for government-backed mortgages reflects their safety, national scope, uniformity of provisions, terms, and, consequently, better marketability than is available on conventional loans.

The secondary market for conventional loans given its sheer size should continue to increase in importance on a national scale as the relatively low risk in single-family mortgages (default ratio less than ½ of 1 percent) and the high, long-term interest rate on newer mortgages make these securities appealing to institutional investors.

Private Financial Institutions in the Secondary Market

Several financial institutions participate in the secondary mortgage market. Savings and loan associations are especially important on the buy side and, in recent years, have been significant in the packaging and selling of mortgages. Mortgage companies, as noted earlier, are significant factors in packaging mortgages. A newer attraction for mortgage investors is the mortgage-backed pass-through certificates issued by some banks. These securities differ from those backed by government agencies in that the issue is handled entirely by the private sector. The pass-through certificates have 5 percent of the mortgage amount privately insured and a loan-to-value ratio of 80 percent. These issues are offered by brokers and are sold in denominations to attract large investors.

Mortgage Yields

The data in Table 12–6 and Figure 12–1 provide mortgage yield information from 1960 through 1978; the figures compare the averages of conventional and FHA mortgages and the yields on long-term corporate bonds. The data reveal the annual variations in mortgage yields when conditions in the capital market change. Tight money conditions in 1970, 1974, and 1978 are indicated in the mortgage series and in the bond rate. Yields on FHA mortgages (for purchases of new homes) were less variable than those on conventionals because of standardization and the fixed nominal rate. The first column in the table illustrates the recent variability in the FHA rate from allowing more flexibility in the fixed contract rate. Using annual averages, comparison with the second column reveals that FHA mortgages have sold at a discount in the secondary market. Before declining, their average market yield reached over 10 percent in December 1978 against a nominal yield of 9.5 percent. In order to encourage the flow of funds into mortgages the nominal or contract yield on FHA mortgages was raised to a then all-time high of 10 percent in April 1979, and to 11½ percent in October.

Conventional yields on new homes were consistently above the FHA rate until 1966. Since then, conventional loan rates (with higher risk) have often been below FHA market rates. This inconsistency can be explained in part by the relatively low default risk on conventional homes, the buyers' market that has existed in FHA/VA loans, and the propensity of lenders to prefer conventional loans—causing lower rates—over FHA loans, with their extra paperwork and time delays.

In 1974, mortgage yields reached all-time highs, with yields above 10 percent on single-family homes and 11 percent on commercial and multifamily units. This compared with the prime rate of 12 percent on short-term loans and 9¼ percent on long-term high-grade bonds. In addition, a peculiar difficulty faced some would-be borrowers: where market yields on mortgages equaled or exceeded the usury ceilings in some states, new mortgage financing had to await changes in legislation. Despite unprecedented home building, interest rates generally declined throughout much of the intervening years from 1974 through 1977. Plentiful funds and a recession worked to keep the rates well under previous highs. The persistent problem of inflation, the general rise in interest rates, and a continued boom in construction, however, forced mortgage rates above the 1974 level, to 12 percent or more in October 1979.

In comparing the open-market rate on high-grade corporate bonds and on conventional mortgages, a lag in the rate of change in the latter due to the lack

TABLE 12-6. Yields on Mortgages and Bonds, 1960–1978

	FHA Mortgages (New Homes)		Conventional Home (New Homes) Mortgages	Aaa
	Contract Rate (%)	Market Yield (%)	National Average (%)	Corporate Bonds (%)
1960	5.75	6.2	6.2	4.4
1961	5.75–5.25	5.7	6.0	4.3
1962	5.25	5.6	5.9	4.3
1963	5.25	5.5	5.8	4.3
1964	5.25	5.4	5.8	4.4
1965	5.25	5.5	5.8	4.5
1966	5.25–6.00	6.3	6.3	5.1
1967	6.00	6.5	6.5	5.5
1968	6.00–6.75	7.2	7.0	6.2
1969	6.75–7.50	8.3	7.8	7.0
1970	7.50–8.50	9.0	8.4	8.0
1971	8.00–7.00	7.7	7.7	7.4
1972	7.00	7.5	7.6	7.2
1973	7.00–8.50	8.2	8.0	7.4
1974	8.25–9.00	9.6	8.7	8.6
1975	8.00–9.00	9.2	9.0	8.8
1976	8.50–9.00	8.8	9.0	8.4
1977	8.50	8.0	9.0	8.0
1978	8.50–9.50	9.7	9.5	8.7
1979 (9 mo.)	9.50–10.50	10.6	11.3	9.4

Sources: *Federal Reserve Bulletin; Aaa* corporate bonds are *Moody's series; The Mortgage Banker* (yellow section).

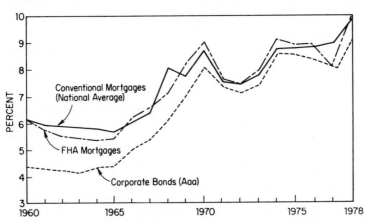

Figure 12-1. Average Yields on FHA and Conventional Mortgages and Corporate Bonds, 1960–1978

Source: *Federal Reserve Bulletin: Federal Home Loan Bank Board, Journal;* U.S. Department of Commerce, *Construction Review.* Aaa corporate bonds are Moody's series.

of a fully national flow of funds is apparent. Changes in mortgage yields appear somewhat more volatile in recent years. The spread between the annual average high-grade bond yield and the mortgage yields widens as mortgage yields rise. Although the FHA yields are now more flexible, there is aversion on the part of institutional investors to paying a price substantially different from par. Even during periods of rising effective yields, many investors are unwilling to move funds into mortgages when yields on other investments are also rising.

Typically, yields on mortgages exceed those on *Aaa* corporate bonds. The pattern remained in late 1978 as the average corporate bond (Aaa) yielded over 8.5 percent versus over 9.5 for the average new conventional mortgage (Figure 12-1). Government programs designed to aid the mortgage market were only partially successful.

In spite of some development of the national mortgage market, geographical differences in mortgage rates exist. Yield spreads exist in the capital-surplus areas of the East and Middle Atlantic regions and in the capital-seeking West and Southwest. The spread narrows to as low as 0.25 percent during periods of credit ease and widens to as much as 0.50 to 0.75 percent during tight money periods.

```
1313131313131313131313131313131313131313131313131313131313131313131313131313
1313131313131313131313131313131313131313131313131313131313131313131313131313
131313131313131313131313131313    31313    313    313    313    313131313131313131313131313
1313131313131313131313131313131    131    1313    313    313    313131313131313131313131313
1313131313131313131313131313131313    3    31313    313    313    313131313131313131313131313
131313131313131313131313131313131    131313    313    313    313131313131313131313131313
131313131313131313131313131313131313    3131313    313    313    313131313131313131313131313
1313131313131313131313131313131313131    131313    313    313    313131313131313131313131313
1313131313131313131313131313131313    3    31313    313    313    313131313131313131313131313
1313131313131313131313131313131    131    1313    313    313    313131313131313131313131313
131313131313131313131313131313131313    31313    313    313    313    313131313131313131313131313
1313131313131313131313131313131313131313131313131313131313131313131313131313
1313131313131313131313131313131313131313131313131313131313131313131313131313
```

Summary: Sources and Uses, and the Yield Pattern

Total Sources and Uses of Funds, 1970 through 1978

IN Chapters 3 through 7, the sources of funds for capital-market investment were itemized for each major institution, together with their purchases and holdings of the various instruments. Chapters 8 through 12 discussed the demand for intermediate- and long-term funds on the part of major users. In this chapter, the overall sources and uses are collated. Four categories that supply funds to the market were not given separate treatment except for the flow of their funds into various instruments as shown in this chapter. These include business corporations, state and local government proper, foreign investors, residual households, and others. Also included in the last category are bank-administered trust funds and minor institutions. Three additional uses included in the master schedule in this chapter are bank term loans to business FHLB loans to credit agencies and foreign securities acquired mainly by institutions.

Explanation of two procedures is again relevant. First, it was noted that except for commercial banks, most institutional funds flow into intermediate- or long-term use. To determine commercial bank sources, data on the actual application of these funds to capital-market use were employed. Second, all maturities of federal and federal agency securities were considered. This procedure was based on two factors: (1) the constant transfer and arbitraging among the various maturities of these instruments, making distinction by maturity somewhat unrealistic; and (2) the lack of reliable data on the maturity composition of the investments of several institutions.

Table 13-1 combines the totals of the detailed data presented in Chapters 3 to 12 into a master array of net flows of capital-market funds for 1970-1978. Details on the variations of the components of the total sources and uses of capital-market funds were presented in previous chapters.

After rising moderately from 1965 through 1969, the total flow of funds into the capital market burgeoned in the 1970s with the total for 1973 almost tripling the amount for 1965, and 1978 more than doubling 1973. The data, although revealing a strong upward trend from 1970 through 1978, was not always reflected in the individual institutional flows. Open-end investment companies, and real estate trusts, for example, often experienced declines in asset values throughout this period. Prime contributors to the dramatic rise in capital flows during this period were commercial banks, savings and loan associations, life insurance companies, state and local governments, and foreign investors.

The capital-market benefited greatly from increased competition in savings deposits, which helped to induce a higher rate of personal savings in the early 1970s. The threat of inflation and continued strong loan demand moderated the personal rate of savings somewhat in the late 1970s, but flow of funds into the capital market remained high. Also the worldwide threat of inflation, coupled with the more stable political and economic atmosphere in the United States, encouraged foreign investors to place funds (especially oil funds) in the capital market in record amounts.

As can be seen in the lower panel of Table 13-1, the primary beneficiaries of the rapid advancement in capital market funds in the 1970s were mortgages, government securities, and corporate bonds in that order. Of the large suppliers, noted earlier, foreigners tended to place most of their funds in U.S. government securities; savings associations favored mortgages, with commercial banks spreading their funds more evenly among federal securities, state and local bonds, and mortgages.

The chief factors of instability in the use of funds have been the fluctuating net additions to outstanding federal securities, and mortgages. Net changes in outstanding federal agency securities have followed a contracyclical pattern, as the agencies tend to step up their financing in periods of restrictive monetary policy. As we have seen, net additions to municipal bonds fluctuate because of special tax influences. Variations in net additions to corporate bonds reflect the pattern of their yields and, more important, the changing reliance by corporations on internal sources of funds.

Capital Flows and Market Yields

The annual yield averages in Table 13-2 conceal the magnitude of interim variations. They are, however, useful in showing the relationship between the

TABLE 13–1. Sources and Uses of Capital Market Funds, 1970–1978 (billions of dollars)[a]

	1970	1971	1972	1973	1974	1975	1976	1977	1978
Sources									
Commercial banks	$26.1	$32.8	$37.7	$32.7	$30.7	$39.1	$34.0	$41.5	$53.5
Federal Reserve banks	5.0	8.5	0.3	9.3	5.2	8.4	10.0	7.2	7.3
Mutual savings banks	3.6	9.4	10.0	4.6	3.1	10.5	11.9	11.2	8.7
Savings and loan associations	10.4	26.0	33.9	27.2	19.1	35.5	49.4	61.9	56.7
Life insurance companies	6.2	10.4	12.9	14.0	12.1	17.6	23.7	27.1	28.6
Property and liability insurance companies	4.0	6.2	6.7	5.8	4.4	5.9	12.4	19.3	19.8 (est)
Private pension funds	6.9	7.4	6.6	7.8	8.1	13.8	12.6	15.6	12.9
State and local government retirement funds	6.2	6.5	8.3	9.1	9.4	11.6	13.4	12.9	14.7
Investment companies (open-end)	2.1	0.7	-1.5	-3.2	-0.4	0.7	-0.1	-2.8	-1.2
Real estate investment trusts	1.9	2.3	4.2	5.6	0.2	-4.8	-3.8	-2.4	-1.0
Federal agencies	8.0	2.3	3.1	5.8	14.7	11.5	4.3	1.5	12.5
Mortgage pools	1.6	4.8	4.9	3.6	5.8	10.3	15.7	20.5	16.5
Non-financial business corporations	-0.5	3.5	-1.1	-3.5	2.9	8.9	2.9	-6.4	-6.3
State and local governments (general funds)	-0.3	-2.3	7.8	7.7	3.8	3.3	14.7	26.3	23.3
Foreign investors	10.5	27.2	10.6	3.6	5.5	13.0	15.3	37.9	33.5
Households and others	4.7	-1.1	5.0	19.0	15.4	20.8	11.0	-4.2	13.9
Total sources	$96.4	$136.3	$149.2	$149.0	$139.6	$206.7	$227.5	$268.7	$293.6
Uses									
U.S. Treasury securities	$12.9	$26.0	$14.3	$7.9	$12.0	$85.8	$69.1	$57.6	$55.1
Federal and foreign agency bonds	8.5	1.9	5.3	17.0	16.7	2.0	3.4	6.5	21.5
State and local government bonds	9.0	15.3	14.4	12.9	11.5	13.0	19.4	25.0	24.8
Corporate bonds[b]	23.3	23.5	18.4	13.6	23.9	36.4	37.2	36.1	32.1
Corporate stocks	10.5	15.0	13.3	9.2	3.7	10.7	11.9	3.8	3.1

(continued)

225

TABLE 13-1. Sources and Uses of Capital-Market Funds, 1970–1978 (billions of dollars)[a]   Continued

	1970	1971	1972	1973	1974	1975	1976	1977	1978
Uses (cont.)									
Mortgages	29.9	52.6	77.0	79.9	60.5	57.2	87.1	134.0	145.9
Bank term loans	2.0	2.0	6.4	8.4	11.0	1.3	-1.1	5.2	10.5 (est)
Agency term loans	0.3	–	0.1	0.1	0.3	0.3	0.5	0.5	0.6 (est)
Total uses	$96.4	$136.3	$149.2	$149.0	$139.6	$206.7	$227.5	$268.7	$293.6

[a]For sources of data, see detailed schedules in Chapters 3 to 12.
[b]Corporate bonds include term loans of life insurance companies. Some columns (of sources) do not add to totals because of rounding.

TABLE 13-2. Yields of Selected Capital-Market Instruments, 1970–1978 (annual averages)

	1970	1971	1972	1973	1974	1975	1976	1977	1978
U.S. Treasury, 3–5 years	7.4	5.8	5.9	6.9	8.7	7.6	6.9	6.8	8.3
U.S. Treasury long-term	6.6	5.7	5.6	6.3	7.0	7.0	6.8	7.0	7.9
Aaa state and local bonds	6.1	5.2	5.0	5.0	5.9	6.4	5.7	5.2	5.5
Aaa corporate bonds	8.0	7.4	7.2	7.4	8.6	8.8	8.4	8.0	8.7
125 industrial common stocks (dividend yield)	3.8	3.1	2.8	3.1	4.5	4.5	4.3	3.8	4.6
Conventional home mortgages, contract rate	8.4	7.7	7.6	8.0	8.9	9.0	9.0	9.0	9.5

Sources: *Federal Reserve Bulletin; Moody's Investors Service.* Bond yields are Moody's series, stock yields are Standard and Poors series; mortgage yields are FHLBB series.

flow of funds into and out of the capital markets and the prevailing rates. First, the general upward- but cyclical, drift in interest rates and divided yields through 1978 is apparent for all security issues, including common stocks. The large spread between bond and stock yields has generally contributed to the stock market weakness throughout most of the period (1970-1978) as investors sought higher current yield investments. The large increase in the average dividend yield in 1974 to over 5 percent and in 1978 was a result of a declining stock market coupled with increased dividends.

As expected, the greatest yield volatility was found in shorter-term securities, particularly bills and notes, and U.S. Treasury bonds with three- to five-year maturities. Corporate bond and mortgage yields exhibited an upward trend, declining only slightly over the business cycle. Although the rise in rates on corporate bonds and mortgages paralleled the increases in other securities, they rose relatively more as the demand for these loans often outstripped the supply of funds. The high rates on short-term instruments contributed to this imbalance. Mortgage yields showed the least variation, reflecting the lack of a truly national competitive market and strong resistence of borrowers to sharply higher rates. Tight money conditions in 1974 and 1979 resulted in an inverted yield curve, where short-term rates exceeded long-term rates.

Annual changes in the bond and mortgage yields series show only an approximate relationship with the change in total supply of, and demand for, long-term funds as shown in Table 13-1. This is partially explained by the fact that the yields in Table 13-2 are yearly averages and hence tend to obscure sharp changes occurring within the year. Second, demand and supply changes tend to be dominated by other factors, such as monetary policy, the fear of inflation, and the rate on personal savings. Third, it is the interrelationship between total demand and supply that determines ultimate interest-rate levels.

In general, when the total sources of funds does not exhibit good growth (around 7 percent or more) over the previous year, tighter money conditions are indicated. This, of course, is only a rough approximation, as tight money does not follow a yearly schedule. Nevertheless, the tight money periods of 1973-1974 and 1978-1979 were characterized by slower growth in total sources of funds.

The differential effects of interest rates on the uses of funds, as applied to each of the representative securities, is revealed in the tables. Given the transitivity and arbitrage process between interest rates, when money is tight, short-term rates tend to rise relatively more than long-term rates and funds tend to flow to the short-term instruments. Consequently, long-term bonds and mortgages are likely to suffer from a lack of available funds, and total amounts committed to these securities will tend to moderate, all other things equal. In 1974 and 1979, tight money periods, total funds flowing to mortgages declined compared to previous years. Funds flowed to mortgages in 1976 and 1977 as interest rates declined, but again the flow fell off in late 1978 because of the high costs of mortgage money and disintermediation from savings banks and associations.

The flow of funds to corporate bonds is a little more difficult to explain. Amounts committed to corporate bonds actually increased in the tight money periods of 1970 and 1973–1974. This reflected the need for funds by businesses and the declining stock market, which made the sale of stock undesirable and left borrowing as the only acceptable alternative for most firms. In this respect, the need for funds by users dominated the preference for short-term securities by suppliers of funds and, as a result, substantial long-term loans were made to businesses at high interest rates.

Rates on municipal bonds showed more volatility and a less dramatic longer-term increase through 1973, but they tended to follow the general market conditions of "overdemand" and "undersupply" in 1974. The effects of the enormous financing needs in all segments of the municipal market in subsequent years and the serious financial problems of large cities caused rates in 1975 to rise to abnormally high levels.

Are changes in long-term yields a result or a cause of changes in the supply of and the demand for capital-market funds? In general, our previous discussion of the individual markets would suggest that both possibilities are true. The question could be handled more explicitly if we were to examine, in addition to the data on long-term sources and uses of funds, the changing liquidity requirements of institutional and individual suppliers and uses of funds as well as changes in personal savings habits. We have equated capital-market sources and uses, but we have not discussed the changes in liquid funds or the impact of total funds devoted to both short- and long-term employed. Also, we have not studied the shifting demand between short-and long-term uses. Unfortunately, our short discussion does not permit such an analysis and the reader should keep in mind the caution suggested in Chapter 1, namely, that a somewhat arbitrary segregation of the flow of long-term funds within the total investment market fails to present a complete picture.

A Concluding Statement

Our study has focused on the institutionalization of savings, the expanding role of institutions in funneling savings into the capital market, and the impact of their investment policies on both the primary and secondary markets for longer-term instruments. We have also shown the demands made upon the markets by individuals, businesses, and governments seeking longer-term funds for a wide variety of purposes. We have measured the combined influence of supply and demand forces on prices and yields, with special attention to the dramatic developments in the 1970s.

The contribution of the capital markets to economic growth and the free flow of funds has increased greatly in the postwar period. The efficiency of the market structure has been enhanced by the expansion of investment banking activity, the broadening geographical range of institutional investment, the development of correspondent systems, the improvement of secondary markets, and the increased competition among financial institutions. But there are still barriers to a free flow of funds. Efficient capital markets require market agencies and organizations that function on a national scale, a minimum of restraints on investment policy, minimum government regulation of prices and yields, and widespread information on prevailing market conditions and prices so that yields can reflect the full play of supply and demand. Much progress has been made toward these goals. However, when pressure for funds in the face of limited supply produces the conditions that prevailed in 1973–1974, and 1978–1979 the virtues of even more efficient markets, in which prices and yields reflect full national flow of and demand for funds, may conflict with national policy. Reduction in defense spending, implementation of domestic programs of great importance, and braking inflation may require business, monetary, and fiscal controls that conflict with the principle of unrestrained markets.

Appendix

TABLE A-1. Yields on U.S. Government Securities, Selected Dates, 1961–1979

	May 1961	Sept. 1966	June 1967	Jan. 1970	Mar. 1971	July 1971	July 1972	Aug. 1974	Dec. 1976	Oct. 1979
3-month bills	2.29%	5.36%	3.53%	7.87%	3.38%	5.39%	3.98%	8.96%	4.35%	10.5%
6-month bills	2.44	5.79	3.88	7.78	3.50	5.62	4.50	9.11	4.51	11.75
9- to 12-month issues	2.72	5.80	4.40	8.82	3.66	5.73	4.90	8.88	4.92	11.54
3- to 5-year issues	3.28	5.62	4.96	8.14	4.74	6.77	5.85	8.64	5.96	11.30
Long-term issues[a]	3.73	4.79	4.86	6.86	5.71	5.91	5.57	7.33	6.39	10.51

[a]Due or callable in ten years.
Source: *Federal Reserve Bulletin.*

232

TABLE A-2. U.S. Government and Municipal Bonds Yields, 1960–1979

| | Long-Term Treasury (1) | State and Local Government | | Spread (1) over (2) | Spread (3) over (2) |
		Aaa (2)	Baa (3)		
1960	4.01	3.26	4.22	0.75	0.96
1965	4.21	3.16	3.57	1.05	0.41
1966	4.66	3.67	4.21	0.99	0.54
1967	4.85	3.74	4.30	1.11	0.56
1968	5.26	4.20	4.88	1.06	0.68
1969	6.10	5.45	6.07	0.65	0.62
1970	6.59	6.12	6.75	0.47	0.63
1971	5.74	5.22	5.89	0.52	0.67
1972	5.63	5.04	5.60	0.59	0.56
1973	6.30	4.99	5.49	1.31	0.50
1974	6.99	5.89	6.53	1.10	0.64
1975	6.98	6.42	7.62	0.56	1.20
1976	6.78	5.66	7.49	1.10	1.83
1977	7.06	5.20	6.12	1.86	0.92
1978	7.89	5.52	6.27	1.62	0.75
1979 (6 mo.)	8.97	5.71	6.52	3.26	0.81

Sources: *Federal Reserve Bulletin; Moody's Bond Survey.*

TABLE A-3. Yields on Corporate and Treasury Bonds, 1960–1979

| | Corporate | | Spread (1) and (2) | U.S. Treasury Long-Term (3) | Spread (2) over (3) |
	Baa (1)	Aaa (2)			
1960	5.19	4.41	0.78	4.01	0.40
1965	4.87	4.49	0.38	4.21	0.28
1966	5.67	5.13	0.54	4.66	0.47
1967	6.23	5.51	0.72	4.85	0.66
1968	6.94	6.18	0.76	5.25	0.93
1969	7.81	7.03	0.78	6.10	0.93
1970	9.11	8.04	1.07	6.59	1.45
1971	8.56	7.39	1.17	5.74	1.65
1972	8.16	7.21	0.95	5.63	1.58
1973	8.24	7.44	0.80	6.30	1.14
1974	9.50	8.59	0.93	6.99	1.58
1975	10.61	8.83	1.78	6.98	1.85
1976	9.75	8.43	1.32	6.78	1.65
1977	8.97	8.02	0.95	7.06	0.96
1978	9.45	8.73	0.72	7.84	0.84
1979 (6 mo.)	10.15	9.34	0.81	8.97	0.37

Sources: *Federal Reserve Bulletin; Moody's Bond Survey.*

TABLE A–4. Yields on High-Grade Industrial Bonds, Preferred Stocks, and Common Stocks, 1960–1978

	Aaa Industrial Bonds[a] (1)	High-Grade Industrial Preferreds[b] (2)	Industrial Common Stocks[c] (3)	Spread (2) over (1)	Spread (3) over (1)
1960	4.47	4.48	3.39	0.1	-1.09
1965	4.25	4.07	2.99	-0.18	-1.26
1966	4.68	4.67	3.45	-0.01	-1.23
1967	5.03	5.13	3.12	-0.10	-1.91
1968	6.12	5.62	3.04	-0.50	-3.08
1969	6.92	6.15	3.03	-0.77	-3.89
1970	7.76	7.03	3.80	-0.73	-3.96
1971	7.16	6.55	2.90	-0.61	-4.20
1972	7.09	6.56	2.75	-0.53	-4.34
1973	7.37	6.65	2.84	-0.72	-4.53
1974	8.04	7.48	4.32	-0.56	-3.72
1975	8.43	7.83	3.87	-0.60	-4.56
1976	8.21	7.37	3.38	-0.84	-4.83
1977	8.10	7.12	4.36	-0.98	-3.74
1978	8.65	7.65	5.06	-1.00	-3.59
1979 (6 mo.)	9.13	8.07 (est.)	5.18	-1.06	-3.95

[a]Standard & Poor's series.
[b]Moody's low-dividend series.
[c]Standard & Poor's 400 series.
Sources: *Moody's Industrials*, Standard & Poor's *Standard Trade and Securities Statistics*.

References

Statistical sources are cited throughout the book. The following list is generally restricted to recent major works and articles.

American Bankers Association, *The Commercial Banking Industry.* Englewood Cliffs, N.J.: Prentice-Hall, Inc., 1962. A monograph prepared for the Commission on Money and Credit.

American Mutual Insurance Alliance, et al., *Property and Casualty Insurance Companies: Their Role as Financial Intermediaries.* Englewood Cliffs, N.J.: Prentice-Hall, Inc., 1962. A monograph prepared for the Commission on Money and Credit.

Board of Governors of the Federal Reserve System, *Flow of Funds Accounts.* Washington, D.C., 1978.

——, *Federal Reserve System: Purposes and Functions.* Washington, D.C., 1974.

Break, G. F., et al., *Federal Credit Agencies.* Englewood Cliffs, N.J.: Prentice-Hall, Inc., 1963. Research studies prepared for the Commission on Money and Credit.

Calver, G. L., ed., *Fundamentals of Municipal Bonds,* 9th ed. Washington, D.C.: Securities Industry Association, 1972.

Colean, M. L., *Mortgage Companies: Their Place in the Financial Structure.* Englewood Cliffs, N.J.: Prentice-Hall, Inc., 1962. A monograph prepared for the Commission on Money and Credit.

Commission on Financial Structure and Regulation, *Report* (popularly called the Hunt Commission Report). Washington, D.C., 1971.

Dawson, J. C., *A Flow-of-Funds Analysis of Savings–Investment Fluctuations in the United States.* Princeton, N.J.: Princeton University Press, 1965.

De Prano, Michael, et al., eds., *Money, Financial Markets, and The Economy.* Belmont, California: Dickenson Publishing Company, Inc., 1970.

Employee Pensions in State and Local Governments. New York: The Tax Foundation, Inc., 1976.

Federal Home Loan Bank Board, *Study of the Savings and Loan Industry,* 4 vols. Washington, D.C., 1970.

Federal National Mortgage Association, *Background and History of the Federal National Mortgage Association.* Washington, D.C., 1969.

Financial Institutions and The Nation's Economy (FINE); compendium of papers purchased for the FINE study, June 1976. 9th Congress. 2d session. Washington, D.C.: U.S. Government Printing Office, 1976.

The First Boston Corporation, *Handbook of Securities of the U.S. Government and Federal Agencies,* 30th ed. New York: The First Boston Corporation, 1978.

Fisher, L., and J. H. Lorie, "Rates of Return on Investments in Common Stock: The Year-by-Year Record, 1926–1965." *Journal of Business,* July 1968, pp. 291–316.

Fraser, D. R., and P. S. Rose, "Bank Entry and Bank Performance." *Journal of Finance,* March 1972, pp. 65–78.

Friend, Irwin, *Study of the Savings and Loan Industry.* Submitted to the Federal Home Loan Board (Washington, 1969).

Friend, I., M. Blume, and J. Crockett, *Mutual Funds and Other Institutional Investors: A New Perspective.* New York: McGraw-Hill, 1970.

Gies, T. G., and V. P. Apelado, eds., *Banking Markets and Financial Institutions.* Homewood, Ill.: Richard D. Irwin, Inc., 1971.

Goldfield, S. M., "Savings and Loan Associations and the Market for Savings: Aspects of Allocational Efficiency." *Study of the Savings and Loan Industry,* Vol. 11. Washington, D.C.: Federal Home Loan Bank Board, 1969.

Goldsmith, R. W., *A Study of Savings in the United States,* 3 vols. Princeton, N.J.: Princeton University Press, 1955–1956.

——, *Financial Intermediaries in the American Economy Since 1900.* Princeton, N.J.: Princeton University Press, 1958.

——, *The Flow of Capital Funds in the Postwar Economy.* New York: Columbia University Press, 1965.

——, *Financial Institutions.* Random House, Inc., 1968.

——, *Capital Market Analysis and the Financial Accounts of the Nation.* Morristown, N.J.: General Learning Press, 1972.

Gup, B. E., *Financial Intermediaries: An Introduction.* Boston: Houghton Mifflin Co., 1976.

Gurley, J. G., and E. S. Shaw, *Money in a Theory of Finance.* Washington, D.C.: The Brookings Institution, 1960.

Henning, C. N., W. Pigott, and R. H. Scott, *Financial Markets and the Economy,* 2nd ed. Englewood Cliffs, N.J.: Prentice-Hall, Inc., 1978.

Hirshleifer, J., *Investment, Interest and Capital.* Englewood Cliffs, N.J.: Prentice-Hall, Inc., 1969.

Homer, S., *A History of Interest Rates*. New Brunswick, N.J.: Rutgers University Press, 1963.

Institutional Investor Study Report of the Securities and Exchange Commission. 92nd Congress, 1st Session, House Document No. 92-64. Washington, D.C.: Government Printing Office, 1971.

Joint Treasury-Federal Reserve Study 9th U.S. Government Securities Market. Washington, D.C.: Board of Governors of the Federal Reserve System, 1969.

Kessel, R. A., *The Cyclical Behavior of the Term Structure of Interest Rates*. New York: National Bureau of Economic Research, 1965.

Klaman, S. B., *The Postwar Rise of Mortgage Companies,* Occasional Paper No. 60. New York: National Bureau of Economic Research, Inc., 1959.

——, *The Postwar Residential Mortgage Market*. Princeton, N.J.: Princeton University Press, 1961.

Kroos, H. E., and M. R. Blyn, *A History of Financial Institutions*. New York: Random House, 1971.

Kuznets, S., *Capital in the American Economy: Its Formation and Financing*. Princeton, N.J.: Princeton University Press, 1961.

Light, J. O., and W. L. White, *The Financial System*. Homewood, Ill.: Richard D. Irwin, Inc., 1979.

Lutz, F. A., *The Theory of Interest*. Chicago: Aldine Press, 1968.

Malkiel, B. G., *The Term Structure of Interest Rates*. Princeton, N.J.: Princeton University Press, 1966.

Meiselman, D., *The Term Structure of Interest Rates*. Englewood Cliffs, N.J.: Prentice-Hall, Inc., 1962.

Melvin, D. J. et al., *Credit Unions and the Credit Union Industry*. New York: New York Institute of Finance, 1977.

Merrill Lynch, Pierce, Fenner and Smith, Inc., *Proposed for a National Market System*. New York: Merrill Lynch, 1975.

Pease, R. H., and L. O. Kerwood, eds., *Mortgage Banking*. 2nd ed. New York: McGraw-Hill Book Company, 1965.

Petersen, John, *Changing Conditions in the Market for State and Local Government Debt;* a study for the Joint Economic Committee, 94th Congress, 2d Session, Washington, D.C.: U.S. Government Printing Office, April 16, 1976.

Piper, T. R., and S. Weiss, "The Profitability of Multibank Holding Company Acquisitions." *Journal of Finance,* March 1974, pp. 163-174.

Polakoff, H. E., et al., *Financial Institutions and Markets*. Boston: Houghton Mifflin Company, 1970.

Prather, W. C., *Savings Accounts,* 5th ed. Chicago: American Savings and Loan Press, 1974.

Real Estate Investment Trusts: A Background Analysis and Recent Industry Developments, 1961-1974. Washington, D.C.: Securities and Exchange Commission, February 1975.

Ricks, R. B., *The Role of Federal Mortgage Credit Agencies in the Capital Markets*. Washington, D. C.: Federal Home Loan Bank Board, 1970.

Ritter, L. S., *The Flow of Funds Accounts: A Framework for Financial Analysis.* New York: New York University Graduate School of Business Administration, 1968.

Robinson, R. I., and D. Wrightsman, *Financial Markets: The Accumulation and Allocation of Wealth.* New York: McGraw-Hill Book Company, 1974.

Securities and Exchange Commission, *The Future of the Securities Market.* Washington, D.C., February 2, 1972.

Smith, P. F., *Money and Financial Intermediation: The Theory and Structure of Financial Systems.* Englewood Cliffs, N.J.: Prentice-Hall, Inc., 1978.

A Study of Mortgage Credit. Subcommittee on Housing and Urban Affairs of the U.S. Senate Committee on Banking and Currency, 90th Congress, 1st Session, May 22, 1967. Washington, D.C.: Government Printing Office, 1967.

Tucker, J. R., *State and Local Pension Funds.* Washington, D.C.: Securities Industry Association, 1972.

Van Horne, J. C., *Financial Market Rates and Flows.* Englewood Cliffs, N.J.: Prentice-Hall, Inc., 1978.

Index

241